The Slave Sublime

STACY J. LETTMAN

The Slave Sublime
The Language of Violence in Caribbean Literature and Music

The University of North Carolina Press *Chapel Hill*

*This book was published with the assistance of the
Authors Fund of the University of North Carolina Press.*

© 2022 Stacy J. Lettman

All rights reserved

Set in Arno Pro by Westchester Publishing Services

Manufactured in the United States of America

The University of North Carolina Press has been a member of the
Green Press Initiative since 2003.

Complete Library of Congress Cataloging-in-Publication Data is available at
https://lccn.loc.gov/2021046366.

ISBN 978-1-4696-6807-9 (cloth: alk. paper)
ISBN 978-1-4696-6808-6 (pbk.: alk. paper)
ISBN 978-1-4696-6809-3 (ebook)

Cover illustration: Stafford Schliefer, *Bars with Stripes and Spanish Jar*
(acrylic on canvas, 2004). Used by permission of the artist.

Portions of chapter 2 were previously published in a different form as "Freeing the
Colonized Tongue: The Representation of Linguistic Colonization in Marlene Nourbese
Philip's and Eaven Boland's Poetry," in *The Black and Green Atlantic: Cross-Currents of the
African and Irish Diasporas*, ed. Peter D. O'Neill and David Lloyd (London: Palgrave
Macmillan, 2009), 131–45; and "Journeys to (Un)dis/cover Silence: A Critique of the
Word in Looking for Livingstone," *Encounters: An International Journal for the Study of
Culture and Society* 5 (Fall 2012): 69–90.

For Savannah and Doris Lettman

Contents

Illustration

Acknowledgments

I'm thankful for the Mellon Mays Undergraduate Fellowship (MMUF) and grants from the Andrew W. Mellon Foundation that helped to kickstart my scholarly journey. Thanks also to the Florida Education Fund for the McKnight Junior Faculty Fellowship, which allowed for a one-year release from teaching and service at Florida Atlantic University (FAU) so as to focus on writing this book. I am thankful also to the Dorothy Schmidt College of Arts and Letters at FAU for the one-semester Scholarly and Creative Award Fellowship (SCAF) granting course releases from teaching that made possible the mental space to finish up the manuscript, albeit during the heights of the COVID-19 pandemic!

I am so appreciative of the wonderful enthusiasm and support that I received for this book project from David Lloyd, John Carlos Rowe, Karen Tongson, and Edwin Hill when it was just an idea. Along the way, as it materialized, I am grateful for the feedback that I received from my former colleagues and friends at the University of Central Arkansas, namely Clayton Crockett, Katelyn Knox, Taine Duncan, and Michael Kithinji. I am thankful also for the other friendships that were nurtured there with Sonia Toudji, Zach Smith, Lori Leavell, Melissa Smith, Melissa Eubanks, and Glen Jellenik. At FAU, I am equally grateful for the collegiality, friendship, and scholarly feedback from Carla Calarge, Ashvin Kini, Stacey Balkan, Sika Dagbovie-Mullins, Regis Fox, Kate Schmidt, Julieann Ulin, and Clevis Headley. I want to thank Eric Berlatsky for his tremendous support while serving as chair of the English department at FAU. My long-term friendships both inside and outside academia have been equally sustaining. Thank you Lori Moses, Sherleyne Zinn, Brian Zinn, Peter O'Neill, Ann Mackenna Mwenda, Allyson Salinger Ferrante, Mariko Dawson Zare, Jean Neely, Michael Cucher, Alicia Garnica, Priyanka Joshi, Vanessa Griffith Osborne, Nora Gilbert, and Debbie Harrigan. Thanks to my family for their support as well.

I am very thankful to the readers who provided such excellent feedback on my manuscript during the blind peer review stage at The University of North Carolina (UNC) Press. I am grateful also for the clear guidance from Lucas Church, my acquisitions editor, and others at UNC Press including Dylan White, Andrew Winters, Valerie Burton, and Elizabeth Ashley Orange for their assistance. I am also very thankful to Elaine Maisner for seeing the manuscript's potential for becoming a book.

I would like to thank the University of the West Indies, Mona, for granting me access to their archives during my research trip to Jamaica. I am thankful to the Schomburg Center for Research in Black Culture in New York City for access to their archival materials as well. Lastly, I am filled with gratitude for the mentorship that I received from Ashraf Rushdy, Monique Sulle, and Krishna Winston while I was an undergraduate student and MMUF Fellow at Wesleyan University where my scholarly endeavors began.

The Slave Sublime

The Slave Sublime

A Jamaican Case Study

Human progress is . . . an attempt to ritualize violence to protect the society's members from mutual destruction. At present the world's formerly colonized societies, regardless of the form of government, can hardly be said to have succeeded in this. Is it possible they contain more latent violence than other societies, which is reflected in their destructive and self-destructive behavior?

—Albert Memmi, *Decolonization and the Decolonized*

Albert Memmi's rhetorical questions are pertinent to Jamaica, as the island is grappling with problems that stem from histories forged in the violent product of contact and systemic oppression under slavery and colonialism. Jamaica has been identified as having one of the highest per capita murder rates in the world. For many years this Caribbean island has consistently ranked third while Brazil, Columbia, South Africa, and Venezuela vied for first or second place, with the exception of the year 2005 when Jamaica actually ranked number one.[1] In fact, in a January 2006 article, the *BBC* referred to Jamaica as the "murder capital of the world."[2] The violence in Jamaica has been attributed to the West Kingston garrison communities, created by politicians during the 1960s and 1970s to shape voting affiliation, which now function somewhat as autonomous, subnational entities ruled by dons (drug lords) because of structural neglect by the nation.[3] During the late 1970s and early 1980s Cold War era, the high influx of firearms into the country, partly engineered as a component of American destabilization of Jamaica's social and political fabric through clandestine operations, along with huge loans from the International Monetary Fund (IMF) and accompanying structural adjustments, had devastating effects on the country and further marginalized the West Kingston garrisons. Since the 1980s, the socioeconomically debased, Third World–esque slum and ghetto conditions in these garrison communities, manifesting in the high murder rates and other interpersonal violence, have been linked to the rise in illegal drug trafficking of cocaine from South America by heavily armed dons who are no longer subject to the authority of the government as they become part of a transnational network.

While these factors greatly contribute to the present problems, the cause has a deeper historical root, especially when one considers that other postcolonial nations in the Americas and Africa are also dealing with violence as a critical social problem. Strikingly resonant about these nations topping the list is one commonality: they all share histories of oppression stemming from slavery or European colonization to a newer form under globalization—neocolonialism, in other words. Given these considerations, this book explores the multifaceted histories and legacies of violence and its transnational formations in the Caribbean—Jamaica in particular.

This interdisciplinary project investigates how Jamaica's legacies of violence are socially articulated in literary and musical texts that reflect upon slavery and its more contemporary manifestations in the era of globalization. Moreover, it illustrates how the violence from the plantation era is now reimagined materially as a means of prolonging slavery into newer forms of oppression. Imperial nations maintain dominance over postcolonial nations such as Jamaica, where there is a refiguration of "social death" and economic dispossession as structural violence that replicates, mirrors, or refigures the slave plantation system. In this book, I look at various forms of cultural production including music, poetry, and novels in order to show how musical artists and writers represent the current iterations of plantation systems, all deeply structured by violence—similar to the way that a language is structured by grammar. I use the term *slave sublime* to contextualize the infinite violence that the imagination endures by discussing the antithetical ideas of *change* and *sameness*. I am indebted to Paul Gilroy's coinage of the term in *The Black Atlantic*. Although Gilroy leaves the term slave sublime undefined, within the context of Jamaica's transhistorical violence I use it to foreground the overwhelming magnitude of awe stemming from unrelenting violence, which, nonetheless, does not override the imagination's ability for representation.[4]

As I argue, for the historical and contemporary slave, the sublime is not only a bodily experience, but also one in which the imagination interiorizes terror—wherein the terror associated with the sublime remains ever-present without transcendence through reason, a contrast to Kantian philosophy. Kant's metaphysical interiority privileges the Cartesian *cogito ergo sum*, "I think therefore I am," which nullifies and thereby transcends a somatogenic notion of phenomenology. Such transcendental possibilities of knowledge, however, overlook the body's importance, which is so central to African and African-diasporic phenomenology. The slave sublime's integration of mind and body suggests also a divergence from the Cartesian dualism that informs the sublime in Western philosophy. The continued deferral of freedom, therefore, connects to the materiality of a Caribbean subject's entrance and embeddedness into a language of violence—the symbolic violence of the slave plantation, its maintenance by slave codes, and its transition to the (neo)colonial order wherein ideological conventions about capitalism, and the institution of hegemonic systems such as the IMF, maintain the sublime presence of slavery as the Real of freedom.

A Prelude to Contemporary Stagings of Violence

Although many contemporary factors have contributed to the high rate of violence in Jamaica, I will argue from an interdisciplinary point of view, taking into account ideas from history, philosophy, psychoanalysis, linguistics, and literary theory, that the current violence is not just a contemporary phenomenon but one that has deeply entrenched sociohistorical roots. Leonard E. Barrett explains that Jamaica—as the crown colony of the British Empire when it reigned supreme—experienced a high degree of brutality because of the disproportionate ratio between the large slave population and few planters. As such, Barrett states that "slavery in Jamaica lacked any vestige of humanity. A handful of greedy planters held absolute power over thousands of slaves. Only through violence could such complete domination by a minority be initiated and perpetuated."[5] Under slavery, as Orlando Patterson notes in *Slavery and Social Death*, "the relation of domination" verges on the "limits of total power" from the master and the "total powerlessness of the slave."[6] Scholars such as Kamau Brathwaite have critiqued Patterson for overlooking the degree of agency many slaves held. Nonetheless, by referencing the extreme forms of violence in Jamaican slave society, Patterson provides an important sociohistoriographical basis for his concept of social death, wherein the "slave's powerlessness" was a symbolic substitute for death on a social level because of the "direct and insidious violence," "natal alienation," and "dishonor."[7] Indeed, since Jamaica was not a settler colony, its sole purpose was as a slave economy that was kept alive by violent means, implemented so as to coerce slave labor. In describing the kind of brute force needed to maintain slavery in Jamaica, Terry Lacey states that the "plantocracy used the British army and a system of parish constables to supplement its own army of professional terrorists—the overseers and slave drivers. Brutality against the slaves reflected a general style of social control."[8]

Linking historical violence to contemporary instantiations of violence as transhistorical repetition, I point out that the modern-day police force has a genealogical relationship as a paradigmatic substitution for the slave drivers or constables who committed acts of violence against both the mind and body—in which the imagination was an important consideration for experiencing the sublimity of terror along with its symbolic and ritualistic staging, as spectacular, theatrical exhibitions in slave society. In this sense, affect was linked to both mind and body, the sensuous aspect that connected to the slave's imagination. This integration of mind and body suggests a contrast to the Cartesian mind/body dualism that informs the Western philosophical understanding of terror and as an instantiation of the sublime in the Kantian formulation, for instance. As I argue, for the historical and contemporary slave, the embodiment of the sublime suggests that the imagination interiorizes terror. Another key difference is that, for the slave, the violence of the sublime remains ever-present without experiencing a transcendence through the faculty of Reason that Kant privileges. It is for this reason that I use the term slave sublime as an aesthetic concept, signaling a departure from the Kantian worldview. Simultaneously, it extends our understanding of social death, moving beyond a historiography of slavery, to consider violence from the perspective of the slave—to show that the sublime is linked to interest, rather than disinterest as Kant asserts. This is particularly important for demonstrating how slaves have found agency no matter how despicable and overwhelming their material existence, thus underscoring the important role of the imagination to a world hinged upon violence.

Suggesting the importance of the imagination to the mechanisms of colonial domination, Aníbal Quijano explains that when we think about colonization, we must be mindful that it entails more than just "subordination" to a European culture as an "external relation." As he argues, we must also consider the interiority, the fact that it involves "a colonization of the imagination of the dominated." Quijano prompts us to understand that conquest of the imagination targets "specific beliefs, ideas, images, symbols or knowledge." It is a mode of "repression" focusing on "the modes of knowing, of producing knowledge, of producing perspectives, images and systems of images, symbols, modes of signification, over . . . instruments of formalized and objectivized expression, intellectual or visual."[9] To put it simply, and by no means providing a reductive analysis of Quijano's comprehensive argument, is to consider the central role that the imagination plays in ideation, whether the creation or reception of knowledge, as in perceptions or worldview, be it in the tangible or supernatural realm. Above all, Quijano echoes Frantz Fanon's idea that the European control over signification (what Quijano refers to as "modes of knowing" and "images and systems of images") has created a realm of psychic violence that distorts colonized people's self-image. The descendants of slaves continue to articulate this experience of the slave sublime in a distorted language (similar to Roland Barthes's discussion in *Mythologies*)[10] that is punctuated with the grammar of violence in which the imagination connects with interest with regard to affect and its mediation.

For the Jamaican slave, sublimity as an affect of violence was integrally connected to the imagination. Historian Vincent Brown points out that physical violence was not the sole principle for instilling fear and authority: "slave masters did not achieve the fear requisite to maintaining control over the enslaved by physical force alone"; it was equally important for them to maintain power by "trying to terrorize the spiritual imagination of the enslaved. To do so, the slave masters projected their authority symbolically through spectacular punishments committed upon the bodies of the dead."[11] Below, Brown describes the "ghoulish" manner in which slave masters targeted the slaves' spiritual imagination as a site of terror:

> Nearly everyone remarked, such ghoulish displays served clear purposes. They used dead bodies, dismembered and disfigured as they were, as symbols of the power and propriety of slave masters. Severed heads stood sentry over the plantation landscape, watching passer-by, white, black and brown, conveying warnings to potential rebels and assurance to supporters of the social order. Such symbols were thought to be effective because they were affective: they harnessed the other-worldly and the sacred to specific bodies, places and narratives, and those to the social power of rulers. These conventions were largely inherited from the British theatre of social control but the Jamaican plantocracy had to re-stage several elements of the exhibition.[12]

This affective strategy was purposive in that it allowed slave masters to exert fear through the symbolic realm by targeting the spiritual imagination of the enslaved, not only by posthumously mutilating and beheading dead bodies as iconic displays of their power, but also by denying proper funeral procedures to prohibit a rite of passage to the afterlife.[13] As theatrical optics of violence, the mutilated body parts would be put on display to serve as a deterrent force. These forms of psychic violence functioned as assaults to the slaves' cosmological beliefs since many slaves believed in a spiritual transcendence to Africa after death. Indeed, such mutilations served to inflict psychic or spiritual violence against the imagination through a symbolic discourse based on the plantocracy's performance of violence. By staging dismembered body parts, these iconic displays of violence functioned strategically for establishing and maintaining authority—within both the spiritual and material worlds.[14] These theatrical displays of mutilated body parts, what Brown calls "carnivalesque dramas," were gruesome means and an affective strategy for dramatizing the plantocracy's power and for conveying the notion that, even in death, freedom as spiritual transcendence was unattainable—that the slaves would be trapped eternally in the material world of their masters.

The display of mutilated bodies that Brown discusses can be thought of in this regard to affect and to the social aspect of the symbolic power of "social death" because it establishes the unquestioned authority of the master over both the present and afterlife of the slave. In his exposition of "natal alienation," a constituent element of social death, Patterson links this form of domination to the cultural realm as "secular excommunication" because the master bases his authority on "the control of symbolic instruments."[15] Patterson connects this element of social death to the "dishonor" experienced by the slave, which demonstrated "the sociopsychological aspect" of the master's dominating power.[16] This symbolic power had "an intellectual and a social aspect": the intellectual facet has a mythic quality much like the "validating" aspects underlying religious dogma, while the social aspect connects to ritualistic practices that are "highly formalized and ceremonial."[17] It was a hegemonic strategy to represent violence as the norm, as the nature of domination that controls both physical death and social death, as both involve dishonoring the slave through the staging, the formalized and ceremonial display of mutilated bodies. Another way to look at it is as coercive domination represented as the norm, which is, of course, established and structured through violence for domination and exploitation.

The intention of ritualistic violence involving mutilation was not only to destroy the slave's cultural beliefs but also to use these cultural beliefs against them to instill fear and terror through the imagination, especially when we consider Elaine Scarry's arguments about torture in *The Body in Pain*. In relation to Patterson's idea of social death, torture can be thought of as similar to the natal alienation and dishonor of the slaves' body and spiritual beliefs. As Scarry defines it more concretely, "Torture consists of a primary physical act, the infliction of pain, and a primary verbal act, the interrogation."[18] In a way, Scarry explores a process involving torture that illuminates a relationship to social death and gestures to the slave sublime concept regarding the embodiment of affect resulting from the repeating histories of violence. On the Jamaican plantation scene that Brown describes, because (social) death was an imperative or objective of the torture, what was done both to the body and spiritual core in the form of public exhibition was a communal mutilation, not just of the individual body but also the collective, bodily corpus, while the interrogation was an inward, private matter. In the context of Brown's work, the purpose was to make the surviving slaves question their spiritual beliefs, thereby rendering the interrogation as an interiorized self-reflective act, as a psychic wounding to destroy the slave's world, their African worldview. Scarry reminds us that "Intense pain is world-destroying."[19] Here we may see a congruence between Patterson's idea of social death and Scarry's idea of mimetic death; for Scarry, it is a scenario in which the "body is emphatically present" and the voice is "so alarmingly absent."[20] In Pattersonian terms, this absence would be linked to the lack of legal protection, for example, the "social excommunication" that renders the experience of social death.

As a concept, the slave sublime extends both Scarry's and Patterson's very compelling arguments. Although Scarry's text focuses on torture, we must also consider structural violence as pertinent to this domain, especially given her description of pain, which is very relevant to the effects of structural violence in the ghetto. Under this theoretical framework, the ghetto, or other plantation structures, can be seen by extension as a torture chamber that symbolizes the embodied violence of its dwellers for whom there is little to no division between the private/individual and the public/collective bodily corpus. Scarry characterizes the torture chamber as the "dissolution of the boundary between inside and outside" that "gives rise to a fourth aspect of the felt experience of physical pain, an almost obscene conflation of private and public."[21] This is because the "prisoner is forced to attend to the most intimate and interior facts of his body (pain, hunger, nausea, sexuality, excretion) at a time when there is no benign privacy, for he is under continual surveillance."[22] Through the sliding signifiers of the slave ship, plantation, prison, and ghetto the transhistorical aspect of the torture chamber becomes clear: there is a glaring substitution of the slave ship for the plantation in which *change* remains *same* even in the modern-day, paradigmatic context of the prison and ghetto. In contemporary Jamaica, the ghetto and prison are likewise bounded spaces, limits within which the poor are kept and are held at the mercy of the police, soldier, and prison guard—the agents of state power. In chapter 4 of this book, I discuss Marlon James's representation in *A Brief History of Seven Killings* of the difficulty of escaping the ghetto, which always seems to move one step ahead of those who try to get out. This is because of the coloniality of power—the mechanisms of colorism, a color-caste hierarchy, and the state apparatus that limit social mobility. It is in many ways a torture chamber that also symbolizes the collective, structural violence to the bodily corpus of ghetto dwellers. In this light, we can consider Scarry's point that "There is nothing contradictory about the fact that the shelter is at once so graphic an image of the body."[23]

Although Scarry maintains that pain is "usually invisible,"[24] I argue that it is perceptible in the structural violence of the ghetto, the lack of privacy in the one-room shacks where otherwise ordinary private matters—shit, blood, soapy water—spill out into the public domain, as represented in *A Brief History of Seven Killings*. Such squalor symbolizes suffering in the ghetto, and with no avenues for escape, it is a virtual prison or torture chamber.[25] We can think further about this structural violence of the ghetto as transhistorical in relation to the impact on the individual body and to Scarry's apt description of the pain that torture produces. Here, we may think about the planned failure of emancipation to preserve the specter of the plantation, especially through the withholding of resources (and lack of infrastructural development) in postcolonial Jamaica as a display of state power as overt agency. In the process of torture, as Scarry observes, "the objectified pain is denied as pain and read as power, a translation made possible by the obsessive mediation of agency."[26] As I argue, this overwhelming aspect of violence that extends beyond the body into the physical environment makes it sublime and its unyielding repetition takes sublimity into the terrain of the slave sublime, a transhistorical experience that violates a division between the public and private.[27] This transhistorical experience of plantation structures is at the heart of this book's exploration of the slave sublime concept—in which terror is not only embodied but ever-present.

With regard to this notion of the slave sublime, there are two crucial issues that I investigate, affect and mediation—that is, the overwhelming realization and the extreme physiological impact stemming from the perpetuation of plantation structures—an experience that challenges a Kantian understanding of the sublime as cognitive and transitory: "Sublimity, therefore, does not reside in anything of nature, but only in our mind, in so far as we can become conscious that we are superior to nature within, and therefore also to nature without us (so far as it influences us) . . . Reason exerts dominion over sensibility in order to extend it in conformity with its proper realm (the practical) and to make to look out into the Infinite, which is for an abyss."[28] In my reading of Scarry's description of the overwhelming pain associated with torture, I see an implicit engagement with the sublime that moves beyond the cognitive basis to suggest its embodiment but also the resulting "political and perceptual complications."[29] With the slave sublime, I extend Scarry's point by suggesting a connection between embodied pain and the harnessing of the imagination as a means of mediating such extreme affect, freeing limitations often associated with expressing physical pain. This productive form of violence (that induces pain) functions also as a language that articulates agency as raw, brutal power: "Nowhere is the sadistic potential of a language built on agency so visible as in torture. While torture contains language, specific human words and sounds, it is itself a language, an objectification, an acting out . . . In the very processes it uses to produce pain within the body . . . it bestows visibility on the structure and enormity of what is usually private and incommunicable, contained within the boundaries of the sufferer's body."[30] As a contrast to the victim, the torturer remains connected to "voice, world, and self" while the "body and pain are absent."[31] It is for this reason that Scarry characterizes power as "fraudulent" because of "its distance from the body."[32] This helps us to understand the masterly discourse that underlies the Kantian sublime and its connection to Cartesian dualism, that is the separation of mind/reason from the body/imagination as a position of power that allows for the overlooking of bodily pain. We must, therefore, consider Scarry's apt question: "How is it that one person can be in the presence of another person in pain and not know it—not know it to the point where he himself inflicts it, and goes on inflicting it?"[33]

We can think about the role of reason in this distancing from the body and the disavowal or unrecognition of the other's pain: "All those ways in which the torturer dramatizes his opposition to and distance from the prisoner are ways of dramatizing his distance from the body. The most radical act of distancing resides in his disclaiming of the other's hurt."[34] We can also think of reason as a weapon, as an instrument of violence, especially in relation to Max Horkheimer's and Theodore Adorno's characterization of it as instrumental reason that is "radiant with triumphant calamity."[35] This mechanization allows for the disconnection from the body in a Cartesian fashion as transcendence over the body in Enlightenment ideology and the basis for the disinterested reason that Kant articulates. This disinterest is false, and this rationalization is what Scarry calls "the vocabulary of 'excuse' and 'rationalization'" that has a "fixed place in the formal logic of brutality."[36] Scarry's focus on the body articulates Edmund Burke's notion of the sublime as a bodily experience in the colonial sphere, where power went hand in hand with violence as a display of agency. The brutal violence in colonial settings, similar to Scarry's exposition of torture, is a sublime experience that targets the body.

Under these theoretical considerations, I explore how Caribbean, primarily Jamaican, writers and musical artists are able to convey the overwhelmingly dire experiences of transhistorical violence, especially because of the politics of denying suffering or pain by state actors (a denial due to pain's supposed invisibility), while paradoxically gaining power and agency from said violence. The victims' harnessing of this complicated agency found within violence is also key to the slave sublime.[37] While Patterson's notion of social death speaks to the slave's circumscribed agency, the slave sublime recognizes a paradoxical agency that is bound up with idiomatic codes that repeat and articulate violence and pain, derived from plantation structures, as both infinite and communal. This is in contrast also to Scarry's implicit engagement with the sublime in which she characterizes pain's "unsharability" as symptomatic of its "resistance to language." Pain, she argues, is resistant to language and "actively destroys it, bringing about an immediate reversion to a state anterior to language, to the sounds and cries a human being makes before language is learned."[38] While the latter rings true to some degree as being ineffable, a key difference from the slave sublime is the issue of shared or communal pain in brutal experiences, whether during the Middle Passage, in slavery, in prison, or in the ghetto. This pain is voiced through the body, the very site of violence. For African slaves and their descendants in the Americas, performance arose from the violence of plantation systems to express and make visible those brutal experiences of torture, what Brown represents as "carnivalesque drama"[39] and which Scarry similarly dubs as a display of power and agency as "a grotesque piece of compensatory drama."[40] In the context of the slave sublime, it is a mimetic language that is transferred to the body through performance.

While the mouth functions most often as the medium for language, the body serves less noticeably as the medium through which the symbolic language of violence is communicated. In *Violence*, James Gilligan states that "behavior can be just as symbolic as words; that like words, bodily behavior communicates meanings, often of astonishing specificity, about matters of life-and-death importance, which can be understood quite clearly, consistently, and reliably by those to whom the behavioral signs and signals are directed."[41] Gilligan identifies violence as rituals between individuals or among groups in which the conscious meanings of the "given [violent] behavior" are not clearly stated in what we regard as "language."[42]

In Jamaica, the violence that forged the historical encounters between the master and slave has been adopted by the latter as a mimetic language—a reenactment of transhistorical plantation violence—and as a nonverbal means of communicating the continued desire for freedom. Extending Frantz Fanon's and René Girard's notions about the mimetic potential of colonial violence, Dane Archer and Rosemary Gartner point out the tenets of social learning theory. As they suggest, violent acts "can provide a model or script, increasing the likelihood of imitative violence," and they explain that "civilian members" of society are "influenced by the 'model' of officially approved'" violence.[43] I argue that this transhistorical violence serves as a script that is reenacted in modern-day Jamaica, not only as illegal practices by the state and citizens, but also through musical performances that function as restagings or repetitions of plantation-era violence.

These mimetic performance rituals involve both pleasure and pain during which the mind and body are essential for the processing and unleashing of pent-up violence. In poststructural theory, *jouissance* is connected to a transgressive pleasure that stems from the subject's splitting. It is Lacan's notion of a special kind of ecstasy that extends beyond Freud's pleasure principle, which connects to the death drive as a futile search for an unachievable whole. It is a paradoxical mixing of pleasure and pain in excess that violates boundaries and that, in some sense, is overwhelming or distressing because of the inability to give form to the experience. In such terms, an underlying element of the sublime is perceptible. In the case of the slave sublime, the split subject can be equated with a double bind, especially given that the slave is a transhistorical subject who is repeatedly alienated from *jouissance*, from freedom, as a result of entering the imaginary, the mirror stage of plantation-derived violence that defines Black subjecthood in the Americas. This subjecthood is marked by the entrance into a symbolic order that is defined by the social construction of racial difference, in which linguistic signification as violence can be read as "the name of the father"—colonial law, language, and culture built upon violence. The "name of the father" (the plantation system supported by various laws, for instance) is that which denies power to slaves, making it difficult for them to resolve the identification process in the formation of subjectivity.

The effect of this power is that the slave (historical and contemporary) is disciplined through the authority of the master and interpellated as a dishonored figure, as constructed through the apparatus of slave plantation systems. In other words, that which is supposed to ensure the formation of the Subject is precisely that which denies them subjectivity. In this sense, I suggest a Lacanian reading of Patterson's notion of social death—the natal alienation, dishonor, and secular excommunication—in order to understand the slave sublime concept in which violence is the Real. If, as Dominick LaCapra suggests, the "repetition compulsion, the death drive, and trauma with its symptomatic aftermath" that is situated beyond the Freudian concept of pleasure principle can be identified as the "real,"[44] then we can think of the repetition of violence as the slave sublime as transcending limits, as excess that is *jouissance*, as an ecstatic negative pleasure that leads to pain rather than pleasure—that is, the disheartening paradox of harnessing violence as a complicated agency, especially in the current neoliberal environment of globalization that further undermines the possibility of freedom, wherein the sublime presence of slavery is reimagined as the Real of freedom.

It is crucial, therefore, that we understand that the violence in Jamaica does not just stem from contemporary factors alone, but occurs also as reenactments of the spectacular violence that was communicated during slavery—which have been repeating during the various stages of Jamaica's history. Decades after formal emancipation was granted, the structural violence evidenced by the scarcity of material necessities and withholding of freedom led to the Morant Bay Rebellion in 1865. A number of historians argue that true liberty was "thwarted" by the efforts of planters in Jamaica, who maintained a virtual system of slavery to flout the English parliament's decision, which ignored their local concerns by abolishing slavery. More specifically, Michael Craton argues that "When emancipated slaves found their aspirations thwarted by their former owners, discontent mounted . . . [A]ll of these major outbreaks were essentially similar to the late slave rebellions, signifying how little conditions had actually changed with formal emancipation."[45] As a response to this reenactment of a slave rebellion, the colonial Jamaican government reacted in kind, with a violence similar in magnitude to the plantocracy's during slavery, killing "nearly 500 people" and "seriously wound[ing]" hundreds more to send a message about what would happen when their power or authority was questioned.[46] Richard D. E. Burton discusses the horrific manner in which the people were killed: "Without a clear strategy or definable objective, the uprising lost momentum and . . . the forces of law and order . . . crushed with a systematic use of violence and terror that even today [beggars] belief. Insurgents and bystanders alike were flogged (often with whips threaded with wire), raped, shot, or hanged . . . [H]uts, even whole villages, were put to the torch."[47] Burton's description of the massacre suggests that the colonial forces maintained a monopoly on violence as the planters did during slavery—a time when rape, hanging, and acts of burning were routine symbolic displays of the master's spectacular power.[48]

As with the current neglect of the West Kingston garrison communities (ghettos) where one-third of Jamaica's population resides, these forms of violence that arose during the post-emancipation period were directly related to the planned structural violence, a way to prolong the experience of slavery and to limit the former slaves' freedom. Gad Heuman and David Trotman argue that rather than providing social mobility through access to education, the colonial government "preferred to place their bets on the coercive promise of the law, police and prison" and "used their continued control of the political apparatus in order . . . to define the responses of the emancipated as criminal activity and therefore to use the brute force of the law to support their efforts to define the limits of emancipation and the meaning of freedom."[49] The planters used "political power to restrict access to land . . . to frustrate the ambitions of the emancipated to define the meaning of their freedom" through legal restrictions.[50] The former slaves' lack of land ownership during the post-emancipation period suggests their transformation from slaves to "reconstituted peasants" and proletarians, as Sidney Mintz argues. As he puts it, the newly emancipated were "doomed to straddle two economic adaptations—as reconstituted peasants and as rural proletarians—neither of which could become economically secure."[51] Thomas C. Holt has argued in *The Problem of Freedom* that emancipation had little to do with personal liberty as it was caught up with the abuses of the newly imposed industrial/capitalist labor system, which needed its own kind of coercion and discipline, similar to a slave economy. Furthermore, this kind of freedom, which fosters self-interest, prompts competition in a society where scarcity is the norm, and this scarcity is utilized by the power structure as a coercive force for motivating work. The structural violence coupled with the state-sanctioned physical violence that was routinely used by the power structure during both slavery and the post-emancipation periods is what maintains the current slum conditions in West Kingston ghettos.

The ex-slave's desire for freedom remained unrequited, what Lisa Lowe calls "promised freedoms" or "freedoms yet to come," suggesting a liminal space between the desire for freedom and its postponement.[52] Neil Roberts offers a similar perspective in his concept "freedom as marronage." Roberts's notion of marronage posits post-emancipation unfreedom as a liminal and relational space between slavery and freedom.[53] While the context of Roberts's argument in *Freedom as Marronage* is slightly different from the issues under consideration in this book, it is worthwhile for understanding the reality of unfreedom in post-emancipation Jamaica, which conflicted with the expectation of complete liberation from one's chains. The reality in the post-emancipation period, however, was that the physical chains were translated to symbolic chains of oppression through structural modes of violence. Of the four elements Roberts outlines as constitutive properties, I appropriate "distance" for understanding the way in which this idea conveying spatiality suggests that the newly emancipated were not too far removed from plantation life and its systems of dominance. Their discontent stemmed from the recognition of the limits that were imposed upon the true acquisition of liberty, because slavery was transformed into structural modes of domination with the transition to a capitalist system.

As a concept, structural violence within a capitalist system not only has a semiotic relationship to slavery and its institutionalized practices as a paradigmatically substituted form of oppression, but, more specifically, it has an underlying semantic dimension as well: "Slavery is one of the more basic forms of structural violence . . . It is structural violence because the violence exists because of the structure of the positions of slave and master or slaveholder. It is because one is defined as a slave that one experiences the violence of a loss of one's humanity."[54] In this sense, the semantic significance of the word "structural," as having its foundation in language, is important. This definition highlights also the issue of interpellation—of being hailed through language and "defined" as a slave, which calls attention to the exercise of power by the speaking or viewing subject. As the definition suggests, the master's verticality and the slave's horizontal position in the hierarchical power structure indicate a semiotic dimension of violence. As I discuss in chapter 2, which deals with NourbeSe Philip's *Looking for Livingstone* and *She Tries her Tongue*, these structural elements of power relate to the operations of language, wherein verticality denotes a paradigmatic aspect of language in which metaphor functions as substitution, while the horizontal element of language corresponds to a contiguous dimension with metonymy. With regard to grammar, there is a clear alignment between violence (a subject of power) as allied with a paradigmatic dimension and subordination (as an object of power) as a sign of contiguity and syntagm, given slavery's unbroken continuum.[55] It is through language and its production of discourse that a person is defined or positioned as a slave, and it is through discursive practices, such as legal statues, that the slave's humanity is denied,[56] thereby providing legitimacy for inhumane brutality.[57]

Mapping this spatial positioning through a linguistic frame reveals how violence is structured paradigmatically. The verticality is perceptible with respect to the hierarchical elements of power wherein the up-down spatiality denotes inequality. This verticality of power between master and slave parallels the Global North's position of power, as displayed by the United States' current international policy-making decisions in which the fate of subordinated countries and their citizens in the Global South is sealed, yet the violence remains unseen as it is cloaked in the rhetoric of bringing "freedom and democracy," to quote Ronald Reagan. Reagan's neoconservative perspective aligns freedom with laissez-faire capitalism and the positivist myth about the linear progression of history. The ideology that informed the practices of slavery and colonialism during the age of empire has been *changed*—but remains *same* in kind as a metaphoric substitution—for the rhetoric of neoliberalism and the free market discourse of global capitalism. Today, despite the legal proclamation ending Jamaican slavery in 1834 and the granting of independence in 1962—signaling the end of slavery and colonialism as formal practices—freedom is continually forestalled as the substituted forms of governance have deliberately masked their violence through rhetorical and discursive practices.[58] Ronald Reagan's 1982 remark that the Caribbean Basin Initiative would bring "freedom and economic vitality,"[59] a mask for the capitalist and neoliberal agenda for American neocolonial domination over the Caribbean, is a reminder that such rhetorical strategies are still being performed in the abeyance of freedom.

I refer to this perpetual substitution as "the changing same" to characterize the historical repetition, the ways in which one system of dominance is substituted for another in a paradigmatic fashion, which privileges metaphor to suggest similarity. With some modification to focus on the mutability of colonial power, I borrow this concept of "the changing same" from Amiri Baraka, Deborah E. McDowell, and Paul Gilroy. In his 1966 essay "The Changing Same (R&B and New Black Music)," Baraka, known as LeRoi Jones at the time, coined the term to characterize the dynamic freedom or "essence" of African American music to "exist (and the change to) in the existing, or to reemerge in a new thing."[60] With special emphasis on R&B music, he argues that, despite its many incarnations, the music has symbolically "remained the exact replication" of Blacks in Western societies for whom this art is a cultural expression of an "un-self" that represents the convergence "of a one-self."[61] Gilroy signifies upon Baraka's definition of the changing same in his 1993 book *The Black Atlantic*, while challenging ideas about ethnic essentialism and pluralism, as a way to reconceptualize Blackness (seeing Blackness as a cultural trope rather than as a fixed social construction). In turn, McDowell in her 1995 book *"The Changing Same": Black Women's Literature, Criticism, and Theory* credits Baraka in her use of the term to characterize the "shifting vocabularies" in literary studies in which "terms and modes of inquiry has remained the same." McDowell cautions, however, that even when sameness seems apparent, when "we look again" we will come to "know with certainty that the ways things stay the same are always changing."[62]

I use the term the changing same as a way of speaking about the metamorphic power of plantation and colonial systems, which seem to change yet remain the same as they assume new forms of domination across historical epochs—and, in response, the shifting modes of resistance, which include articulations exemplified in African-derived religious and musical performances. I draw upon philosopher Achille Mbembe's definition of the Real and power in relation to this consideration of change and sameness: "Faced with a real that is characterized by multiplicity and an almost unlimited capacity for polymorphism, what is power? How can it be acquired and conserved? What is its relationship to violence and trickery? Power is acquired and conserved owing to its capacity to create changing relations with the half-world of silhouettes, or with the world of doubles."[63] Mbembe goes on to explain that "Power cannot be enclosed within the limits of a single, stable form because, in its very nature, it participates in the surplus. All power, on principle, is power thanks only to its capacity for metamorphosis."[64] Essentially, the violence from slavery is now reimagined materially by power structures in the Global North as a means of prolonging social death into a newer form of oppression, namely the neoliberal economic system underlying globalization. In this continued deferral of freedom, I argue that slavery is ever-present, what I refer to as the slave sublime, a reformulation of the Kantian sublime, to characterize the high magnitude of psychic violence stemming from the stark realization that plantation structures continue in Jamaica (changing while remaining the same) to suggest that this instantiation of the sublime has both an imaginative and bodily dimension. This magnitude of the slave sublime prompts the descendants of slaves' mimetic responses to the transhistorical, repeating histories of violence.

Defining Violence: An Interdisciplinary Approach

Slavoj Žižek identifies three forms of violence: subjective, objective, and systemic. The first deals with scenarios in which there are identifiable agents of violence, whether as individuals or representatives acting on behalf of the state's power apparatus. The second, objective violence, is a somewhat abstract form of violence in the sense that it has been shaped by the rise of capitalism and the exchanges between material production and social interaction—what Žižek sees as exemplifying the Lacanian Real, not simply because of its connection to a kind of "systemic" violence of our social order that has "uncanny" undertones, but more so due to the absence of concrete agents that points to the "'abstract,' spectral logic of capital that determines what goes on in social reality."[65] Invisible governments and institutions in the Global North (having military and economic power) exert hegemonic rule over countries in the

Global South. Situated within this power dynamic, the "'abstract,' spectral logic of capital" is akin to the Kantian sublime's devotion to Reason alone to the exclusion of emotions and imagination, which, in turn, suggests the Cartesian dualism that characterizes the Western frame of understanding, which denies and overlooks suffering.

The abstract quality of this violence, as I argue, stems from an ideological dimension that serves as a catalyst, especially when we take into consideration the abstract ideologies of neoliberalism (or neoconservatism) that have given rise to global capitalism but which have a much longer genealogy. This form of "mercantile reason," according to Mbembe, stems from "the emergence of the plantation and the colony . . . during which a new form of governmental reason emerged and was affirmed." Mercantilist reason also underlies "The expansion of liberalism as an economic doctrine and a particular art of governance . . . at a time when European states, in tight competition with one another and against the backdrop of the slave trade, were working to expand their power and saw the rest of the world as their economic domain and within their possession."[66] Neoliberalism has now become the dominant economic ideology, mainly because it has entered a "decontested" terrain, as Manuel B. Steger suggests. Because of this "decontestation," it has become narrativized as a master-narrative that has been grounded as a "strong discourse" servicing economic rationality as reasonable and objective truth.[67] In a way, Steger is pointing to the mechanism through which neoliberalism has been distilled into a myth. As Roland Barthes defines it in *Mythologies*, a myth conceals its identity by associating itself through similarity with other signs, while at the same time disguising its underlying ideology to become naturalized. Thus, through this process of naturalization, neoliberalism as the ideology underlying globalization becomes naturalized as a myth in the association of markets with the concept of freedom—in effect, erasing the significant historical genealogy of colonialism through distortion. This political strategy and mode of thinking has produced catastrophic, "systemic" consequences for Caribbean people because of the disregard for how so-called objective abstractions from imperialistic nations such as the United States affect the lives of real people who have been objectified in the ongoing pursuit of capital gains, reminiscent of the days of slavery and its own carnivalesque dramatization of violence. As Žižek suggests, it is crucial that we pull back the curtain from the center stage of the obvious display of physical violence to look at what is not as easily perceptible,[68] along the lines of Scarry's idea that pain is mostly invisible.

As an example of the invisible form, symbolic violence occurs within the structural and discursive elements of language; most notable is its power to produce and impose meanings—similar to my aforementioned argument about the discursive or semiotic elements of violence. Žižek explains that "there is a 'symbolic violence' embodied in language and its forms." He elaborates further by explaining that the "relations of social domination reproduced in our habitual speech forms . . . [are] a more fundamental form of violence still that pertains to language" and the "imposition of a certain universe of meaning."[69] As such, we may take into account also Steger's rhetorical notion that neoliberalism's "language has resulted in enhancing . . . political power to shape the world largely according to . . . ideological claim" because of the semantic link, the "ideological chains" that connect "'globalization' and 'market' to the adjacent concept of 'democracy.'"[70] Consider that the free market and invisible hand discourses of global capitalism—and its imposition in developing countries such as Jamaica with austere structural adjustments during the 1980s—had a clear relationship to worsening poverty and electoral waves of violence, which resulted in the deaths of at least 800 people. The CIA's intervention to destabilize the economy and to undermine the democratic election during this time certainly negates the discursive linkage of "freedom and democracy." It becomes a question, then, of whose freedom and democracy was at stake. The resulting gains in the U.S. economy during this period of recession provide a clue about the judging subject's identity. That the imperial power justifies its neocolonial relationship to Jamaica through recourse to the language of democracy—that is, (market) freedom, humanitarian militarism, etc.—is actually more revealing about the imperialist's desires and material investments. Certainly, this was an uncanny repetition of the Morant Bay Massacre: in this case, the capitalist imperative of the neocolonial master was threatened by Jamaican Prime Minister Michael Manley's perceived alliance with Fidel Castro. Time and again, we've seen the destabilization of countries in the Caribbean and Latin America, such as Nicaragua under the Sandinista government or Grenada under Maurice Bishop, which the United States perceived as a communist revolt against its capitalist hegemony. These interventions contradict the United States' neoliberal myth in which freedom is aligned with the market and its natural noninterventionist forces. These examples articulate on a profound level Žižek's third notion of violence as "'systemic' violence, or the often-catastrophic consequences of the smooth functioning of our economic and political systems."[71] In many ways, Žižek contemporizes our understanding of violence by pointing to the notion that violence has both a concrete and an abstract element, that it even exists within the recesses of discourse that legitimize violence—such as the catastrophic consequence of maintaining the vertical relations of power, the economic and political structures in the Global North, at the expense of subordinated nations in the Global South. Under such circumstances, power is derived from and maintained through systemic violence.

In *Critique of Black Reason*, Mbembe provides us with a compelling, poetic definition of power that he attributes to a skillful performance of evading identification because of its changeability, its metamorphic power: "Power comes to those who can dance with the shadows, weave tight links between their own vital strength and other chains of power always situated in an elsewhere, an outside beyond the surface of the visible. Power cannot be enclosed within the limits of a single, stable form because, in its very nature, it participates in the surplus. All power, on principle, is power thanks only to its capacity for metamorphosis."[72] This metamorphic ability connects to the changing same of power as a paradoxical and antithetical idea that *change* can remain the *same*. One way to understand this concept more fully is in relation to Paul Ricoeur's concept of *idem* identity, which suggests a self-constancy as unchanging sameness.[73] It is the recognition of the *self* as *self* despite change or mutability to suggest the permanence of the self throughout time. In a manner similar to Ricoeur's *Oneself as Another*, the power that Mbembe describes has "the goal of becoming another . . . while remaining the same, to marry new forms of life and constantly enter into a new relationship." Not only does Mbembe's characterization of power fuse Ricoeur's concept with Žižek's idea about subjective violence's catastrophic force that leads to "destruction, loss, and death," but it is useful also for understanding the discursive or rhetorical force of mercantilist reason and its transhistorical genealogy—"to give and receive forms" and simultaneously to "escape existing forms" as it changes or morphs over time "while remaining the same."[74] This paradigmatic power betrays its continued colonial ethic of violence, and of this identifiable trait, Mbembe states, "Colonialism cannot be understood without the possibility of torturing, of violating, or of massacring"; it "is a grotesque and brutal power that in theory brings together the attributes of logic (reason), fantasy (the arbitrary) and cruelty."[75]

I use these ideas to contextualize the changing same concept and the power that infuses it—the paradigmatic chains that rely on substituting one discursively driven economic principle for another while remaining the same in its practices. The pernicious nature of such power, to quote Mbembe again, is that is "situated in an elsewhere, an outside beyond the surface of the visible."[76] This is what makes it the Real, in the sense that it cannot be pinned down. It is amorphous and metamorphic. It "danc[es] with the shadows"[77] as a display of its tantalizing essence. With regards to mimetic desire and the replication of this tantalizing violence, metamorphosis is like-wise the key to Anancy's subversive power in Caribbean folklore, and when utilized as aesthetic strategy and display of agency by Caribbean writers and musical artists—as mimetic power—it provides endless signifiers that convey distortion and ambiguity because of the amorphous and changeable charac-teristics. It is a symbolic "dance of possession," à la Fanon, that in some ways is a subversive reenactment of power and the violence that is endemic to this kind of metamorphic ability.

From a psychoanalytic point of view that predates Žižek's work, Fanon's work on the Algerian Revolution in *The Wretched of the Earth* also presents three modalities of violence: physical, structural, and cultural. Žižek's work connects to the underlying Hegelianism in Fanon's work, specifically the rela-tionship between language and subject formation and between objective and subjective violence. In other words, Fanon's work highlights the racism en-demic to the colonial order, its reliance on master discourses that reposition a colonized subject as object. Fanon's notion of physical violence points to the function of the military and police as agents of violence in the colonial system, in a manner similar to how the Jamaican slave and colonial regimes operated as a way of maintaining these institutions.[78] For Fanon, structural violence operates in binary ways, as Manichean divides, to instill inferiority and incite subordination. The withholding of basic resources such as proper living conditions—in the ghetto, for instance—and access to education are elements of this structural form of violence. Negating a colonized person's cultural identity and belief systems brings about cultural violence, similar to the Jamaica plantocracy's mutilation of dead bodies so as to negate the slave's spiritual belief in the possibility of transcendence after death. Together, these three forms of violence that Fanon outlines have a psychic dimension that demand release when internalized. However, this release, as Fanon explains, oftentimes occur in self-destructive ways, as misdirected political agency. He characterizes these violent acts as "collective autodestruction" and "fraternal battles," the means of releasing the "muscular tension" of "colonial frustration." As an additional means of releasing the pent-up violence, Fanon points out that the colonized will stage a dance of possession with "symbolic killings, fantastic rides, imaginary mass murders."[79]

At the core of Fanon's argument is the idea that colonized people will claim and repeat that same language of violence as their own as a means of purging the colonial system. But before that occurs they will be involved in a kind of "autodestruction," an internalized violence against fellow sufferers as a means of releasing the tensions from the ongoing colonial oppression. In Jamaica, the *sufferahs* as the descendants of slaves are the poorly educated, unemployed or unemployable, and economically challenged lower-class stratum of society who enact the daily routine of violence against the establishment—and, in particular, against each other—in a manner that complicates agency as a misdirected political activity. Sartre explicates Fanon's idea best in the "Preface" of *The Wretched of the Earth* when he states that the "thirst for blood" is never quenched because the real enemy remains unavenged. Driven by their "delirium," what they have done instead is appropriate the learned language of terror against each other. Sartre explains further that the dance of possession is colonized people's means of counteracting their "humiliation and despair" and that the ancestral spirits provide an outlet for their violence as they go into trances and exert themselves until their tensions are released. In other words, they revert to a kind of ancestral religion as another way to combat colonialism.[80] I explore these issues in the first and last chapters of this book in my discussion of Pocomania worship and the performance of dancehall music, respectively. The implication is that performance practices function as a deterrent force, allowing colonized people to repress their conscious and unconscious desires as a preliminary stage before engaging in a bloody revolution to overturn the systems of violence.

In this Fanonian context, violence against the colonizer is rendered *justifiable* because it is retributive justice and, consequently, seems to vacate the moral responsibility, as Christopher J. Finlay points out. For Fanon, decolonization is a historical process and is, therefore, a "natural phenomenon; and since violence is seen as an essential part of this dynamic" it nullifies "moral responsibility," displacing it "from the individual to a natural process."[81] In this context, the retributive violence against the colonizer is "presented as a necessary part of the preparation of true revolutionary subjectivity." By expressing violence toward the colonizer rather than a "surrogate victim," this third stage allows for the (re)emergence of subjecthood from under the yoke of colonialism.[82] As Fanon himself points out, decolonization "transforms spectators" into "privileged actors" who "bring a natural rhythm into existence . . . and with it a new language and new humanity . . . [T]he 'thing' which has been colonized becomes man during the same process by which it frees itself."[83] It is "at the moment that he realizes his humanity ['that he's not an animal'] that he begins to sharpen the weapons with which he will secure his victory."[84] As Sartre points out in the introduction of *The Wretched of the Earth*, colonialism is a mechanism that dehumanizes its subjects so as to give legitimacy to domination. As a mode of reversal, revolutionary violence provides agency to the economically and socially dispossessed—those whom Fanon identifies as the "wretched of the earth."

Despite his privileging of a male subject, there is strength in Fanon's argument, as suggested by its congruence with René Girard, who argues that the pent-up violence must find an outlet or else it will have devastating consequences for the individuals involved. But as Girard warns, "the mimetic character of violence is so intense that once violence is installed in a community, it cannot burn itself out."[85] In this sense, Girard's observations of colonized, indigenous Brazilians exemplify Fanon's ideas about the mimetic aspect of colonial violence that does not disappear once unleashed. Although Fanon's and Girard's arguments are pertinent to the situation in Jamaica, questions about the limitations of their thesis for a society in which there is no historical point of origin to return are certainly pertinent. A major problematic for Afro-Jamaicans is the overwhelming dislocation from traditional ancestral beliefs and the adaptation of an alien belief structure due to the dual legacies of slavery and colonialism. The disruption caused by the colonial experience manifests itself as a psychic and ontological break, as Paget Henry has discussed at length. While there are retentions of the African ancestral practices, including West African–derived traditions that inform spiritual practices such as Pocomania (as well as Rastafari), another way of considering this dilemma is to view the decolonizing process in Jamaica as a kind of liminal journey back to the originary violence of conquest and slavery—which provides the script for reenactments of violence, whether as a mimesis of colonial violence, "auto-destruction," or as a dance of possession.

A number of Caribbean scholars argue that the dance of possession (exemplified in Pocomania religious ritual) provides momentary outlets for pent-up violence. Gordon K. Lewis points out that such dances provide "emotional release from the ordinary frustrations of lower-class life" and that the dance tradition in Afro-Jamaican culture follows what he calls a "historical continuity unbroken by the great oppressive forces, economic and political reorganization."[86] There is a great degree of persuasiveness in what Lewis argues, given the fact that after the abolition of slavery, Pocomania rituals served as cultural artifacts from the slave era to function as a temporary antidote for colonial oppression because of their ability to reinvigorate the African spirit. Since slavery, it has continued to serve a similar purpose in relation to newer encroachments upon freedom to signal the *sufferah's* dislocation from sites of power. Edward Seaga echoes this viewpoint when he explains that the symbolic acts of possession in Jamaican Pocomania, which developed during slavery, provide a "spiritual, social and, at times, economic aid which was to them available in an acceptable and satisfying form."[87] Even during the more recent post-independence era, Pocomania practitioners still "are mostly outside the socioeconomic framework of the middle-class" and in Kingston many are "not employed on a full-time basis; when they do work they are usually laborers, higglers, household helps, fishermen and tradesmen's assistants, port-workers; rarely do they own land or property."[88] The more contemporary emergence of dancehall music out of the impoverished garrison communities, the ghettos in West Kingston, during the 1980s and its connection to the imposed structural adjustments by the IMF in many ways suggest that the music functions similarly as an opiate for the masses, despite the artists' engagement with and reflection on violence. Given these *sufferahs'* low socioeconomic status and dislocation from the power structure, they channel their (neo)colonial frustrations and engage (through music and religious possession) with the very forms of violence used against them and their ancestors, as a way of communicating their unconscious desires for freedom.

Connecting to reggae superstar Bob Marley's own reenactments, the more current engagement in symbolic murders/killings suggest that these performances from various Jamaican dancehall artists provide momentary cathartic release—not only for the individual artist but also for the community, the other *sufferahs*—to dispel violence rather than to create it. The actual catalyst for violence can be located in the three elements that Žižek and Fanon outline. In addition to the affect corresponding to the slave sublime, this book, therefore, investigates not only how historical violence can be memorialized and sociality articulated but also how best the mimetic aspect of violence can be adequately mediated, whether in literature or music, and represented in the face of ongoing state-sanctioned, systemic violence (à la Žižek) in which discourse such as the letter of the law is used paradoxically to justify unjust violence.

Extreme Violence and the Sublime

As further explication of the term slave sublime and its relatedness to the high magnitudes of terror and violence, I locate the Black body as an object and site of violence and pain, and I investigate how the judgment of that violence can be effectively communicated or represented by the descendants of slaves. Therefore, of primary concern is the identity of the judging subject and the form(s) of representation in literature and music with which they engage. I interrogate Immanuel Kant's and Edmund Burke's notions of the sublime by pointing out the applicability and the limitations of these two Eurocentric lenses, perspectives from which a masterly judgment can occur. Burke's sublime lays emphasis on the corporeal effects of certain perceptions as opposed to Kant's derivation of it from the cognitive faculties.

Kant's ethical and aesthetic ideas about sublimity in *The Critique of Judgment* and its effects are problematic when considering the judgment of violence within the (post)colonial sphere. There are two aspects of the Kantian sublime, the mathematical and the dynamic: the first is a contemplation of greatness that is not inhibited by limitations, while the second concerns an aesthetic judgment of nature "as might that has no dominion over us."[89] Kant regarded the sublime as a transitory mental response to an object of terror rather than the feeling of terror itself, a process during which Reason transforms displeasure to pleasure: "the Sublime as that of a like concept of Reason" and it "can be found in the mind; for no sensible form can contain the sublime properly so-called."[90] The Cartesian dualism that underlies the Kantian sublime is apparent. He separates the mind (reason) from the body (sensible).

In Kantian terms, the imagination is linked to the sensible and is aligned also with the beautiful, which he separates from the sublime. As Rundell explains, "Within the category of the beautiful, the imagination has a precise function. It is one of the indispensable, yet intricately linked dimensions through which the feeling of pleasure arises when we witness the form of nature, its purposiveness without purpose. Imagination and the understanding combine in a free play that does not presuppose a determinate concept."[91] Kant argues that disinterest is a moral quality of the judgment of beauty, its fundamental condition, since only the disinterested subject can be adequate to the universal subject who judges as if for all humanity. The sublimity of violence, which is also based on a moral judgment of disinterest, would actually be the ultimate expression of interest, of immediacy or gratification, and is antithetical by virtue in the attempt to produce a suspension of violence in the colonial sphere. Because of its magnitude and because Kant believes the mathematical sublime lies beyond our representative faculties, he suggests that it does "violence to the Imagination" and "violates" purpose: "the sublime . . . may appear as regards its form to violate purpose in respect of the Judgment, to be unsuited to our presentative faculty, and, as it were, to do violence to the Imagination; and yet it is judged to be only the more sublime."[92] For Kant, the sublime can be characterized as the experience of tension that results from the antagonism between the imagination and reason: "Sublimity, then, is the condition where reason and imagination co-exist in a relation of disequilibrium where both pleasure and displeasure are simultaneously expressed."[93] For this reason, Kant argues that it poses a challenge to the systems of representation because of its "formlessness."[94]

Thus, for Kant, there is a principle of pleasure that accompanies the pain of the mathematical sublime because of the challenges that it poses to representation: "The feeling of the Sublime is therefore a feeling of pain, arising from the want of accordance between the aesthetical estimation of magnitude formed by the Imagination and the estimation of the same formed by Reason. There is at the same time a pleasure thus excited, arising from the correspondence with rational Ideas of this very judgment of the inadequacy of our greatest faculty of Sense; in so far as it is a law for us to strive after these Ideas."[95] The paradox is evident, and for Kant the pleasure that underlies the pain comes from realizing the inadequacy of estimating magnitude with a "correspondence with rational laws."[96] The idea is that there are no adequate systems or modes available for representing it. Yet Kant locates pain only as an aesthetic judgment of the sublime: "The *quality* of the feeling of the Sublime is that it is a feeling of pain in reference to the faculty by which we judge aesthetically of an object, which pain, however, is represented at the same time as purposive."[97] He acknowledges that it is "impossible to find satisfaction in a terror that is seriously felt."[98] Pleasure or satisfaction comes from knowing that one is safe and "The Sublime is what pleases immediately through its opposition to the interest of sense."[99] In this way, again, Kant's formulation of the sublime suggests a mind/body dichotomy in which the mind and faculty of Reason are privileged. Kant's shortcomings stem from his problematic approach: the separation of "pure" theoretical reason from "practical" reason. Kant's philosophy centers on the *a priori* noumenal realm of reason rather than the phenomenal realm of feelings.[100]

Although Saidiya Hartman does not explicitly use the word sublime in *Scenes of Subjection*, part of her argument is essentially a critique of sublimity, more precisely a critique of the judging white subject who holds a masterly perspective. Implicitly, Hartman calls into question the pleasure/pain paradox that Kant identifies, as well as the very notion of disinterest that he posits as central to the sublime judgment. Hartman refers to the pleasure/pain paradox as the "complicated nexus of terror and enjoyment."[101] With a focus on slavery, what concerns her is "the spectacular nature of black suffering and, conversely, the dissimulation of suffering through spectacle."[102] She adds that the "dissimulation of suffering" is greatly due to the "fungibility of the commodity."[103] In the legal and commercial sense, the word "fungibility" points to the exchangeable or substitutable value of a commodity—the Black body, for instance, during slavery.[104] Hartman argues that the "relation between pleasure and the possession of slavery, in both the figurative and literal senses, can be explained in part by the fungibility of the slave," which is "the joy made possible by virtue of the replaceability and interchangeability endemic to commodity" and "the augmentation of the master subject through his embodiment in external objects and persons."[105] As Hartman explains further, what "makes the captive body an abstract and empty vessel vulnerable to the projection of others' feelings, ideas, desires, and values" is that "as property, the dispossessed body of the enslaved is the surrogate for the master's body since it guarantees his disembodied universality and acts as the sign of his power and dominion."[106]

What is significant here is that Hartman refutes Kant's ideas, although implicitly, critiquing his claims that sublimity involves disinterest and that the pleasure/pain paradox is relegated to the mental faculties of the judging subject. The problem with Kant's sublime is the Eurocentrism, as is evident by the Cartesian dualism between mind and body. Hartman gives significance to race in her reading of the sublime within the nineteenth-century context of slavery, a time when the taxonomic discourses about race developed. For Hartman, the Black body, in the economic sense, given its exchange or substitutive value, is nothing but of *interest* to the judging subject of that time period, a material factor that overrides moral judgment. Furthermore, as a corporeal being—rather than an abstract object for sublime judgment—the "beaten and mutilated [Black] body presumably establishes the brute materiality of existence" yet "the materiality of suffering regularly eludes (re)cognition by virtue of the body's being replaced by other signs of value, as well as other bodies."[107] To fully understand the significance of Hartman's critique, we must take into account the prevailing perspective of the nineteenth century, which denied the Black body's subjecthood—and thereby its ability to incite the affective or empathetic response of pain in others—because of its linkage to commodity value. In the following quote on mercantilist reason, Mbembe helps us to more fully understand the stakes in Hartman's argument: "Merchandise had value only to the extent that it contributed to the formation of wealth, which constituted the reason for its use and exchange. From the perspective of mercantilist reason, the Black slave is at once object, body, and merchandise."[108] In addition to unmasking the economic basis—its foundation within Eurocentric reason, which informs the judgment of the Black body as a sublime object, a materiality that negates moral disinterest—Hartman asks, in a manner that echoes Scarry, "how does suffering elude or escape us in the very effort to bring it near?"[109] As Hartman seems to suggest, the answer lies in the (re)cognition of terror and its physiological impact, not to mention the materiality or the embodiment of pain. What is implied also is that the consideration of sublimity cannot be disentangled from the identity of the (racialized) subject, a problematic that is apparent in the disinterested Kantian subject and his Eurocentric standpoint. Hartman's discussion about the "fungibility of the slave" informs my definition of the slave sublime, which, given the importance of the embodiment of pain, suggest a closer alignment with the physiological, Burkian sublime rather than the transcendental, Kantian sublime.

Burke's exposition of the sublime in *A Philosophical Enquiry into the Origin of our Ideas of the Sublime and Beautiful* focuses on a physiological dimension, the effect on the body and the subject's realization of corporeal or bodily limitations, a difference that greatly contrasts with Kant's notion of moral or spiritual transcendence. Burke situates the sublime within the context of terror during eighteenth-century colonialism in Ireland and moves toward a physiological understanding of the sublime in which perception not only registers in the mind but corporeally as well. Kant actually critiques Burke's formulation of the sublime as being too "physiological"—that is, not founded on a notion of the formal person or subject, but on the individual corporeal frame and its responses. Burke explains that "Without all doubt, the torments which we may be made to suffer, are much greater in their effect on the body and mind, than any pleasures."[110] Similar to the Kantian framework, the Burkian sublime is concerned with greatness to an infinite degree, which is beyond measurement or imitation, suggesting its ability to challenge modes of representation, but a key difference again is the bodily dimension, the relationship between bodily pain and the sublime: "Of *Feeling* little more can be said, than that the idea of bodily pain, in all the modes and degrees of labour, pain, anguish, torment, is productive of the sublime; and nothing else in this sense can produce it."[111] In addition to terror and pain functioning as the core basis for the Burkian sublime, Burke suggests that "power derives all its sublimity from the terror with which it is generally accompanied."[112] This argument that links power to the sublime can be read in relation to my earlier discussion about the Jamaican plantocracy's iconic and spectacular displays of mutilated body parts to instill terror and to articulate the immensity of their power. This notion about the connection between terror and power, therefore, is central to his formulation of the sublime, and "Indeed terror is in all cases whatsoever, either more openly or latently the ruling principle of the sublime."[113]

Burke's formulation of the sublime is applicable to the understanding of violence in the colonial sphere, and Luke Gibbons explicates the aesthetic-political nexus in Burke's reaction to the excessively violent and theatrical spectacle of executions during the Whiteboy movement. Referencing Burke, Gibbons reflects upon the legacy of colonial violence in Ireland and argues that the "oppressed is charged with the disruptive force of the sublime" mainly because the "ordinary violence of conquest has never been put to rest."[114] He coins the term, the "colonial sublime," which, as he explains, is "a fraught, highly mediated response to the turbulent colonial landscape of eighteenth-century Ireland."[115] It is very fitting that Gibbons uses the phrase "ordinary violence of conquest" as way to suggest that colonial violence has a naturalized mimetic potential: "This is the prospect raised by the spectre of the colonial sublime. In the absence of the tranquilizing effects of tradition, Burke's great fear was that the transformative power of terror would pass from master to slave, in keeping with the logic of the sublime whereby the endangered subject appropriated to itself part of the force which threatened to overwhelm it."[116] The "disregard for self-preservation can be attributed to the debilitating rather than the empowering effects of the sublime. Instead of internalizing or privatizing the power with which we are confronted, the individual looks to solidarity or 'imitation.'"[117] As such, solidarity with or imitation of the colonizer's violence points to the mimetic potentials of colonial aggression, which brings to light Fanon's and Girard's arguments.

Challenging Boundaries: Lawlessness of the Slave Sublime and Associative Imagination

I use the term slave sublime to foreground the mimetic responses to the ongoing histories of plantation violence in Jamaica. And although the slave sublime deals also with the issue of overwhelming magnitude, it does not override the imagination's capacity for representation. While Kant disciplined the imagination in his movement from the beautiful to the sublime, the slave sublime reverses this directionality, moving from the sublime to the beautiful as it privileges the imagination. As a concept, the slave sublime suggests that there is no permanent transformation of displeasure to pleasure in the contemplation of violence. Nonetheless, there is an element of aesthetic pleasure involved in the creation of and attention to the works of literature and music, even if it doesn't redeem the suffering of the oppressed. The historical accounts of slavery, apprenticeship, and colonialism are now reimagined materially as neocolonialism/globalization as a means of prolonging social death into new social forms of oppression. Even though my definition of the slave sublime connects to the corporeality of Burke's sublime, similar to Gibbon's explication of his concept the "colonial sublime," it moves beyond these formulations, given that race is an important consideration. It is important that judgment comes from the perspective of the descendants of slaves, whose ancestors were denied subjectivity and relegated to the status of objects. Moreover, Gibbons's concept of the "colonial sublime" does not explore the issue of representation and mediation through performance and does not take into account the issue of aesthetics in accordance with how histories of violence can be socially articulated and memorialized—a key reason as to why I explore, reformulate, and depart from the Kantian sublime, in particular, as well as the Burkian sublime because of such limitations.

The slave sublime, a reworking of Kantian and Burkian notions of the sublime, points to the dissonance between plantation rationality ("mercantilist reason") and the imagination in an antagonistic manner. Despite the dissonance, there is beauty in the slave sublime: the way in which the imagination retaliates against plantation-derived reason through subversion as a kind of lawlessness. Beauty remains tethered to the slave sublime in which the imagination's relationship to understanding remains intact while maintaining a paradoxical tension with reason by presenting the aesthetic of beauty, for instance, in the mimetic reenactment of violence as form and as derivative of plantation reason. That is to say, as a contrast to the way in which the Kantian aesthetics of the beautiful stem from the understanding's relationship to the imagination, providing "lawful freedom,"[118] the beauty in the slave sublime corresponds to agentive liberation from disinterested judgment and universalism as a complicated willfully unlawful agency. As I contend, the body and the imagination are crucial to the representation and performance of the slave sublime. In the slave sublime, the beautiful and the sublime are not separate and are actually wedded together in the same way that the mind/body split is repossessed, especially given the centrality of the imagination and body in performance (both religious and secular) and its aesthetic and semiotic codes.

The imagination fosters a subversive process by challenging ratiocentric and hegemonic systems. The associative imagination, in particular, links together the various plantation structures that it re-creates and re-produces through performance as a mode of creative (re)presentation. This liberatory display of the imagination seeks to break down boundaries, such as discursive formulations from which power is derived or historically specific time periods, despite the mutability of paradigmatic plantation structures across time. In other words, the associative imagination perceives time as transhistorical—making links, despite power's amorphous quality and ability to hide its presence by "danc[ing] with the shadows." It is the associative power of the imagination that forms relations between the past and present to identify the changing same. Thus the associative imagination has three key aspects: its empirical character, which is informed both by the sensible and intangible worlds; its power, which relies upon observations, intuitions, senses, and feelings so as to form images and perceptions; and its cognitive ability, which forms patterns and associations and seeks to break down existing systems of representation or to challenge existing boundaries.

The slave sublime is linked to dissonance and the beauty in chaos or disharmony between the imagination and reason because of the imagination's defiant expression of the desire for freedom.[119] In Jamaican music, for instance, part of the power of the slave sublime is derived from the associative imagination's modes of communication that correspondingly occur on three different levels: somatic, emotive, and cognitive. The first involves dancing, the second is associated with the emotional response, while the third deals with the cerebral or mental perception that results.[120] In particular, the somatic level is significant because it is the medium through which "nondiscursive" elements "operate on a physiological mode which affects the human body."[121] Here we can think about the dissonance of reggae, its accentuated downbeats that communicate directly with the body. Luke Ehrlich attributes this nondiscursive mode of communication to reggae's drum language, the "bass riddim, low in pitch and under the arrangement" which "moves past the intellect and communicat[e]s directly with the heart by massaging it in rhythm." The contrast of this "music of the heart" with keyboard sounds as an ensemble is where the sublime can found.[122] I discuss these elements in chapter 3 in my exploration of Bob Marley's reggae music, particularly notable in "Concrete Jungle" and "Rastaman Chant." To extend Ehrlich's point, I argue that reggae's power lies in its transgression of boundaries, communicating somatically, emotively, and cognitively with a discourse that shatters the Cartesian dualism and instead privileges both the body and imagination in its enunciation of the slave sublime rather than the Eurocentric sublime with its racist underpinnings that disregard Black agency, subjecthood, and powers of representation.[123] In Rastafari nyabinghi drumming, for instance, the body is important also for the reenactment of violence, a performance in which the aesthetic appreciation for the beautiful cannot be severed from the sublime judgment. These considerations suggest the need for reformulating the Kantian sublime, a limitation that stems from Kant's indebtedness to

Cartesian dualism and prescriptive subordination of the body to the supposed superiority of reason.

Calling for "thinking through sound" in his book *Sonic Bodies*, which seeks to reorient logos with sonic sensibility, Julian Henriques gestures toward the slave sublime concept when he embraces the imagination and challenges the dualistic understanding of knowledge and rationality that eschews the body in favor of the mind. As Henriques puts it, "the multi-sensory and multi-media apparatus of the dancehall session demands a different kind of understanding of the nature of rationality itself—as a challenge to what are conventionally considered the limitations of embodiment. This is one of the major rewards for thinking through sound."[124] Henriques not only prompts us to consider the significance of the imagination to what he calls "embodied knowing," primarily when immersed in the "excess of sound," but also the secular religiosity of dancehall music that "brings you to yourself, to and through your senses."[125] He provides an important discussion about the relationship between sound and the body, particularly the ways in which the dancehall experience allows the imagination to be guided on a sonic journey that is "both earthly and spiritual."[126] It is a ritualistic journey through sound, toward fleeting moments of catharsis and the reawakening of the self as "Self rather than Other" amidst the pleasure/pain paradox of excessive sound and bodily stimulation. Within this mode of sensory experience, the music functions as a "trigger for the memories, feelings and associations the crowd already holds."[127] What Henriques outlines are tenets of the slave sublime's embodiment and relationality to excess and repetition—and for which the imagination is crucial for making associations across time despite the overwhelming affect. Moreover, the recursive principles that underlie echo, delay, and reverb within the dub aesthetic of Jamaican music culture that Henriques highlights are noteworthy musical representations that encode mimetically the changing same—that is, "an understanding of identity, continuity and the constitution of phenomena in terms of difference, variation and propagation, as well as similitude, consistency and being."[128] This mimesis is not static, however, as dub enacts a challenge to hegemonic powers through sound as noise or "sonic disturbance." In essence, the changing same concept underlying the slave sublime can be discerned from Henrique's discussion about rewind and remix, which maintain principles of repetition as same and difference, what he calls "repetition with difference" that occurs as "*both* same *and* different in a system of analogue variation."[129] Building upon Henriques's ideas, I argue that the empirical knowledge derived through "thinking as sound" makes possible the associative imagination's cognitive ability to identify repeated modes of oppression that signal an echoing of slave plantation structures—their transhistorical recurrence—which maintains the slave sublime experience through violence.

As suggested in the various literary and musical texts that I explore, the imagination provides agency as a means of transcending boundedness, symbolically violating the limitations and boundaries imposed by reason, whether in terms of Eurocentric generic traditions in music and literature or master-narratives such as (neo)liberalism in economics. For instance, the Pocomania religious practices that I discuss in chapter 1 in relation to Andrew Salkey's novel *A Quality of Violence* can be read as representative of the discord with Christianity vis-à-vis the colonial regime's suppression of African spirituality in the transition from a plantation economy to a modern, capitalist structure based on classical liberalism. As an aesthetic of the slave, the slave sublime conveys an understanding of the nature of subjectivity in this sense, the seizing of agency, despite the fact that Caribbean identity and experience are framed by the violent histories of slavery and colonialism and its prolongation in the current era of globalization. Indeed, in this milieu, there is no rendering of "displeasure" as "pleasure" in the superiority of Reason over the sensuous Imagination, and because the *magnitude* of colonial violence is never permanently resolved, despite fleeting moments of catharsis, it perpetuates as it did during slavery. In the continued abeyance of freedom, there is no resolution. And in the absence of resolution, a key feature of many Caribbean novels, this slave sublime aesthetic suggests that the experience of terror is ever-present.

This overwhelming realization and awe that plantation structures continue is at the heart of the slave sublime affect wherein this aspect of the changing same of violence calls for mimetic responses. Although the slave sublime is both an embodied experience of terror and an aesthetic contestation that attempts to break the various forms of mimesis, at times the *sufferahs* as descendants of slaves engage in performative modes of violence that function as forms of distortion, mediation, and mitigation. While the Kantian sublime defies representation, dancehall music, for instance, strives toward representation by engaging with the structures of historical and contemporary violence as a codification of the slave sublime. In many ways, such performances bring into focus a mirroring of past violence—that is, a reflection of colonial culture as a regime founded upon and maintained by violence. With regard to the aesthetic judgment of the slave sublime, there is no long-term transformation of displeasure to pleasure in the contemplation of (post)colonial violence, insofar as slavery is ever-present. As a reaction to and representation of this traumatic state of being, the slave sublime challenges and calls attention to the various modes or forms of representation, whether generic, linguistic, or performative, as writers and musical performers engage with the very structures of historical and contemporary violence by harnessing the imagination's subversive power.

I investigate the modes of communicating and representing violence in the Caribbean, primarily in Jamaican literature and music. My investigation of genre is a means to understand the purposive aspect of representing violence and additionally the effective ways in which it is communicated back to the society. Inquiries about audience and reception are thus important. I explore whether one particular form of representation (literary or musical) is better or less well poised to represent the dimensions of violence, and to what degree that is dependent on who has taken up the task of representing violence, both in the historical and contemporary sense. Specific questions that I explore include the following: What kind of literature or music is produced within this context of violence, and how do sign systems of representation operate within the linguistic elements of violence, whether symbolic, literal, or performative? What are the functions of imagination and body in such representations? If we accept that modern-day political and economic arrangements are refigurations of the plantation system, then how do musical artists such as Bob Marley and Mavado or authors such as Andrew Salkey, M. NourbeSe Philip, and Marlon James engage with the tension between the sublime and its representation? How can art mediate and mitigate violence, and what tensions exist between the presumed high culture of literature and the low-class status of popular forms such as music? What are the aesthetics of violence that undergird the slave sublime? Are there connections between the slave sublime, morality, and (the desire for) freedom?

Chapter 1 focuses on Andrew Salkey's novel *A Quality of Violence* and addresses narrative voice and genre. More specifically, it explores the suitability of realism as a novelistic mode of representing the slave sublime elements of the post-emancipation era in Jamaica that replicates rhetorical strategies such as the rationalistic, humanist, and onto-epistemological discourses of slavery. The novel is set during the decades following the nineteenth-century abolition of slavery in Jamaica, a time when human autonomy was defined in relation to the ex-slaves' emancipation—essentially their freedom—from an African self-identification. As the novel suggests, Christianity was the colonial tool that represented the potential for transcendence toward the ideal of freedom from the supposedly irrational and superstitious world of African spirituality. This was a realm of belief that the colonial administration considered to be steeped in the imagination of Africa, which, in their view, necessitated a transition to the world of reason and logic, to Europe as the sign of civilization and humanization. This was a two-fold process of linguistic significations involving the enculturation to British cultural ideals with the use of the law to discipline and shape behavior in accordance with an emerging capitalist order. The expansion of the British Empire to Africa during this period of the nineteenth century coincided with the reemergence of religious censorship in Jamaica to fit into a larger colonial narrative about bringing the irrational beliefs of Africans (and African-descended peoples) into the fold of a rational Europe. As such, I argue that violence is also located in the discursive elements of power, wherein Western ideological formulations (such as Christianity and capitalism) maintain the sublime presence of slavery. Salkey's novel serves an important function in its attempts to portray the originary violence of the slave plantation: the ways in which this violence transcends the marginal space of the plantation; the challenge it presents to our cultural/ artistic imaginaries through its uncanny familiarity; its immense ability to disturb continually the consciousness of the slave's descendants; the challenges it poses to representation and attendant sign systems; and its slave sublime quality as slavery proves to be ever-present. Essentially, Salkey depicts colonial violence as the uncanny trans/scripts that are adopted from the slave plantation. In his representation, he attempts to move away from textuality toward the performative (music and rituals of Pocomania possession), suggesting the limitations of the realist novel as a genre and its incapacity to represent the extant nature of violence in post-emancipation Jamaica. Salkey writes this novel within the trickster tradition to maintain ambiguity so as to disguise his counter-hegemonic critique of rational self-consciousness. Ending the novel at the pinnacle of rising action and the spilling of the plot into the epilogue without resolution point to a notion of the sublime as transcendent surplus.

Chapter 2 explores issue of violence and social death within a larger Caribbean context to demonstrate the broader significance and applicability of this study and the slave sublime concept—beyond the narrow confines of a Jamaican case study. In this chapter, I explore boundary crossing as an element of the slave sublime aesthetic in the work of Trinidadian-Canadian writer M. NourbeSe Philip. Philip moves away from the realistic novel toward an exploration of poetic forms in order to investigate and subvert the paradigmatic quality of colonial violence, language structures, and narrative forms. She uses magical realism in *Looking for Livingstone* to represent symbolically the violence of colonization in nineteenth-century Africa and the related hegemonic discourses (as the racialized discourses embedded within colonial languages and Christian ideology), which undermine an African person's on-tological and epistemological frames of reference. Another text, *She Tries Her Tongue*, completes the work of *Looking for Livingstone*, as Philip opens up an-other angle on the questions of colonialism and violence within language structures. Her formal experimentation offers readers a way to think about how violence might enter into language art, and her writing, both in the ge-neric disruption and in the formal assault on standard English that it fore-grounds and thematizes, makes possible an engagement with the legacies of violence, both colonial and gendered. She draws upon the Rastafari privileg-ing of the letter "I" in words for giving "tangible form" to what she calls the "i-magination" to highlight the important role the imagination plays in ide-ation. By calling attention to the ways in which language as master discourse grammaticalizes, encodes, and regulates attitudes that subjectify Black iden-tity (which Fanon has characterized as the shattering of the Black imago), Philip subverts the negative constructions or substitutions of the Black i-mage within colonial languages. Because of the paradigmatic or the meta-phoric structure of state-sanctioned violence that relies on substitution, Philip uses the Trinidadian demotic as a means of destructuring through an oppositional syntagmatic (metonymic) process that violently disturbs the paradigmatic (metaphoric structure) of the colonial English language.[130] In essence, she messes with syntax or metonymic chains by the grammatical misapplication of verbs, nouns, and adjectives as she goes against the grain of their proper linguistic function and positioning so as to counteract symboli-cally the paradigmatic quality of (post)colonial violence and its vertical rela-tions of dominance, namely between masters and slaves. Even though Philip starts with a problematic quite similar to that of Kamau Brathwaite's "History of Voice," she rejects his notion of "nation language," which, as she suggests, is embedded in the masculine construction and discourses of the nation. None-theless, Philip, too, reaches a kind of deconstructive limit, able only to engage in the deconstruction but not in the construction of a positive alternative.

Chapter 3 discusses oral poetry as the counter-hegemonic potential of the first-person bodily discourse in Bob Marley's music and the ways in which performance offers a more viable medium for memorializing the histories of violence that are rooted in slavery. While Kant wants the sublime to keep Imagination in its place, to discipline it with Reason, Marley liberates the imagination to evoke historical memory and draws parallels between the po-litical landscape during slavery and that of his lifetime. I contextualize the slave sublime as an infinite violence that the imagination endures by discuss-ing the antithetical and paradigmatic idea of *change* and *sameness* in relation to "I-an-I," the embodied, plural Rastafari speaker in Marley's music who endures and calls to mind transhistorical memories of violence. As I argue, Bob Marley's music captures the repeating experience of slavery, but it changes this *same*, and repeats it differently in its aesthetic and political expression. It's not just a representation; it's a restaging and reenactment. These instances of repetition, therefore, are elements of the changing same that are inherent components of the slave sublime in its transcendence of time and space as what philosopher Paul Ricoeur calls *idem* and *ipse* identity. Such elements of *idem* and *ipse* identity are identifiable in Marley's representation of himself as a "bounded" slave despite emancipation.

Chapter 4 examines the significance of the imagination, beauty, madness, and Manichean despair in the ghetto as represented in Marlon James's novel *A Brief History of Seven Killings*. Giving an account of the political and social turmoil in Jamaica, Marlon James suggests the importance of the imagination to the slave sublime in his Marley-centric Man Booker Prize–winning novel. He describes Trench Town, a West Kingston garrison community where Marley once lived, as a "Third World slum" that "defies beliefs or facts"; it "immediately leaves the real to become this sort of grotesque" within the "imagination." James describes Trench Town in ways that underscore the central importance of the imagination—and the fact that he is articulating the focal idea of the slave sublime, the imagination, validates the urgent need for this term as an aesthetic, critical tool and vocabulary. And capturing even more profoundly the slave sublime and the centrality of the imagination for experiencing the infinite violence that is associated with the pervasiveness of plantation structures, James adds, "Beauty has infinite range but so does wretchedness and the only way to accurately grasp the full, unending vortex of ugly that is Trench Town is to imagine it."[131] Using a Foucauldian lens, I explore the issue of madness in relation to this slave sublime experience stemming from the logic of capital and the pervasive Babylon system. In essence, I explore how the ghetto as a plantation structure is a space of confinement depicting Babylon's Manichean divisions and use of the Jamaican police—who have a genealogical connection to slave drivers and constables during slavery and apprenticeship—in efforts to contain the so-called unreason linked to Blackness and poverty.

Chapter 5 explores the ways in which Jamaican dancehall music harnesses the slave sublime aesthetic as a complicated agency, specifically the paradoxical and subversive power of the Yoruba god Ogun, in their resistive art-form and as a mode of articulating democratic autonomy via the body through codes that blur the boundaries between literal and symbolic representations of violence. The deejay's active role in the process of mediation can be seen as a necessary part of making meanings and values in the political and social process of polysemic signification through language. A clear distinction between reflection and valorization (as a form of mediation) is very difficult to evince, as both the social practices of violence and the symbolic and actual expressions of it occur simultaneously and ambiguously. Certainly, what has been absent until now is a reading of dancehall as a metalanguage in which structures and form are imperative—both as discrete and dynamic polysemic entities that capture the ineffable aspects of language. Signs are taken at face value, thus overlooking the system of distorted meanings, its polysemic character and symbolic disguise, strategies that are inherited from slavery to disguise encoded meanings from the master class. In this light, Jamaican dancehall music can be seen as a subaltern weapon initiated at the level of both sound and textuality; it serves as part of a long performative tradition in Jamaica in which a revolutionary dialectic "waltzes" with nihilistic violence, performing (at times destructive) responses to state-sanctioned modes or forms of violence. While, in my opinion, music more readily and forcefully gives voice to different types of violence than the literary text, allowing the musical agents to receive and deliver violence, it is critical to investigate how much of this has to do with (and thus plays into or still manages to resist) the construction of Black music as violence (noise). As I contend, certain aesthetic forms prove inadequate to the representation of (post)colonial violence because forms inherited from the West—the realist novel, for instance— demand a particular kind of representativity and resolution. Dancehall, on the other hand, assumes the dissonant material of contemporary violence into its form which it signifies by its very refusal of resolution; it is not merely mimetic, as it does involve a reflection on form and history.

As the first book to use linguistic and semiotic theory to map violence on the paradigmatic (vertical) axis of language, *The Slave Sublime* suggests that in the Caribbean context violence is not only located within language, but that it is structured also as a language. The underlying idea in this book is that regardless of the immediate causes of violence, it is structured—both in the grammar of its practices and in the systems of representation that account for it—by a longer historical continuum than can be accounted for by present sociology or criminology. Contemporary disciplinary knowledges such as sociology and criminology explain away the persistence of psychic, physical, and structural violence through racializing discourses of pathology. In some ways, such disciplinary limitations are precisely what necessitates the rigorous interdisciplinarity work in this book. Thus, this book draws attention to the metaphorical importance of violence while encouraging readers to look beyond the narrow confines of its material affects. Indeed, my reference to the language of violence calls attention to the extent to which the structural logic of violence has infiltrated the immaterial realms of consciousness characteristic of the cultural universe of Caribbean daily existence. Furthermore, the book deals with the political economy of violence insofar as the structural logic of neoliberal economic theory represents the continuation of exploitative social and economic arrangements—current repetitions of slavery. Overall, the book is an analysis of physical violence, metaphorical violence, and their relation to the numerous vocabularies and cultural forces—literary, aesthetic, political, philosophical, religious—that confront it.

The Slave Sublime provides an interdisciplinary understanding of the current violence in Jamaica and participates in a newly developing scholarly conversation about present-day asymmetrical power structures and their historical origins. Recent works such as Michelle Alexander's *The New Jim Crow* (2010) and Robert T. Chase's *We Are Not Slaves* (2020) focus on the prison complex and justice system in the United States and its link to forced labor as it was under slavery. Christina Sharpe's interdisciplinary book *In the Wake* (2016) deals with the continued impact of slavery. Her concept "the wake" in its multiple meanings functions as a metaphor for the hauntological conditions surrounding life and death in the African diaspora and the various artistic modes of resistance. Likewise, Frank B. Wilderson III's combination of philosophy and memoir in *Afropessimism* (2020) speaks about the racialized structures that exist in which Black death is a spectacle and in which Blackness assumes a structural position in the continued experience of social death. *The Slave Sublime* addresses these very important Afro-diasporic issues within a Caribbean context by shedding light on the affective and representational elements that codify this experience as a response to iterations of plantation-derived violence. In her book *Exceptional Violence* (2011), cultural anthropologist Deborah A. Thomas argues that contemporary violence in Jamaica stems from the structural legacies of colonialism and underdevelopment, but she dismisses the cultural characteristics of violence that have been handed down in the society. From a literary perspective, Amy Clukey and Jeremy Well's special journal issue on "plantation modernity" in *The Global South* (2016) traces the reorganization of colonial systems (into modern-day sweatshop economies, for instance) in various places around the world, but none of the articles focus on the refiguration of slavery in the Caribbean. Although Gwen Bergner and Zita Christina Nunes's special issue of *American Literature*, entitled *The Plantation, the Postplantation, and the Afterlives of*

Slavery (2019), includes a chapter on Haiti and focuses on the biopolitics of the plantation structure (the mechanisms of power over knowledge and subjectivation), the various essays do not engage with the sublime and the linguistic or semiotic dimensions of violence that I explore. What further distinguishes my work is its interdisciplinary, comprehensive focus on violence, along with a theorization of the affective, aesthetic, and representational responses to the continuity of plantation structures and violence, what I conceptualize as the slave sublime, thereby codifying Gilroy's original concept. This term is distinguishable from Irish literary scholar Luke Gibbons's term the "colonial sublime" in *Edmund Burke and Ireland* (2003), which takes into account the embodiment of colonial violence per philosopher Edmund Burke but does not consider the importance of the imagination, which, as I pointed out, was a defining aspect of the spectacular characteristic of violence in Jamaican slave society.

Previous groundbreaking scholarly works on the issue of violence in Jamaican popular culture have not addressed adequately the aesthetic forms of representation, not to mention identifying contemporary violence and its representation as expressions of the slave sublime. In *Sound Clash* (2004), Carolyn Cooper casts the recurring themes of sex and violence in dancehall music as the expression of "primal" and "basic instincts" and argues that dancehall functions as an outlet for ritualized drama.[132] Although Cooper offers a phenomenal and well-intentioned response to critics who vehemently dismiss dancehall music, arguing that it contributes to a culture of criminality and misogyny, her retort suggests that she sees dancehall merely as an expressive outlet, not as a reflective medium that interrogates form. The agency that Donna P. Hope's *Inna di Dancehall* (2006) confers to both the creators and consumers of dancehall music who take control of their own representation is very compelling. What is missing, however, from her pioneering work, as some critics have pointed out, is an exploration of spiritual practices that codify violence. Focusing on the spatial and embodied practices of dancehall music, Sonjah Stanley Niaah's *DanceHall: From Slave Ship to Ghetto* (2010) offers a persuasive interdisciplinary approach from geography, sociology, and cultural studies. Rightly so, Stanley Niaah positions dancehall as part of an Afro-diasporic expressive medium, which she links to the experiences and practices of ghetto life that connect back to the plantation and slave ship. In a previous essay, "Dis Slackness Ting," Stanley Niaah questions whether the carnivalesque aesthetic can "explain the multi-dimensionality of DJ art in its sphere of production."[133] Although Stanley Niaah argues that the linkage of slackness in 1980s dancehall music to a political economy enacts a master-narrative, one cannot simply disregard the economic, political, social milieu out of which a particular representational form emerges. As I argue, one has to consider the counter-hegemonic potentials of the carnivalesque aesthetic and the ways in which it makes possible a subversion of meta-narratives, such as slavery, colonialism, and globalization.

The scholarship on Jamaican oral/scribal continuum is growing, accompanied by extant nonacademic publications, not to mention the ever-expanding outputs focusing specifically on Bob Marley's music, which build upon Kwame Dawes's innovative work *Bob Marley: Lyrical Genius* (2002). The new scholarly titles on reggae and dancehall music include many edited books, namely *Dancehall: A Reader in Jamaican Music and Culture* (2020), *Reggae Stories* (2018), *Reggae from Yaad* (2015), and *International Reggae* (2013). However, none of these books are concerned with the breadth of issues surrounding violence and the sublime that I raise in *The Slave Sublime.* In addition to the focus on violence, this book also continues the discussion about the significance of logos vis-à-vis sound/speech in the oral-scribal continuum of Caribbean literary and cultural criticism as theorized by twentieth century writers such as Kamau Brathwaite, Edouard Glissant, and Patrick Chamoiseau, among others. Carolyn Cooper's *Noises in the Blood* (1993) and Mervyn Morris's *Is English We Speaking* (1999) are early pioneers, with more recent books extending these earlier publications into interdisciplinary scholarship including Carol Bailey's *A Poetics of Performance* (2014) and Njelle Hamilton's *Phonographic Memories* (2019).

The Slave Sublime is distinguishable from previous publications as it attempts a paradigm shift in Caribbean literary criticism, as well as historiography, by breaking with naïve realist representations of slavery as mechanical violence by displacing the tendency to interpret slavery as merely a history of recrimination and dispossession. Put differently, the project initiates an end to the stasis of positivism in efforts to critically work through the historical implications of slavery in Caribbean literature and culture by advancing an aesthetics of slavery. In addition to challenging dogmatic assumptions about how best to understand Caribbean literature and culture, this project engages in a decolonization of aesthetics. In particular, it directly challenges Kant's conception of the sublime as, among other things, transcendence through disinterested reason. As such, the book seeks to reconfigure the sublime along the lines of the embodiment of terror and not as being primarily married to disinterested contemplation. It should be noted that, in addition to critically engaging dominant philosophical notions of the sublime, the book also critically intervenes in Afro-Caribbean philosophy. Although there are two dominant schools of thought in Afro-Caribbean philosophy (Poeticist and Historicist), neither school has focused on the significance of the sublime, particularly from the perspective of the slave in an uncompromising interdisciplinary approach. By grounding this project in the perspective of the slave, the book challenges assumptions about the mechanical effects of slavery in rendering the slave as lacking in agency and subjectivity. Even if slavery was a form of social death, such a condition need not entail that slaves lacked a complex and deep inner life, or that they were absolutely incapable of forging creative responses to the peculiar circumstances of their everyday existence. Accordingly, this book project explores areas others have traditionally ignored.

CHAPTER ONE

A Trickster's Challenge to Rationalism

Andrew Salkey's Discourse of the Imagination
in A Quality of Violence

Reason exerts a dominion over sensibility in order to extend it in conformity with its proper realm (the practical) and to make it look out into the Infinite, which is for it an abyss. In fact, without development of moral Ideas, that which we, prepared by culture, call sublime, presents itself to the uneducated man merely as terrible.

—Immanuel Kant, *Critique of Judgment*

Let us note this rather special inscription of a judgment programmed in nature, needing culture, but not produced by culture. It is not possible to *become* cultured in this culture, if you are *naturally* alien to it. We should read Kant's description of the desirability of the proper humanizing of the human through culture within this frame of paradox.

—Gayatri Chakravorty Spivak, *A Critique of Postcolonial Reason*

Western metaphysics has traditionally defined the human in terms of the possession of language and reason. In effect, there is no humanity without language. Reason in particular confers on the human being a generic identity, a universal essence, from which flows a collection of rights and values . . . The exercise of this faculty generates liberty and autonomy, as well as the capacity to live an individual life according to moral principles and an idea of what is good. That being the case, the question at the time was whether Blacks were human beings like all others.

—Achille Mbembe, *Critique of Black Reason*

Set during Jamaica's colonial era, Andrew Salkey's realist novel *A Quality of Violence* focuses on Pocomania in order to suggest a religious sensibility grounded in Afro-Jamaican spiritual imagination. As the novel indicates, Pocomania and other African-derived religious practices conflicted with the British colonial and emancipation project founded upon liberalism's ideals of labor as moral Christian duty, a scheme for transforming slaves into the proletariat of an emerging capitalist order while preserving the coercive mechanisms and ideologies of the slave plantocracy. The paradox is that ex-slaves were barred from the true acquisition of freedom during Jamaica's emancipation project—as freedom, a philosophical ideal, was a domain of liberty reserved for the so-called rational human subject. The terms of emancipation in Jamaica following the 1834 abolition of slavery rested on ex-slaves' socialization to a European worldview that involved a disavowal of African-derived religious practices. This was a realm of identity that the colonial administration believed to be steeped in the imagination and superstition of Africa, which, in their view, necessitated a transition to the world of reason and logic, to Europe as the sign of civilization and humanization. The expansion of the British Empire to Africa during the mid- to late nineteenth century coincided with the reemergence of religious censorship in Jamaica since the era of slavery to support a larger colonial narrative about bringing the irrational beliefs and superstitious practices of Africans and African-descended peoples under the civilizing forces of Christianity and into the fold of a rational Europe. In essence, the socialization to British culture involved a kind of cultural assimilation that was coupled with the notion of humanization. As African philosopher Achille Mbembe explains in Critique of Black Reason, this assimilation was necessary for African peoples to be "perceived and recognized as fellow human beings" so that their "humanity would cease to be indefinable and incomprehensible."[1] Mbembe references Joseph Conrad's The Heart of Darkness implicitly to signify his critique of colonialist discourse. His critique resonates with Chinua Achebe's essay "An Image of Africa" and its in-depth critique of Conrad's novel, which links Africa to the primitive "other world" and calls into question the humanity of Africans.

During the age of empire, European philosophers posited the idea that the human was defined by a predilection for rational thought, and moral and mental value judgments were ascribed to this capacity for reason. The taxonomic classification of races that emerged during this period of history espoused a biological determinism that was specific to each racial category that they devised. The British imperial project during the nineteenth century was grounded in the so-called civilizing forces of Christianity, believed to be central in moving Africans toward the onto-epistemological category of the human. These convictions foreground not only the contradictory aspect of the emancipation project in Jamaica, but also the belief in European racial and cultural superiority in order to rationalize dominance. The belief was that the socialization to reason would confer human attributes to Blacks who were perceived to exist outside the human domain, as given in this chapter's epigraphic quote from Mbembe.

An adherence to a fragmented African ancestral culture, which includes religious practices, during the post-emancipation period in Jamaica signified in this colonial context the lack of human socialization. The socializing imperatives of the emancipation project meant it was akin to a humanization project involving "the entry through language into a given cultural world" of "significations."[2] This perspective correlates with Jacques Lacan's idea about language and subject formation. The point that Gayatri Spivak makes in *A Critique of Postcolonial Reason*, also quoted in this chapter's epigraph, is likewise of utmost importance as it points to an irresolvable paradox: that one cannot "*become* cultured" in a culture to which they are believed to be "*naturally* alien."[3] Caribbean psychoanalyst Frantz Fanon captures the essence of the incommensurability between colonial society and the Black psyche in *Black Skin, White Masks* when he speaks about the empirical, ontological, and epistemological violence as the formation of a triple consciousness, shattered bodily schemata, and distorted mirror image that result from this colonial encounter and its disciplinary mechanisms for making a compliant colonial subject. In the context of Jamaica, the colonial administration held the belief that former slaves could be disciplined by reason and its symbolic function as the law to facilitate their movement toward a human subject position.

As a result, the terms of emancipation in Jamaica were informed by the colonialist and rationalistic discourse of the nineteenth century. Blacks were seen as incapable of reason and, therefore, were regarded as not deserving liberty because they were not human; they could be emancipated, however, which would inculcate them with human characteristics. There is a certain limit imposed upon this kind of emancipation; such emancipation belies the notion of Black people's postponed humanity—a humanity in the process of becoming that socialization would engender in the assimilation to British cultural ideals. This makes sense within the context of what Sylvia Wynter suggests in "Unsettling the Coloniality of Being/Power/Truth/Freedom" about the emergence of racial ideologies to signify difference, which coincided with the rise of European political states and their imperial activities. Drawing upon Michel Foucault's ideas, Wynter argues that the early modern period marked an epochal stage in the development of a Western humanist discourse about "Man's" coming into being, his transcendence from "human" to "Man," with the latter proffering the imperial ideologies that would aid in the transformation of non-European peoples into the "Human Other."[4] As Wynter suggests, Man, in this sense, is to be considered as a ratiocentric, transcendent subject who left behind a lower form of human identity whose irrationality stemmed in part from profound sensual drives—and who was regarded as "sinful by nature." This transcendent, European "Man" was believed to be in possession of reason that made him "lord over the senses," enabling him to "to rule over a 'lower order of reality.'"[5] Because the imagination is aligned with sensation within European epistemology, it is perceived to be an unreliable mediator of reality, given its role of mediating between the "senses and intellect."[6] Sensuality was aligned with Black identity, which correlated to the assumption that Black people lacked reason. This premise allowed European philosophers to make the argument that Black people were ruled by bodily sensations, which they believed created an "enslavement" to passions" or "particularistic desires."[7] This is similar to Kant's notion of the sublime in *Critique of Judgment* in which "Reason exerts dominion over sensibility."[8] Here, Kant echoes the Cartesian dualism that espoused a disjunction between mind and body.

Although Wynter does not identify Kant in her essay under consideration here, we can see a deep connection between Kant's work and the emerging racial ideologies of the time that linked reason to aesthetic and imperial discourse about freedom. Mbembe calls attention to the modern European perception of Africa or Blackness as unrepresentable, that it poses challenges to language's capabilities, given its perceived sublimity: "Africa and Blackness have, since the beginning of the modern age, plunged the theory of the name as well as the status and function of the sign and of representation into deep crisis . . . Every time it confronted the question of Blacks and Africa, reason found itself ruined and emptied, turning constantly in on itself, shipwrecked in a seemingly inaccessible place where language was destroyed and words themselves no longer had memory."[9] Kant's formulation of the sublime can be seen as not only involving a European aesthetic belief but also having a foundation in moral virtue, both of which were based on the invention of race. In addition to Wynter's ideas, which help to bring to the fore the underlying racial ideologies in Kant's work, David Roberts offers a point that helps to contextualize Wynter's claim about "Man," who alone was in possession of the reason that enabled his transition from particularity to the freedom of "universal autonomy":

> The humanity of man becomes the question of the nature of his socialization . . . or his naturalization. For the Enlightenment, naturalization signified alienation or dehumanization, since man becomes human and regains his birthright of freedom only by breaking out of enclosure in any particular society or tradition. Man is the maker of his own humanity and the supreme norm is individual autonomy, whose preservation demands the eternal vigilance of reason, which must scrutinize all "natural" conventions and replace them by self-critical norms. Essential humanity thereby

emancipates itself from all particularism to emerge as the project of universal autonomy made possible by man's right to think and judge for himself. The humanization, i.e. the denaturalization of man, is the task of reason.[10]

Reason was perceived as a prerequisite, not only for the emancipation from particularism but also for inclusion within universalism, that endows "Man" with the power of discourse so as to "judge" for all humanity, not just "himself," as Roberts suggests.

Echoing Wynter, Mbembe provides a similar point that during slavery, Europeans believed that Black people "lacked the power of invention" and the universal freedom that reason endows. This "lack" may suggest Lacan's idea about the relationship between desire and the subject's lack of being, which leads to the deployment of a neurotic or irrational desire.[11] If this lack, as desire, is believed to precede subject formation, then this perspective provides the grounds for denying one's humanity and claim to universal freedom. In the context of such imperial discourse, as Mbembe suggests, this "being-apart" led to the legal exclusion of colonial subjects. The assumption was that "they had nothing to contribute to the universal"[12]: "The period represented the Black Man as the prototype of a prehuman figure incapable of emancipating itself from its bestiality, of reproducing itself, or of raising itself up to the level of its god. Locked within sensation, the Black Man struggled to break the chains of biological necessity and for that reason was unable to take a truly human form and shape his own world. He therefore stood apart from the normal existence of the human race."[13] For this reason, eighteenth- and nineteenth-century political theories, premised upon the racialization of human subjects, defined race in relation to discernible physiological traits that were believed to be intrinsically connected to moral attributes.[14] These theories suggested that Black people not only lacked the moral capacity that reason provides to establish their humanity but that they also lacked the intellect to "shape" their "own world." The ideas that Wynter and Mbembe articulate help to unearth the ideologies and objectives that undergirded the emancipation project in Jamaica. From this perspective, the slave embodied the sign of the irrational, while the emancipated moved toward the rational, away from "passions," "particularistic desires," and African primitivity as guided by moral laws and legal statutes.

In Jamaican post-slavery society, Christian missionaries believed in the important role that Christianity would play toward the ex-slaves' acquisition of moral virtue, which would serve as the prerequisite for freedom. This was only a guise, however. Jamaica was caught at a crossroads between these changing ideas about the role of religion, which merely came to function as a tool of colonialism in the transition from a slave economy to a capitalist system. That is to say, in nineteenth-century Jamaica, this ethic of emancipation through Christianity was aligned also with the ex-slave's labor in the pivot from the slave plantation to a modern capitalist system. William A. Green explains that in Caribbean post-slavery society "religious instruction was deemed a noble device for uplifting the human spirit, controlling passion, and preserving the prevailing social order. The planters were quick to recognize the disciplinary values of religious education." Showing the hegemonic social function of Christian religious education to preserving the social structure, Adam Smith, a key architect of classical liberalism, supported Christian education as a way of stultifying revolutionary consciousness among subordinated groups of people.[15] European liberalism, as Mbembe explains, echoing Green's point, "was forged in parallel with imperial expansion. It was in relation to expansion that liberal political thought in Europe confronted such questions as universalism, individual rights, the freedom of exchange, the relationship between ends and means."[16] Freedom or liberty as defined in Western philosophical and political discourse contrasted with the Jamaican ex-slave's purported emancipation. The introduction of Christianity in post-slavery Jamaican society, and during the period of apprenticeship, clearly suggests its function as a hegemonic tool. Missionaries "identif[ied] themselves with the white minority in Jamaica and tended to support the planter view that manual work on the plantations was a 'christian duty.'"[17]

In this context of post-slavery Jamaica, salvation, paradoxically, not only held religious significance but also the drive to salvage a capitalist system that relies upon disciplined workers, especially if we believe as Niklas Luhmann suggests that modernity is "defined by labor" and that modernity "serves to orient only functional systems of society, e.g. economic rationality in the relation of means and ends."[18] Perceived as a fabric of economic rationality, Black labor was used as "means and ends," suggesting that emancipation was not a break from previous historical periods but rather a continuation of that oppression and preservation of the status quo. Nonetheless, the emerging capitalist economy and the exploitation of Black labor were represented as the facilitator of emancipatory freedom. It was also a question of freedom posed differently, filtered through modernity's dependence of white peoples' liberty upon the exploitation of Black labor. Consider, for instance, liberty in the Euro-American context, which relies upon the unfreedom of others and conveys the racialized, taxonomic, and humanist discourse about "Man," the

European, imperial subject that Wynter's essay highlights. Positioned outside the social contract, Blacks were barred from attaining this "liberty" that was held as a sacred right for "all men" in the "Declaration of Independence." For one to become truly human and to transcend the enslavement to particularistic drives, believed to be endemic to Black identity, salvation had to be earned through modern conceptions of labor.[19]

Pocomania as Resistive Religious Practice

Salkey's novel *A Quality of Violence* demonstrates that African-derived religious practices such as Pocomania functioned as a sign of primitivity, which led to its ambivalent position in Jamaican society primarily due to the cultural values that were steeped within British imperial and Christian ideologies during the colonial era. Moreover, Revival practices such as Pocomania were at odds with the transition to capitalism. The capitalist system called for disciplined colonial workers, but Pocomania practitioners necessarily subverted the conventions of the so-called modern, civilized state. Their religious practices, primarily their hours of observance, conflicted with a routinized work schedule; they disavowed the regimented work week that was necessary for the capitalist workforce by prioritizing spirituality over work. Under these circumstances, it is safe to say that the post-emancipation prosecution of Pocomania and other Revival practitioners was more about disciplining Jamaican ex-slaves to the newly imposed capitalist order: "Employers and members of the elite repeatedly complained about . . . Revivalists' prioritization of religious worship and community above employment. This was only the tip of the iceberg of arrests and prosecutions of religious leaders. A range of other legislative powers, from laws against vagrancy, 'night noises', and disorderly conduct to laws against practising medicine without a license and, of course, laws against obeah, meant that people who worshipped in ways that included catching the spirit, trances, and drumming, and people whose religious practice included spiritual healing, were subject to prosecution and other forms of state harassment."[20] As Walter Mignolo explains, "Religions would be tolerated as far as they do not interfere with THE political economy and THE political theory that rules the world."[21] One may also may consider the law's symbolic function as reason, given its power to sublimate the decolonial and revolutionary spirit accompanying African-derived religions, deemed to be a projection of the imagination.

Another issue that undermined the capitalist system was that these religious groups created underground banking systems, outside the proper structures, in which resources were pooled for communal use by those in dire financial straits.[22] Pocomania was, therefore, a triple threat to the emergent capitalist system. Most significantly, the various Revival practices of this time period were regarded as threatening, as having the potential for igniting a revolution: The "Myal outbreak" caused fear and even the Jamaican Governor "complained that it led to 'the laborers in a body abandoning their work, and devoting themselves entirely to the celebration of the Myalist rites.' Although there were no indications that Myalism involved attacks on the power structure of Jamaican society, the *Falmouth Post* nevertheless feared that it would lead to overt rebellion: state action to suppress the movement was necessary, or the colony from one end to the other, may be lighted by rebellious torches."[23] The trope of fire is clear here in Diana Paton's reference to the newspaper article, and it serves as a metonym for the slave rebellions that occurred in Jamaica, where the chief practice was to burn down the masters' estate. The suggestion that suppression was needed due to the fear that the "colony" would be "lighted by rebellious torches" articulates the Myal and other Revival forms' counter-hegemonic violence and revolutionary potential. In Jamaica, Obeah, which was a catchword for all Revival practices, was perceived as "dangerous power that might be mobilized against one."[24] To understand the revolutionary significance of Obeah, it should be noted that the practice was proclaimed as illegal during the pre-emancipation years, and it was such a potentially incendiary offense that even a free person caught practicing Obeah could be "enslaved through judicial decree," according to religious scholar Dianne M. Stewart.[25] Orlando Patterson reminds us that the slave population's "danger lay in their capacity to offend supernaturally" and that the "master's task" was to "defuse the potential physical and spiritual threat" and to "secure extracoercive support for his power."[26] As historian Randy Browne notes also, "in Jamaica . . . colonial authorities first constructed obeah as a distinct crime and linked it to slave rebellion and other attacks on whites." There were severe punishments for practicing Obeah if convicted, and those punishments included "transportation," which was "deportation and sale into the overseas slave trade."[27]

This autonomy was threatening for the Jamaican colonial state, especially in the context of postrevolutionary Haiti, where Dutty Boukman, a "transported" Jamaican slave, led the incendiary Bois Caiman ceremony that would spark the Haitian Revolution. Despite the various tactics by France, the United States, and England to stifle Haiti's political sovereignty and economic growth because the revolution had challenged their ideas about the interplay of Blackness, humanity, and reason, Vodou became a scapegoat and the central reason used to explain Haiti's continued underdevelopment. Pointing to the practice of Vodou, Haiti was believed to be "locked within sensation" and was therefore thought to be incapable of self-rule.[28] Vodou's threatening power led to the discursive castigation of and legal enforcement against African-derived religious practices in Jamaica. Since the nineteenth century, the perception of Vodou as a negative religious sign has extended to African-derived spiritual practices and cultural identity in the Caribbean as a "a signifier for African Caribbean backwardness."[29] The church was to play an important role—to humanize and inculcate moral virtues—especially alongside the expansion of the British Empire in Africa, which cloaked itself in the rationalization of the White Man's Burden ideology and belief in the necessity of bringing light to the heathens in order to civilize them from their dark, primitive condition.

This colonial mindset about African primitivity is articulated by Cousin Biddy, a brown character in *A Quality of Violence*, specifically in her notion that Haiti is "the land of duppy and Voodoo" as well as "black art and nastiness."[30] Not only does she articulate a Eurocentric critique that links African-derived religions to the irrational, but she views it as evidence of Black people's inability to self-rule. She states, "they working this voodoo and everybody still poorer than ever. You watch out, Mr. Marshall! Watch those countries that have black art and all those strong, strong religion business, they always have plenty poverty and misery."[31] Cousin Biddy links Haiti's "poverty and misery" since the revolution to Vodou, which captures a prevalent belief about Haiti's unpreparedness for freedom and for self-rule. There is no recognition of Vodou's decolonizing practices, its importance to the Haitian Revolution, or its preservation of ancestral knowledge and spiritual agency in the pervasive experience of coloniality. Brother Parkin attempts to provide a more positive regard for Vodou but in a somewhat ambiguous manner. He tells Marshall that "the Jamaican celebration of Pocomania closely resembled Haitian Voodoo and that Pocomania was only a rather feeble tower of Babel that certain Jamaicans had erected in order to get nearer the truth of the power of the Almighty."[32] Although validating Pocomania to a certain degree as a legitimate mode of religious expression that enables believers to "get nearer the truth of the power of the Almighty," Parkin's ambivalence can be seen in his ambiguous use of the word "feeble," which undermines Pocomania at the same time. Unlike Parkin, Marshall's critique of Pocomania is one of certitude. He is of the opinion that the ceremony is nothing but a "sham": "There must be some sort of bad deep reason for the sham actin' and all that. Anybody can see that the whole fat set-up is one big coonu-moonu affair."[33]

Sharing Marshall's critical stance, Cousin Biddy sees Pocomania and Vodou as the antithesis of Christianity: she juxtaposes polytheism with monotheism, evil with goodness, and death of an enemy with brotherly love. Paton reveals that "For a long time obeah was the ultimate signifier of the Caribbean's difference from Europe, a symbol of the region's supposed inability to be part of the modern world."[34] She explains that, along with other African-derived religions, "obeah is the most vivid and enduring symbol of and inheritance from Africa within the Anglo-creole Caribbean; for both, it marks out the Caribbean's difference from Europe and thus helps—despite all the evidence—to position Europe as rational and anti-superstitious."[35] Euro-derived sensibilities and Christian biases inform the Marshalls' and Parkins' cynicism toward African-derived religious practices. This disavowal of Africa was a crucial thing for many brown, middle-class Jamaicans who conformed to colonial ideologies at the time.

Part of this perception about backwardness stemmed from the fact that Christians did not understand the ecstatic possession trances that are central to the Revival practices in Jamaica. As Edward Seaga notes in his research on Pocomania and other Revival practices, "The Christian Church in its orthodox and accepted form . . . frowns upon more emotional manifestations of the spirit,"[36] as can be seen in the following description that Salkey provides in his novel, which highlights the somatic and emotive aspects of Pocomania: "There were about twenty-five people gyrating and uttering Pocomaniacal prayers. They all wore turbans and white gowns of calico. Some women were stamping the ground and jumping up and down and grunting. Some were squirming in the dust and frothing at the mouth. Most of the men were clapping their hands and shouting hymns of praise to candles on the table. A small group of musicians hovered over the bowl of rooster's blood and played and sang while the three women in the spirit tore at their calico gowns and screamed for release from the devil."[37] Indeed, the perception was that these "emotional manifestations of the spirit" were irrational—tied to a "lower order" faculty such as the imagination that contrasts with reason. In other words, these spiritual practices were regarded as "more animated than reflective."[38] This is because of the drumming, dancing, and possession trances that are central to Pocomania's spiritual practices.

This discursive stance overlooks the body's importance as a somatogenic mechanism, which is so central to African and African-diasporic phenomenology. Rather than the individualistic Western phenomenology, it is a phenomenology that prioritizes collective or communal ties. African-centered phenomenology, as Esiaba Irobi defines it, is a "philosophical construct that examines how the human body is the primary source and interpreter of all significations: desire, sexuality, power, freedom, presence, intelligence, aliveness, spirituality, joy, grief, anarchy, etc."[39] Speaking about Jamaican dance performances, "H" Paten explains that the body serves as a communicative medium for knowledge and language that utilizes the "senses, symbolic gestures and kinaesthetic" that enable meanings engendered from corporeal semiotics that "reunite the physical body, reason and emotion," which, in turn, reanimates the body and spirit.[40] Paget Henry explains in *Caliban's Reason* that the "gravitational pulls of non-being" that result from slavery and colonialism have created an "ego-implosion in the Caribbean."[41] This is what Fanon describes as the "Fact of Blackness" in *Black Skins, White Masks,* "a triple consciousness"—as the ontological experience of "being for others"—as he became "dislocated" and removed from his own presence and made into "an object."[42] Here, Fanon describes the Black experience in the colonial encounter and the ensuing negative, racialized discourses about Blackness and the supposed link to primitivity and cannibalism, for instance. Performance modes such as Pocomania religious rituals provide a basis for "self-relationality" to the African ego as "originary freedom."[43] It is a symbolic pursuit of liberation fostered by contesting the colonialist imperatives that underlie emancipation. As such, Pocomania practitioners reclaimed the body, if only momentarily, in practices that cultivate ego regenesis.

Even so, Salkey does not essentialize the embracement of Africa as naturally occurring among the lower class of dark skin Jamaicans. He depicts some of his lower-class characters as having a false consciousness as well because they, too, have internalized colonialist attitudes about Africa: "we going to learn her what it mean to lead people into darkness. Must be back to Africa she must be want to lead we!"[44] Mother Johnson, however, the object of that comment, embraces her African heritage: "Me and you and the rest-a-people in St. Thomas all belong to the days that pass by when slavery was with land. Everybody is a part of slavery days, is a part of the climate-a-Africa and the feelings in the heart is Africa feelings that beating there, far down. Dada did know that, I know that, too. We all come down from Ashanti people who did powerful plenty, and we have the same power-house brains that them did have."[45] This was a response to Miss Mellie's disavowal of her African identity: "We is people who live on the land in St. Thomas, not Africa. You hear? We is no slave people, and there is no Africa in we blood the way you would-a like we believe."[46] Under the colonial system in Jamaica, the population were taught to distance themselves from Africa. Nonetheless, Mother Johnson is a self-proclaimed African who reclaims the African sign as an expression of decoloniality as connected to her practice of Pocomania. As Stewart explains, "Kumina people are self-identified 'Africans.' They do not refer to themselves as Black, Jamaican, Afro-Jamaican, or even African Jamaican. They conceive of their African identity exponentially."[47] Mother Johnson symbolically rejects her colonial Jamaican identity for an African ancestry. Overall, she offers a number of compelling ideas, including the affirmation of Black people's capacity for reason with the acknowledgment of having "power-house brains," but because the reader and the characters have no political allegiance to her at this point in the plot, the effectiveness falls short.

As Salkey's novel demonstrates, during Jamaica's colonial era, Africa functioned as a sign of primitivity, which led to its ambivalent position in the society primarily due to the cultural values that were steeped within British imperial and Christian ideologies. The irony was that even those of African ancestry (as we've seen in Salkey's characterization of Cousin Biddy and Marshall) had an ideological affiliation with the planter class of enslavers when they perceived African religious forms such as Obeah and Pocomania as inherently evil. It was a belief that those who continued to hold on to those African practices had refused the redeeming influences, morality, and salvation offered by Christianity. While Stewart argues that the rejection of Obeah stems primarily from "Afrophobia" or "Anti-Africanness,"[48] for Paton it is more than cultural rejection alone; it is also about Obeah's link to criminality, given the law's discursive representation of its practices as a criminal offense.[49] As the ultimate sign of reason, the colonial law presupposes its own legitimacy, especially given the social contract that is supposed to exist in a modern, civilized state. These rules were put into place because of the continued threat that Obeah posed to the colonial system; the Obeah laws, therefore, became a means by which Obeah's illegitimacy would be curtailed, and the law allowed for the legitimate use of violence against the perceived threat to its authority or power as a way to sanction and censor illegitimate power.[50]

When one considers the emancipation project as a "rational" and political experiment, one may also refer to this prescriptive representation of the law as reason, a way to sublimate the decolonial and revolutionary spirit accompanying the African-derived religions, deemed to be a projection of the imagination. Paton reminds us that the "renewal of the obeah laws also took place in the context of the expansion of British imperial power, and in particular the colonial encounter with indigenous religion and healing practices in new colonies, especially in Africa."[51] The British colonial venture into Africa was facilitated by the recycling of old discourses about the importance of civilizing Africans through conquest, a veneer for capitalist exploitation of African resources and people with the long and strong arm of British law. Moreover, conceptions of the human, rationality, and civilization cast Africans and Afro-Jamaicans as the logical recipients of the British civilizing mission. As such, Obeah and other Revival practices were effectively criminalized in Jamaica to augment this civilizing project and its rhetoric of salvation.

What the British perceived as the need for strict laws to police Obeah and other Revival practices in Jamaica had been informed by their imperial activities in Africa and those indigenous challenges to their power. This concern, as Paton argues, "set the scene for a substantial expansion and harshening of obeah law in the 1890s and the first decade of the twentieth century across most of the Caribbean region."[52] This was necessary because, as a subaltern religious expression, Obeah had an underlying radical consciousness and potential for revolt—a source of trepidation for Jamaica's colonial administration, especially given Vodou's role in precipitating the Haitian revolution. Through a colonial lens, Obeah and other related African spiritual practices were seen as a potential weapon and, therefore, were criminalized as a way to censor and punish practitioners. There were "cases where obeah was explicitly considered as a potential charge, but where the defendant was ultimately charged with another crime: larceny or practising medicine without a license."[53] The prosecution of and penalties for practicing Obeah, such as flogging, were designed so as to stress the "significance of obeah convictions as a sign that state power was stronger than the power of obeah."[54] As historian Thomas C. Holt argues in *The Problem of Freedom*, criminal behavior is at times redefined as a means of control, and new laws are framed as a way to regulate behavior. Those who reject the power structure's regimentation and control are labeled as criminals. The ability to regulate behavior in this particular sense ensures the continuation of systemic domination.

This points to the significance or the power of discourses through the law as a symbol of reason, to discipline the spiritual imagination, as this was a discursive and legal tactic to lower the reputation of Revival leaders. Because of the way Revival practices were sensationalized by the laws during this time period of *A Quality of Violence*'s setting, the third-person limited narrator passes judgment as well and conflates Dada Johnson's Pocomania practices with Obeah by describing him pejoratively as "an obeah man who preferred to be called a 'spiritualist and healer of the afflicted and the discontented.'"[55] Suggesting even more bias against Dada Johnson, the narrator states that he (Dada Johnson) was "fear[ful] of being exposed as a confidence trickster with a police record, and of his haunting anxiety about the progress of the drought" and that "Brother Parkin was the only person in St. Thomas who knew that

Dada Johnson was a confidence trickster. He knew, too, that he had been to prison, twice; he had served six months for obeah, and he had served two years for larceny. But, Brother Parkin considered him to be a small-time business man."[56] This narrative perspective is unreliable and lacks objectivity because the narrator passes judgment at times, even using the word "rass" to reveal his emotional state and to suggest how deeply he objects to the issues under consideration.

Salkey bends the realist literary tradition by presenting a narrator who is not omniscient. The narrative point of view is third person limited, similar to an unnamed character in the story. By violating the presumed objectivity of the realist tradition, the issue of verisimilitude in relation to a Western gaze, Salkey undertakes a counter-hegemonic narrative strategy. The pathos-driven narrative perspective betrays the rhetoric of disinterested judgment that supposedly informs understanding. This counter-hegemonic strategy that undermines rational self-consciousness is similar to what Mark McWatt identifies as the "language of the imagination," specifically in regard to Caribbean writer Wilson Harris's work.[57] As McWatt explains, "The language of the imagination seems to rely very little upon processes of the intellect, for such processes require a certain detachment and distance from the thought or feeling, which would dilute the experience and change the reader's role from that of participant to mere observer."[58] In a related way, Salkey unsettles the realist novel tradition in A Quality of Violence by presenting a narrator who is not omniscient and who conveys a narrative perspective that is emotional rather than objective. By departing from this key feature of the Western realist novel convention, Salkey violates distinctions, undermining the logos-driven objectivity of the omniscient narration so prototypical of the genre. The objectively driven omniscience of realism suggests detachment and disinterest, of being closed off from emotions without having a connection to "thought or feelings." Rendering the narrator with emotions makes her a participant in discursive violence, especially when the narrative gaze conflicts with the characters' subject position and their supposed alignment to sensation.

In the brief essay "Rereading A Quality of Violence," Mervyn Morris offers a compelling explanation that the "narrative eye of A Quality of Violence is an outsider's"—especially given the way in which the rituals are regarded as a "sensational spectacle." It is for this reason, as Morris explains, that the "narrative tone is often distant and critical."[59] What Morris is suggesting is that the narrative perspective can be described as a central consciousness that pervades a text. It is a perspective that is usually connected to "an external, third person narrator who tells the story from a distinct point of view . . . revealing that character's thoughts and relating the action from his or her perspective."[60] In the context of Salkey's novel, the central consciousness of the third-person limited point of view is problematic as it seems to endorse class- and color-based hegemonic values. This limited point of view, for instance, doesn't provide the detail that Dada Johnson's charges for larceny were most likely trumped up, that this was usually a penalty for practicing Obeah.

One has to question, however, the authorial decision to maintain ambiguity in the novel, as it is very evident that Salkey is signifying upon Jamaica's long history of criminalizing the practice of Obeah, which became the catchword and sign for criminalizing all African-derived spiritual practices. As a mode of censorship, Pocomania leaders were oftentimes arrested and charged with larceny because their religious observance undermined the emancipation project and its presumed moral, Christian, and capitalist imperatives, as we've seen in the narrator's comment in the aforementioned quote—that Parkin considered Dada Johnson "to be a small-time business man." While the middle-class characters dismiss Dada Johnson's credibility by seeing him as a profiteer, Stewart explains that "African religions, like all religions, offer their leaders opportunities to capitalize on the beliefs, fears, and anxieties of their adherents. However, African religions are often scapegoated as predisposed toward the abuse of power when compared to Christianity."[61] Dada Johnson addresses this concern in a conversation with Parkin, although in a somewhat ambiguous manner: "It can't matter if I am a rass or not, Brother Parkin; because I know that is what you thinking, right now. It can't matter at all." He goes on to say, "All I do, that is bad, is collect a little 'dues' off them, and that is my living. And for that collection, I give them hope and faith."[62] Dada Johnson's critical reflection suggests that he honestly believes in the goodness of his Pocomania practices and that he has a profound understanding of the spiritual void in his followers' lives, left unfulfilled by Christianity, and that he does not merely exploit them as outsiders are led to believe. This is certainly a contrast to Cousin Biddy's point that what the people get in return for their dues "is a dirty glass of belly-wash lemonade mix up with coolie-foot sugar."[63]

The letters that Dada Johnson receives attest to the success of his alternative therapies, which fill the "void" left by Western institutions, including the church and medical establishments, as he explains to Parkin:

> These letters can prove that I am a great healer among men . . . Well, this
> one is from a man who used to go the hospital for a sore on his back
> which he had for over three years. It just wouldn't heal and the doctors try

all sorts of things on it. In the long run, he start to get poorly and he lose a lot of weight and look like death self. He come to me, one day when I was holding meeting in the yard, and ask for treatment. So I say yes. And we arrange some "dues." The wife and me give the man some bush baths over two weeks' period and the man begin to get well like magic take him. The sore dry up more and more . . . In a month from time to time he come to me, he fix up nice as ninepence, ole man. He was so happy in him mind that he write me this letter thanking me for what I do for him. In the letter he tell me how I am a doctor that should get Government help to establish a Poor Hospital in St. Thomas.[64]

Peter Nazareth interprets this letter from an ex-patient as evidence of Dada Johnson's duplicity as a conman.[65] Even so, if we consider this very compelling argument from Nazareth, we should also think about the multiple narrative voices in the text that either support or challenge the central consciousness. This aesthetic can best be characterized as a cunning authorial strategy whereby Salkey plays tricks on the reader and the very issue of signification. It is very possible in this case that Salkey intends to send some readers in the critical direction that Nazareth suggests. But there is also evidentiary information supporting another reading of the text—the possibility that Dada Johnson is not actually a fraud, an interpretation that conflicts with the novel's "central consciousness" and the values of middle-class characters such as Parkin. This is the other face of the "Janus coin," so to speak, which reveals the novel's ambivalence, its double voice. The lens through which Dada Johnson is rendered negative is from the perspective of the law wherein healing is the sole domain of licensed epidemical doctors. Parkin reminds Dada Johnson about the law's power to define him: as a perceived Obeah man, he is in contention with the law, and is, therefore, considered a criminal. Parkin's response, for instance, conveys his belief in the authority of "code and custom," the law's power to regulate licensure:

Yes. That is good evidence, all right. But still and still Dada, you are considered an obeah man and as such you are breaking the law. In this modern world, you have to have a piece of paper which gives you authority to heal people. A doctor is a man with such papers, and an obeah man is the other kind of healer. All the good that you feel that you doing for the people in St. Thomas, all the faith and hope, all the contentment of mind, all the blessing that you are handing around, might just as well be curses and crosses for your own neck. If you going to do good for people, you have to do it according to code and custom. You can't cook up your own

idea of doing good and dish it out as you like without the stamp of
approval from the people who are in charge of code and custom.[66]

In the modern world, as Parkin suggests, the law dictates one's ability or privilege to engage in healing practices. Dada Johnson's healing competes with the medical establishment and its scientific backing and, therefore, its link to reason. "Code and custom" can be read as a metonym for the colonial system as a whole—and a realization of the entrenched specter of the plantation structure and its suppression of cultural practices. In considering the ideas from Paton and Holt, there's a clear connection between radical religious practices, their criminalization, and the figuration of the slave sublime—that is, the ways in which practitioners contest colonial law (and the attendant assumptions about rationality and the human) through an irreverent expression of the spiritual imagination.

Transhistorical Reenactments of Plantation Violence

The heteroglossia in *A Quality of Violence* complicates the novel, suggesting the author's ambivalence in representing the way in which Pocomania practices mime the plantation-era violence as a transhistorical script for symbolizing a challenge to the circumscribed freedom during Jamaica's post-slavery period. At first glance, the central consciousness seems to privilege a brown, middle-class perspective because the Marshalls and Parkins provide the dominant voices in the novel, conveying their critical distance from the lower-class Black characters. These two families are "small planters," and this is a decisive word choice by Salkey for conveying a contrast to "small farmers."[67] The Marshalls' and Parkins' mixed-race, brown identity connects them to the power structure from slavery, and as small planters they are significantly above the station of the peasant class in the post-slavery capitalist economy.[68] In essence, Salkey's word choice suggests a concerted effort to highlight the historical continuity between the Marshall's and Parkin's post-slavery planter class status and the institution of slavery. Marshall had "inherited 'family land,'" which Salkey places in quotation marks.[69] As the novel reveals, the Marshalls have a "family history" that has made possible their "progress on the land," "aloofness," and "security."[70] The political language of the post-slavery era aligned land ownership with freedom and the virtues of citizenship to the extent that the colonial administration proposed measures for "diminishing the facilities of obtaining land."[71] This tactic preserves the association of freedom with white (or near white) property ownership as it was during slavery.

The Marshalls' planter class status is confirmed by their positive regard for the Number Seven, the brutal heat of the midday sun, serving as a symbol for slave drivers. Suggesting a deep intimacy and conviviality with this iconic figure of violence that serves the plantocracy's interests, the narrator divulges that "there were times when Marshall laughed with Number Seven. He was proud of the company, the acquaintance, the harmony they enjoyed because of their mutual power and ambitions."[72] Because of the Marshalls' identity as mixed-race brown people, Mother Johnson believes that they have internalized the attitudes and values of the slave era: "Those Marshall people is always a funny set of false-pride people. They going on like they different and born to play the boss-man on everybody. My Dada, bless the dead, always used to say that the Marshalls was people who born with the wrong sort of skin colour. They don't have to open their mouth before you get the feeling that they believe that they is superior and all that rass!"[73] There are repeated references to them as putting on "big house style on people"[74] or as being "house-enemy,"[75] suggesting a class difference between field slaves and house slaves, a basis for conflict that oftentimes rested on a color differential. Mother Johnson makes the prediction that brown people will eventually rise to power as part of the *ancien régime* that preserves the race-based power and attitudes of the slave plantocracy: "Those Marshall people always trying to do those things that I just tell you 'bout. Making time is what they doing, like they know that the day will come when they going to take over the place and govern total everybody like them bad foreign landlord with plenty estate."[76] Mother Johnson insinuates that the lingering effects of slavery result from the continued presence of plantation-derived ideologies that confer power based on race: "The days of slavery still sounding in most of we ears."[77] By suggesting that they "burn down houses and canefields," Mother Johnson calls for a slave rebellion, of sorts, against the Marshalls, especially because she aligns them with the plantocracy.

Mother Johnson experiences the slave sublime awe, the dreadful affect that comes with a transhistorical encounter with slavery. She "stood and stared. The women around her heaped themselves closer to her chunky, blowzy body. They, too, stared, silent and full of dread."[78] The word "dread" captures the overwhelming terror that is associated with the slave sublime experience, which can be defined along the lines of what Neil Roberts characterizes as the "trepidation and knowledge of a confirming reality" and an "encounter with history" that is "awesome and fearful."[79] In the context of the novel, this slave sublime affect as "dread" leads to the reenactment of plantation violence as a form of resistance. There is a ritualized element to this mimicry of plantation-derived violence, particularly the spectacular forms of punishments that were scripted by slave masters. As part of the plantation-era script for violence, slaves were oftentimes hung from trees after several rounds of flogging, then had chili peppers rubbed into their wounds. Salkey's novel reveals that these dramatizations of power would be recreated by the descendants of slaves when Parkin is punished for his perceived affinity with the plantocracy and is thus scapegoated as the maleficent force responsible for Doris's death: "The same addict picked up the rope and tugged it venomously as he took aim and threw it back over the branch. The force of the rope sliced into the rawness of Brother Parkin's neck."[80] Instead of hot peppers, the three addicts apply red ants to Parkin's groin area, where the phallus stands as a symbol of (white) male power when we think about sexual violence against women. In this pantomime of plantation drama, Mother Johnson reverses the power dynamic, both in terms of gender and race, when she directs the scripted violence. By assuming the discursive stance of a slave master, Parkin is able to reverse his fate by suggesting that Mother Johnson illegitimately inhabits a position of power: "You want power to enslave the people of St. Thomas; to exploit their emotions; to live on them like a bloody, fat parasite. A day's honest work in the fields would straighten you out."[81] The linkage of labor to disciplinary measures and as a prerequisite for socialization, for the acquisition of morality, comes up here in Parkin's statement. Revealing his ideological alignment with the plantocracy, Parkin insinuates the important function of Black labor while suggesting his exemption from such work because his skin color grants the masterly privilege of being a parasitic usurer. Other elements regarding the restaging of plantation life are discernible in the novel, including the flogging that occurs as part of the Pocomania ritual that Dada Johnson reenacts to stop the drought: "If skin is to cut with lash, then come we lash the skin till water come down and wet the land. If the skin is to break with lash, then come we break the skin till water come down and wet the land. If man must dead with the lash, then come we dead and make water wet we and the land."[82] These replications remind us of the bloody, brutal punishments slaves endured as their blood nourished the land. Salkey is not alone in this literary representation of the repeating forces of history in which practices of violence replicate the scripted violence from slavery.

In his book *Surviving Slavery in the British Caribbean*, Randy Browne not only provides historical evidence about the mimicry of plantation violence but also demonstrates the ways in which this learned language of violence is handed down from masters to slaves, who repeat these primary instantiations of violence in their religious rituals: "The types of physical violence that Hans and Willem used—floggings, beatings, and the application of hot peppers—were among the methods favored by slaveholders for torturing and punishing enslaved people. That most of these forms of violence were absent in African rituals designed to identify suspected witches and poisoners or combat powers suggest that the Minje Mama dance was a creole, Caribbean phenomenon, not a watered down African survival. Its cosmological origins lay in various slave exporting regions of Africa, but the brutal violence that characterized its practice had been learned on West Indian plantations."[83] As Browne notes, the "centrality of violence" in these reenactments "suggests that white colonialists were not the only people who recognized the efficacy of violence and terror for projecting power."[84] What follows is the point Browne makes about the intensification of violence when replicated by (ex-)slaves as a symbolic display of and mimetic desire for power: "the Minje Mama dance and other healing practices—even when they incorporated features of African cosmologies—came to include extreme violence when configured in the plantation environments of the Americas, where physical violence was central not only to the masters' exercise of power but also in structuring power relationships among enslaved people themselves."[85] Browne's findings provide historical evidence supporting the notion that the violent nature of plantation settings in the Caribbean are responsible for transforming African-derived spiritual practices into extreme forms of violence.

What is discernible also is a basis for understanding the mathematical aspect of the slave sublime—the magnitude of violence, its augmentation when reenacted as mimetic desire and as scripted violence. Similar to the Minje Mama dance becoming violent by miming the slave master's sadistic power, Anancy, too, is transformed within the historical context of Caribbean slavery. Emily Zobel Marshall argues the following regarding the metamorphosis of Eshu in Akan culture to Anansi (Anancy) as a violent figure in Jamaican folktales: "His actions seem even more violent and remorseless and many elements of plantation life enter into the tales as Massa, the whip and the cane fields."[86] Through the violence of the plantation world, Anancy loses his connection to the world of spirits as he morphs into a symbol for "the black slave trapped in a social system in which negotiation was an impossibility. In his Jamaican setting, Anansi was breaker rather than tester of the chains. He becomes a symbol of creative chaos and longed for freedom in a tyrannical and coercive order."[87] The desire for freedom underlies the restagings of violence that serve as symbolic projections of power, particularly by amplifying the original instantiation of violence.

As a demonstration of the mathematical aspect of the slave sublime, the above bears similarity to Pocomania and the plot's rising action in Salkey's novel, when the people dance and chant in a procession that culminates in killing Mother Johnson: "The procession entered a long lane. It was much darker and rougher than the Parochial Road. The shadows were uglier and they criss-crossed even more irregularly. Shadows were curtains. Shadows in a long lane were the curtains that were dropped in front of the procession's penultimate act in a drama of drought and insanity."[88] Salkey's use of the words "uglier" and "more irregularly" denote the comparative forms of the original adjectives, which may suggest the magnification of violence when re-enacted by oppressed people. Most significantly, the trope of plantation-derived violence as scripted drama is very evident in Salkey's word choice of "curtains that were dropped" in a "drama." The word "shadow" points to the reenactment of the original plantation-era drama, to the reflection of an image, as an imitation of an original, or as a remnant of something having an omnipresent influence. Both the connotation and denotation of these words suggest that the "shadow" is more ominous than the original—that the reenactment is a vestige of slavery that is comparatively an augmented form of plantation violence in this "penultimate act in a drama of drought and insanity." Given this reenactment and amplification of the master's power as the sublime's transcendent surplus, it is worth noting Mbembe's point that "Power comes to those who can dance with the shadows, weave tight links between their own vital strength and other chains of power always situated in an elsewhere, an outside beyond the surface of the visible. Power cannot be enclosed within the limits of a single, stable form because, in its very nature, it participates in the surplus."[89] Salkey's novel demonstrates implicitly Pocomania's efficacy for collective revolt whereby the oppressed are moved by an intangible and powerful spiritual force—a potential subaltern weapon for fighting against oppressive figures and systems of thought by harnessing the spiritual imagination.

From Parkin's purview, however, the Pocomania practitioners were not addressing rational approaches to the problem, while having a radical consciousness. For Parkin, the violence leading to Mother Johnson's death is irrational given that he can no longer appeal to the people "through sentiment or logic."[90] Parkin assumes an ideological stance that aligns the Pocomania worshippers with sensuality and emotions. It is a contrast to his characterization in the novel as "big-brains Parkin," in which the descriptor serves as a metonym for reason and its linkage to moral contemplation. This is another way in which Salkey links him to the plantocracy, given the European belief in their intellectual and moral superiority. Shortly after Parkin is called "big-brains," a woman asks: "Is what you trying to set yourself up as? Slave boss-man, yes? Is white man you playing on we with all you big moves and thing? Like say you thinking we is still on the white man plantation, yes?"[91] Parkin's response suggests a Eurocentric alignment, one that separates him morally, intellectually, and racially: "You're heading for murder. All of you!" Pointing to Miss Gatha he continues by saying, "This is the only person who has been able to see things my way. She understands even though she's one of you."[92] Parkin aligns himself with Eurocentric ideals of reason, which create a gulf between himself and the community of peasants in the novel. This distinction as class-color hierarchy would then point to the supposed link between race and reason.

It is important to consider the way Parkin, as a central character with a brown, middle-class background, functions as a trope for the colonial belief system in Jamaica that belies a Kantian frame of thinking. This can be thought of in regard to Parkin's quandary that the Pocomania practitioners were not harnessing reason and therefore plunged into committing immoral acts. It is a critical stance that calls attention to the emancipation project's failure since it was supposed to socialize the ex-slave from their irrational and particularistic desires. By not harnessing reason, within a Kantian framework, the underlying idea is that they are not prepared for "human" citizenship: "Kant posits a subject who critically reflects. This subject also stands in relation to others, often in a mutually hostile and antagonistic way. Yet these subjects must solve together the problem of antagonism and hostility. For Kant, the solution is the universalization of the regime of practical reason, which he terms *citizenship*. It has its own institutional form (the conceptual republic) and norms of good conduct (civic virtues)."[93] The preceding quote helps to explain the tension between Parkin and the other members of the community. If citizenship is linked to the human subject, then the central issue that can be gleaned from Parkin's point of view about the "unsociable sociality" of the community is that they are incapable, or not fully ready, for the moral responsibility that comes with freedom and the entitlement of citizenship—they haven't been transformed from their "enslavement" to "particularistic desires" and are, therefore, not ruled by reason, which would allow them to put the needs of the country first. Parkin believes that the Pocomania practitioners have undermined not only colonial authority, "code and custom," by taking matters into their own hands but also the common good because of the possibility of spreading a contagion to the rest of the island. Below, Miss Gatha articulates Parkin's belief that this irrational violence will spread: "I tell you already that is St. Thomas we have to save. Not Mother Johnson, really. Brother feel that the news going to spread and cause plenty other bloodshed . . . this thing is bigger than Mother Johnson . . . If a few people get the taste of blood in them mouth, then the taste bound to spread like fever. Before long, the whole of Jamaica will be going on like it is one big St. Thomas, mix up and blood up from top to bottom."[94] The fact that the violence in the novel oversteps its symbolic containment, literally overflowing into the epilogue, suggests the lack of resolution to this instantiation of the mathematical slave sublime.

Salkey uses Parkin as a foil for Eurocentric modernist inquiry into the nature of synthetic judgment, given that judgment has the role of determining truth or falsity in relation to knowledge derived from cognition. We should take into account also Kant's notion of "pragmatic judgment" and the "universality of reason," a principle endowed only to *human* subjects. Kant distinguishes between "what might be termed pragmatic judgment which proceeds by trial and error (and which contains a naturalistic assumption about the presence or absence of a capacity for judgment" as that which "proceeds from an anthropological principle of the universality of reason, that is, a reason 'with which every human being is endowed.'"[95] This is the politico-ethical dimension of reason that Parkin engages in as a form of inquiry. Parkin's modernist premise is about the transcendental nature of a moral aesthetic with its foundation within reason and logic, which he believes would define a universal notion of freedom. As Kant suggests, if we recall from earlier in this chapter, race is a qualifier for having this moral aesthetic, and, therefore, one's identity as a human subject. Kant's eighteenth-century ideas are far-reaching, and, as Mbembe explains, for Europeans in the nineteenth century, humanity was defined by the capacity to reason, which in turn dictated one's rights, one's liberty and autonomy—and one's ability to live "according to moral principles."[96] Parkin believes in this perceived superior moral position that is in line with a Eurocentric privileging of reason, and he articulates a worldview that clashes with the poorer, dark skin characters especially because his rationalistic discourse undermines the validity of the sensory and somatic experiences of the imagination on which the Pocomania spiritual practices are based.

Bill Carr was certainly on the right track when he suggested, but unfortunately dismissed, the rationalistic elements of "free inquiry" that underlie Parkin's mode of thinking in his 1968 essay "A Complex Fate: The Novels of Andrew Salkey." As Carr puts it, Salkey "subjects everything to liberal enquiry."[97] This liberal inquiry that Carr highlights is an intimation about the rationalistic discourse, an appeal to deductive and intellectual reason, that pervades the brown, middle-class character Parkin's line of thinking. Carr was correct also when he suggested that Salkey "does not intend that his readers, European or West Indian, shall make a simple moral identification with . . . Parkin. This is the complex irony of the book. The limitations of Parkin's enquiring rationalism."[98] The departure from this productive line of thinking is not a fault that lies solely with Carr. One also has to take into account Salkey's ambivalent and paradoxical approach toward his subject matter about the sociohistorical inquiry into African-derived religions as to its cultural significance as objective phenomenon because of the multiple audiences that the novel serves. As a result, the issues are situational, varying according to different perspectives presented in the novel, and they are subject to change at any given time, thereby displaying aspects of ambiguity, where certainty is ever-shifting and is more about relativism. Accordingly, Salkey's novel represents an ongoing tension between rational judgments and the spiritual imagination.

The novel's heteroglossia and related ambivalence stem from Salkey's attempts to speak to different audiences simultaneously, perspectives that conflict with those of his Pocomania characters. This balancing act is easily overlooked. Salkey certainly has a deep appreciation for and understanding of the Pocomania adherents' worldviews—apparent in the first-person perspective we get from Dada Johnson and the space he gives to Linda's high regard for Pocomania and even Mother Johnson's embracement of Africa as home and her ability to see the spirit of her dead husband Dada Johnson on two separate occasions. None of these perspectives are validated, however, neither in the world of the characters nor in the world of the reader. Dada Johnson is overwhelmingly represented as a con artist, Linda is perceived as a child whose opinions can be easily dismissed as childish fantasies, while Mother Johnson is cast as a usurper of power.

This issue of ambiguity corresponds also to audience and reception, given the time period of the novel's publication. In his 2011 essay "So Differently from What the Heart Arranged," Victor L. Chang discusses *A Quality of Violence* alongside two other novels, John Hearne's *Voices Under the Window* and Vic Reid's *New Day*, and argues that these texts "demonstrate a nationalistic impulse" in the anticipation of decolonization. To this end, as he argues, it "also meant that the fiction was used for social, cultural and political ends" but, in retrospect, these objectives were not met in relation to these particular novels.[99] He explains that "Salkey was motivated by his belief that focusing on the African retentions in rural Jamaican society would validate that section of the society which had always been oppressed and victimized by colonial structures."[100] However, as Chang argues, the failure stems, on the one hand, from Salkey's miscalculation of what "the response would be to his detailed rendering of pocomania ritual and practice" and, on the other hand, from not "strik[ing] the responsive chord he had hoped for as there is a danger of the mystification of Africa rather than a representation that makes it more legitimate and familiar." Chang argues further that Salkey made it difficult for "readers to identify with" Dada Johnson and Mother Johnson because of his negative portrayal of them.[101] In light of the issue that Chang raises, that we must consider the great importance of the sociopolitical context of the novel's publication, we should consider also Paton's point about the upper classes' "populist politics" during this time period. During the independence era, there was a major debate over the status of Obeah because of the desire to construct a national identity that would ground Caribbean culture in its African heritage while doing so in a manner that would seem "respectably modern and rational."[102] This sociopolitical context of Salkey's novel suggests also the ambivalence about Jamaica's bourgeoning national identity—of being at a crossroads, in the transition from colony to independent nation that, nonetheless, maintained colonial ideologies about being "modern and rational."

This issue of being at a crossroads, a turning point, is at the heart of the sublime and by extension the slave sublime. Kant's theory of the sublime reflects a turning point as well—that is, the transition from Enlightenment to Romanticism, "which foregrounds the whole problematic of the relation of reason and imagination."[103] In relation to the political milieu in Jamaica, the slave sublime can be considered also as a theory of the crossroads or threshold that is associated with the West African trickster Anancy, known for his verbal wordplay and distortion of signs—the underlying reason for Salkey's overwhelming textual ambiguity.

Salkey's Anancy Strategies

Given the African-derived religion's discursive position as a floating signifier, Salkey had to consider the reception of his book in the United Kingdom, Jamaica, and the wider Caribbean region. There is a limit to what he could represent because of the restrictions that publishers often impose upon writers. By distorting signs through double voice, Salkey in his position as a Caribbean writer assumes a trickster identity as embodied in Anancy. This distortion results in ambiguity, primarily because of the real-world issue of book marketing: he had to enact a skillful "dance" so as not to alienate his readership, so as to turn a profit for the publisher. But this is just one aspect of the multilayered dissimulation that explains the novel's wavering reception, the dearth of scholarship, and the reason why it is currently out of print. Mervyn Morris's concluding remarks in his essay "Rereading A Quality of Violence" explain the changing reception of the novel from positive in the late 1950s to negative in the 1970s, mainly stemming from Edward Seaga's 1969 seminal work, which provided deeper understanding of the significance of "Pukkumina."[104] Morris adds that a trenchant critique came from Sylvia Wynter, who argued that the novel "involves a middle-class exploitation of cult religions, folklore."[105] Salkey's novel is not just a side-show critique of "folklore" in Jamaica, the contention that lies at the heart of Wynter's condemnation, especially given his remark that folklore topics were popular among publishers at the time. Carr points out that in 1961 Salkey found himself under the gun when he faced allegations that he "presented a false picture" of Jamaicans in England and that he had "serve[d] up what English publishers require." Salkey did not make matters easy since he had cynically suggested that *A Quality of Violence* was "written to catch the market for 'peasant' novels."[106]

At the time of the novel's publication, Salkey had to consider the twentieth-century desire for the exotic in literature and the exploration of rational inquiry. According to Mbembe, the twentieth century was a period when artists expressed a deep interest in cultures that were regarded as "exotic," a perception that was fostered by a link between materialism (in both politics and science) and positivism (in philosophy). This interest suggested "an anticolonial critique within aesthetics and politics" which led those in the surrealist movement to reconsider "Africa's contribution to the project of humanity to come."[107] It is worth noting Mbembe's approach to unsettling the belief that the humanity of Africans had not yet been achieved, that it was in the future—in a state of becoming.[108] He does so in order to highlight the perseverance of eighteenth- and nineteenth-century colonialist ideologies in the post-WWII era, despite the anticolonial sentiment held by supporters of primitivism in the surrealist movement:

> Their aesthetic criticism . . . had an ambiguous quality. On the one hand, it depended heavily on reflections about the "African soul" and the supposed essence of "the Black" Man that were fashionable at the time. But such speculative constructions were inherently directly Western ethnographies and philosophies of history that dominated the second half of the

nineteenth century. They were based on the idea that two forms of human society existed: primitive societies which were governed by the "savage mentality," and civilized society governed by reason ... The so-called savage mentality was not adapted to the processes of rational argumentation.[109]

There is a clear linkage of primitivity and savagery to Africa, whose population was believed to have "not adapted to the processes of rational argumentation." These are the issues about the absence of Black reason and morality that Parkin articulates in the novel. His critical consciousness is tied to these beliefs that "There were indigenous qualities inscribed in the blood of each race"—that in "the blood of the Black ran instinct, irrational impulses, and primal sensuality" and that the "power of the universal imagination was linked to a 'melanin principle.'"[110] In a very problematic way, Blackness in this sense was believed to have an aesthetic proclivity not grounded in reason but rather in the imagination, which was considered to a be lower faculty. It was seen as primal, instinctual, and sensuous. Mbembe explains that this avant-garde aesthetic did not critique colonialist discourse; instead, it drew heavily on "colonial myths and stereotypes that it sought to invert. It did not call into question the existence of the cannibal or of a fundamentally irrational and savage Black world."[111] If *A Quality of Violence* is an exploration of primitivism, does Salkey undermine or destabilize this Eurocentric perspective? If so, why does he seem to take a distant position, merely providing the lens through which to represent colonial ideologies, given the multiple and conflicting narrative points of view?

The answer is that he uses language as a political strategy for conveying ambiguity. At the heart of this is the issue of boundary crossing, what Salkey does by using the veneer of drama and by using surrealist ideas of the twentieth century while critiquing them from within. Salkey was writing in 1959 within an already established tradition that presented Black bodies and culture as a spectacle of primitivity. Among the theatrical stagings during the 1950s were Bim and Bam's plays, which focused upon the spiritual and folk traditions of the island. Many of their plays, such as *Duppy Biznezz*, were comedic representations of Pocomania and other Revival practices: "the central focus of comedy was thus a Revival/Pocomania 'Mother' and her community, along with the threat of supernatural stone-throwing. Mother Banner's movement of the 'Pocomania drums' was played for laughs, relying on the audience's sense that it knew what a real 'Pocomania' dance involved. These comedies relied on the audience's knowledge to emphasize its distance from the events depicted."[112] Comedic stagings such as *Duppy Biznezz* can be read as an attempt to police through ridicule and social disavowal the behaviors of the lower class—which certainly has a history in the carnivalesque theater of violence from the slave era when body parts were gruesomely staged to deter subversion and resistance to the master's will. It therefore makes sense that this form of cultural censorship would likewise be staged as it builds upon an existing colonialist practice.

Although Salkey was signifying upon an already established generic tradition, he subverts this narrative by superimposing contrasting voices and perspectives that create a sense of both authorial and textual ambiguity. Salkey inverts what was represented as comedy, fodder about primitivity, into a serious issue for deep consideration, albeit in an ambivalent manner. In his ambivalent stance, while gesturing toward a performative basis of representation with his prologue and epilogue, Salkey enacts a degree of boundary crossing by using the realist novel, and subverting that genre, as an internal mechanism for staging a tragic drama, which is a decisive departure from the comedic stagings of that time period. Because the comedic lens existed already in the popular consciousness, Salkey wanted to suggest the seriousness of his subject matter. While his departure from the comedic lens signals a different political attitude toward the subject matter, the ambivalence suggests a failure—at first glance.

A closer reading of Salkey's novel provides an explanation for the shift in reception that is not solely about the context of readership, but also having to do with a fundamental paradox that underlies the text—the paradox of the slave sublime's ability to mask and create confusion over signification, given the simultaneous and conflicting meanings within its sign system. Salkey continuously distorts signs, the underlying reason for the ambiguity, not only to mask his political distance from Eurocentric beliefs, but also as a ploy to ensure a financial return on his creative endeavor as a writer. In *Anancy in the Great House*, Joyce Jonas suggests that Caribbean writers have to assume a trickster identity because the publishing industry maintains a master-slave power dynamic over Black writers:

One aspect of the applicability to the Caribbean writer is in the matter of publication. The contemporary marketplace experience for the Caribbean artist is the margin where Western commerce meets the creative artist's expressivity—a publisher and global distributor of his work are necessities. And since the marketplace of literary exchange (despite progress made in the establishment of publishing houses in the black world) is still ruled by publishers, universities, and big business, the artist must create and present his fictive message in such a way that the House will be persuaded to invest. Clearly, to shape a marketable fiction that exposes the rottenness of the Great House requires the artist as trickster in a very commercial sense.[113]

In essence, Jonas argues that the publishing industry maintains a paradigmatic plantation structure in its hegemonic relationship over Black writers. On the issue of his readership and market share, Salkey had to consider his work's marketing viability, so he filters the novel's central consciousness through the mixed-race middle-class characters, the Parkins and Marshalls, while subverting it through ambiguity. This ambivalence or double voice is what Jonas calls an "Ananse-fashion" of subverting authority: "It is from the wild, untamed realm of paradox, uncertainty, ambiguity, and imagination beyond the fixed certainties of Western norms that the Caribbean artist, Ananse-fashion, brings the brokenness of folk experience together into a web of meaning and exposes the folly and danger of assuming a position of final authority."[114] As Jonas points out, Caribbean writers, when faced with decisions about the marketability of their work, usually become a trickster and "the trickster becomes a perfect image for the black artist who, confirmed to the margins of Europe's inscribed text, nevertheless presides, godlike, over the marketplace of linguistic exchange, signifying upon authority's text in endless wordplay and deconstruction."[115] The trickster has the ability to transform through the imagination's power: the central work or occupation of the trickster is wordplay, using language to mask subversion. Jonas attributes this trickster strategy of Caribbean writers to Anancy, the spider figure in Caribbean folklore. It is important to take into account again Emily Zobel Marshall's point that Anancy in a Jamaican context is a strategist who metamorphosed as a response to the violent nature of the Massa's whip to become "a symbol of creative chaos and longed for freedom in a tyrannical and coercive order."[116] Like Anancy, Caribbean writers caught in a master-slave dynamic have felt the whip and have sought ways to subvert aesthetically and politically the publishing industry's authority.[117] Peter Nazareth argues persuasively that Salkey's author note in *Anancy's Score* "provides us with clues as to how to read" *A Quality of Violence* as a display of Salkey's Anancy strategy: "I have plucked my Anancy from the great folk tales of West Africa and the Caribbean, and I have made him inhabit both worlds, the old and the new, locked deep in my own imagination . . . He holds no reservations; makes only certain crucial allowances; he knows no boundaries; respects no one, not even himself, at times; and he makes a mockery of everybody's assumptions and value judgments."[118] As additional support for his argument, Nazareth points to a letter that he received from Salkey, in which the author writes openly about his intentional display of "ambiguity" as a narrative strategy: "With your glimpse of my penchant for ambiguity and ambivalence, I would have thought you might have twigged to my method of characterization and narrative. Yes? No?"[119]

Salkey's intentional ambiguity highlights the signifying elements of the Anancy strategy of conveying double voice, which is associated with the slave sublime's contestation of plantation structures through the imagination. As a writer, Salkey was the ultimate trickster figure who thrilled in the art of dissimulation in his concerted efforts to confuse and distort signs. Salkey challenges the Massa's authority, the publishing industry, by using the imagination and Anancy strategy for inversion, as a bodily/carnivalesque aesthetic that dabbles in paradox, ambiguity, masking, doubleness, verbal wordplay—a hermeneutic challenge to hegemonic power structures. Richard Priebe highlights a key passage in his review of *The Trickster in West Africa* that captures author Richard Pelton's notion that "the trickster is hermeneutics in action, creating language out of his own body like a spider spinning its web . . . probing ceaselessly all opacity for hidden designs, and forever rejecting every form of muteness. One is permitted to believe that he, like every hermeneut, is doomed to failure, but not before immersing oneself in the specific language of his dance."[120] The trickster's language is performative—it is a dance that renders language as opaque, a reason why Salkey's novel was regarded as a failure and the issue underlying Nazareth's statement in his 1978 review of the novel that "Salkey's work is not obtained easily as cracking a nut; instead it is like peeling an onion."[121] At the heart of this painstaking "dance" involving opacity, to conceal and convey layers of distorted meanings, is the imagination's display of power, if we consider Lawrence Sullivan's review of Pelton's book as well: "Pelton tells us that the trickster is the quintessential master of irony . . . The use of irony is always an imaginative act . . . The trickster is a master of words. He employs them in an ironic and, hence, imaginative way."[122] Another scholar, Mary N. MacDonald, when reviewing Pelton's book, suggests that the imagination seeks to break down and overturn barriers and boundaries. Left free to roam, it can challenge the rules of language and syntax, time and space, hegemonic systems of ordering that are socially imposed.[123]

In a manner similar to the way in which Salkey harnesses the imagination's power as a display of the slave sublime aesthetic, Mark McWatt provides a compelling analysis of Wilson Harris's critical essays, arguing that in "The Phenomenological Legacy" Harris's articulation of "the imagination is concerned with the transcending of barriers and categories of all kinds—with looking 'beyond the fortress of self-created things toward a paradoxical womb . . . the true complex of one's time is open and transformative, rather than static.'" Harris's language of the imagination conveys "possibilities of . . . genuine freedom" that involve a process of "reading and writing . . . from the margins."[124] Here, not only do we see an echoing of Pelton's ideas about West African trickster and mythic irony that challenge boundaries but also Jonas's idea that Caribbean writers enact a trickster strategy to challenge those boundaries from the margins, particularly with regard to the publication of their work. McWatt describes also a process at the heart of Harris's oeuvre that involves what he calls the "language of imagination" that seeks liberation: "Here the language of imagination can be seen as an interior dialogue or dialectic—the growth, through conflict, of a seed of doubt into a structure of delicate balance whereby the position is held and the position dangerously glimpsed for the first time both assume a new dimension of uncertainty and freedom and cancel out the urge to destroy the alien in order to preserve the known and comfortable. Within this lies the haunting spectre of genuine liberation."[125] The slave sublime points to liberatory strategies, confronting limitations and seeking agency, especially by unshackling the imagination from reason's oppressive hold. These imaginative strategies suggest the metaphoric freedom that comes with the slave sublime's breakdown of boundaries—the very element of the imagination's subversive power that Kant wanted to censor in his exposition of the sublime.

The imagination, in this sense, "confronts the limits" of the representation of sublime in its boundlessness, yet it connects to the beautiful—capturing the essence of the slave sublime.[126] Kant initially acknowledged the important function of the imagination and its transcendental power, but he conformed to the dominant ideas of his time by relegating the imagination to a subaltern position.[127] This is what happens in the first edition of the *Critique of Pure Reason*, which Kant later rewrote to downplay the role of the imagination in our knowledge of objects.[128] Central to this dismissal is the linkage of the associative imagination to "chaos and indeterminacy," which Kant believed were "*not* the nature of the imaginary life and its power." There is a political or radical undercurrent to the imagination in that it only exists in the "context of human unsociable sociability, and that this context permanently raises problems and tensions."[129] It is out of such milieu that the slave sublime emerges to contest the various colonial practices of violence. While Kant dismisses the potential exercise of the associative imagination as a transcendental power on the basis that it "would remain concealed within the mind as a dead and to us unknown faculty,"[130] it is what lies at the heart of the slave sublime's embracement of the imagination as subversive power.

The ambivalence in Salkey's work points to the play of the imagination so that the text remains open to serve multiple audiences. As Salkey's text demonstrates, left free to roam, the imagination in its symbolic form as narrative voice defies and resists logic because of its foundation within "Man's" Enlightenment discourse. Thus, the slave sublime's embracement of the imagination energizes its oppositional force—making it subversion to reason and logic in the figurative back and fro swing of the pendulum from certainty to uncertainty. After all, as McWatt suggests about Harris's work, "the language of imagination . . . must speak to, and [involve] seemingly implacable opposites in order to bridge the gap between them and to enter the chasm, however terrifying, of hostility between peoples and cultures, between matter and spirit."[131]

CHAPTER TWO

Language and Social Death

*Boundary Crossing and the Grammar of Violence
in NourbeSe Philip's Prose and Poetry*

The progenitors of Caribbean society as it exists today created a situation
such that the equation between i-mage and word was destroyed for the African.
The African could still think and i-mage, she could still conceive of what was
happening to her. But in stripping her of language, in denying the voice power
to make and, simultaneously, to express the i-mage—in denying the voice
expression, in fact—the ability and power to use the voice was effectively
stymied . . . To speak a language is to enter another consciousness, that of
their masters, while simultaneously being excluded from their own.

—NourbeSe Philip, "Introduction," *She Tries Her Tongue*

This brings us to the second constituent element of the slave relation: the slave's
natal alienation . . . on the control of symbolic instruments. This is achieved in
a unique way in the relation of slavery: in the definition of the slave, however
recruited, as a socially dead person . . . Slaves differed from other human beings
in that they were not allowed freely to integrate the experience of their ancestors
into their lives, to inform their understanding of social reality with the inherited
meanings of their natural forebears.

—Orlando Patterson, *Slavery and Social Death*

What accounts for the marginalized voice of Africans during the violent acts
of colonization and enslavement under Europeans who privilege the written
word? The problematic, as NourbeSe Philip demonstrates in *Looking for Livingstone* and *She Tries Her Tongue*, results from the unbalanced power relations in the production of knowledge and the epistemic violence that occurs
with the intrusion of European culture during the colonial encounters in Africa and the Caribbean. The opposition between speech and writing serves
as a major focal point in Philip's texts, and she presents silence in contrast to
logocentric and hegemonic Western values that convey a rationalistic worldview through image-making to legitimize colonial violence.[1] The silencing of
Black subjects is created by the social and cultural systems that are embedded

in Western language, such as the negative images, ideologies, and discursive violence through which Black identities are interpellated and dishonored.

In this chapter, I shift from a narrow focus on the Jamaican case study to demonstrate the broader applicability of the slave sublime concept to the Caribbean as I explore the undermining of narrative verisimilitude in *Looking for Livingstone* and the poetic subversion of logos in *She Tries Her Tongue* by Philip, a Trinidadian-Canadian writer. As an aesthetic of the slave sublime, the often colliding and multiple layers of signification that Philip's works portray constitute a concerted effort to undermine the stability and power of Western ideas and to represent the violence and social death that ensue from all facets of colonization, which include the linguistic, ontological, and epistemological. Oftentimes the masculinist colonial discourse renders colonized subjects, whether male or female, simply as feminine and passive bodies. As such, Philip depicts "the Word" as masculine and as a floating signifier for the phallus, Christianity, and Western ontology, while "Silence" represents the feminized Black body and the African continent. In *Looking for Livingstone* Philip uses the architecture of the nineteenth-century travel narrative to represent a Sankofan[2] journey throughout Africa, back in time before the infusion of Western ideas—"the Word"—and its related hegemonic power. This boundary-crossing text fuses together travelogue and poetry to undermine the travel narrative form because of its pretense to realism and historical accuracy.

In *She Tries Her Tongue*, Philip points to the difficulties of dealing with a negative self-image and the loss of the mother tongue as forms of "natal alienation" that foster social death. By miming the process of creolization, she performs violence on the colonial English language, and doing so functions also as a means of recouping both a lost mother tongue and the silences that result from colonization. The dislocation from the mother tongue has had long-lasting psychological ramifications for African descendants in the New World. One approach, according to Philip, for countering these ramifications is to voice the problems of cultural fragmentation and disconnection from the African ancestral homeland by using the idiosyncratic, demotic variant of colonial languages to undermine the inherited colonial language. Thus as a poetic model in *She Tries Her Tongue*, Philip destructures the colonial English language by miming the process of creolization, and by using the creolized, demotic language she taps into a racially relevant semantic universe and experiments with what she considers an appropriate language for poetic expression. She cites in the introduction the Rastafari privileging of I-words (what she interprets as an "i-magination" process to denote the centrality of the imagination to ideation) along with the Trinidadian demotic language as generative models for her own forms of creolization, thus showing the importance of language in the construction of social identity and in the resistance to colonial domination.

It is equally important for Philip to find an appropriate narrative genre in *Looking for Livingstone*, which follows loosely the nineteenth-century travel narrative genre or historical narrative. Caribbean historian Michel-Rolph Trouillot argues "that the historical narrative bypasses the issue of truth by nature of its form."[3] As such, the travel narrative genre has a tautological function: it is a genre in which narrative form suggests truth, and truth is further substantiated by the narrative form itself. This circular logic is what, unfortunately, also gives credence to the colonialist explorer/travel writers, such as David Livingstone and Henry Stanley. Pointing to the "structures of knowledge and power" that are embedded in the colonist travel narrative (or travelogue) Ali Behdad explains that as a generic feature the narrative oftentimes "begins with prefatory remarks that raise and address the general questions of who speaks, in the name of what, and for which particular reasons." In the rendering of a heroic tale from an autobiographical, first-person point of view, relevant information such as institutional affiliation is divulged as a way of legitimating the discourse and providing textual authority for the realist, linear narrative.[4] For Behdad, such a first-person point of view provides also a "unifying function" and a "centralized, consistent, and unique subject of enunciation." In this sense, the first-person subject functions as the "site of an act of interpretation," that is, as one who makes sense of the native culture—in essence, one "who is authorized to *make* meaning."[5] Notwithstanding, this realist perspective is a masquerade and, as Abdul R. JanMohamed explains, "the colonialist text is in fact antagonistic to some of the prevailing tendencies of realism."[6] In a way, realism is rendered as complicit with the colonial project and its rationalistic discourses that depend upon erasures.

By the same token, Mary Louise Pratt points out that the task for explorer/travel writers was to produce what they, subjectively, considered to be "information." Pratt goes on to say that "these subjects positioned themselves in their discourse . . . as invisible, passive, and personally innocent conduits for information," despite the fact that their narratives enact a process of "self-effacement" that fosters "silences." In other words, silence functions as a symbol of erasure for the actual violent circumstances that resulted from the contact between European and native peoples. Conflicts were an "endemic" occurrence, Pratt argues, and "[r]elations were constantly breaking down and erupting into violence, constantly being renegotiated or enforced by brutality" and "the Europeans in this domain of struggle were charged with installing the edifice of domination and legitimizing its hierarchy."[7] As Pratt points out in yet another text, native "voices are almost never quoted, reproduced, or even invented" within the colonial space of the travel narrative.[8] And as further elucidation, Steven Slemon adds that colonization, whatever precise form it assumes, initiates a kind of "double vision" or "metaphysical clash" that "emerges in the space of incommensurability between inherited notions of imperial history . . . in which the silenced, marginalized, or disposed voices within the colonial encounter themselves form the record of 'true' history."[9] Such silences and marginalization equate with social death.

Philip politicizes travel writing's embeddedness within colonial structures, particularly the silencing of the native voices. By posing her travel narrative within the aesthetic of magical realism, Philip questions the supposed truth and facts of that genre as she transforms it and recoups the silenced voices by including their versions of history. In this light, the transformation of genre for Philip involves both political and aesthetic implications. As a female and postcolonial writer, Philip cannot ignore the colonialist and masculine rhetoric endemic to the travel narrative genre. It comes as no surprise, then, that she draws attention to the way in which the travel narrative genre is "complicitous" with "structures of knowledge and power."[10]

In *Looking for Livingstone*, Philip transforms the travel narrative genre through her use of magical realism, an aesthetic that transfigures realist literary conventions and empowers marginalized voices whose social and political subject matter exceeds the capabilities of the genre. Unlike literary realism, which is useful for conveying banal, ordinary life, the magic realism aesthetic is able to embody "experiences of extremity—or random victimization, of powerlessness, of hysteria and panic before unmanageable events,"[11] such as the violence that ensues from colonization, slavery, and colonialism. These forms of violence exceed the capacity of literary realism, often engaging with elements of the (slave) sublime and the aesthetic and political missions of Black writers in the Caribbean. That is to say, by utilizing magic realism, Philip expresses overtly her aesthetic departure and political difference from colonial writers, and by means of the new genre Philips departs from the mimetic tendencies of some postcolonial writers. While it has been argued widely that magical realism "diverges from the logocentric tradition of mainstream Western thought and literature,"[12] it should be noted also that it foregrounds "two opposing discursive systems, with neither managing to subordinate or contain the other" and that this "sustained opposition forestalls the possibility of interpretive closure through any act of naturalizing the text to an established system of representation."[13] Border crossing or liminality between the realistic and the magical is what empowers this aesthetic in its ability to gravitate between, yet to exist simultaneously within, two separate worlds. It is a mode of boundary crossing that conveys the slave sublime aesthetic in its radical interweaving of form and formlessness.

Looking for Livingstone straddles two terrains: the boundaries between the realistic and the magical. Although bearing the generic features of a novel, this text oscillates between poetry and prose and history and fiction. The latter category opens up the closed field of the purported rationality in the scientific-historical approach of colonialist writers. Likewise, in the former, the pairing of the poetic with prose functions as a form of border crossing that permits a counter-hegemonic intrusion on prose narrative, thereby allowing an open field of interpretation with its gaps and fissures. As with the poetic structure that intrudes upon prose narration, the episodic narrative structure in this text allows also for fissures and gaps in narration. In doing so, it forestalls a closed interpretation and drives narrative form and language to the fringes of indeterminacy. A great deal of the indeterminacy of Philip's magical realism, to convey the slave sublime aesthetic, stems from the genre's familial relation to the fantastic genre. The key difference, however, is that in magical realism the reader accepts that the "real" and the "magical" coexist conjunctively even though s/he may hesitate, but in the fantastic the "real" and "magical" are disjunctive temporalities because the reader hesitates in deciding which to accept.[14]

Because of the critical and political aspect of magical realism in *Looking for Livingstone*, Philip's critique must be grounded in the possibility of having both supernatural and rational explanations, even with the appearance of ghosts in an otherwise realistic setting. Philip achieves hesitation when she obliges the reader to decide whether to accept literal explanations for supernatural occurrences, denoted by time shifts, the appearances of ghostly figures, the presentation of magic as commonplace, and the fantastical epic battle fought over the primacy of words or silence. In this sense, Philip disavows Enlightenment rationality, which would dismiss the occurrence and the importance of the supernatural, the imaginary. The magical further intercepts the realistic framework of the text when the first-person narrator, The Traveller, announces that she is searching for the long-dead David Livingstone and the intangible Silence. This text calls constantly for supernatural explanations in its critique of rationality and systems of truth. Philip voices her political views about colonial narratives, ideologies, and the language that both sustains and validates these discourses, as well as the problematic of ascertaining historical truth about precolonial cultures, given the colonist legacy of David Livingstone and Henry Morton Stanley who were two nineteenth-century European explorers of Africa. This enduring legacy of colonialism, which reconfigured all orders of indigenous African societies (ethnic, social, economic, linguistic, etc.), remains as coloniality of power even though "colonialism as an explicit political order was destroyed."[15] Livingstone's and Stanley's appearances as ghostly figures function as metaphors for the sublime haunting of history because their colonial legacies are ever-present—the legacies persist despite the end of colonialism as a formal practice.

While on a journey among the LENSECI people, The Traveller sees David Livingstone appearing as "a ghostly shape standing tall and thin among the stalks of cane," but as she "reached out to touch him" and "shaped" her "lips around his name—'Dr. Livingstone'—and as quickly he was gone."[16] The ghostly appearance and description of Livingstone as "pale, gaunt and naked" suggest the naked truth about British explorations in Africa and his living, historical legacy. As The Traveller journeys to other places she is plagued with dreams about Livingstone and continues to see his ghost everywhere. The phantasmagoria, which the narrator calls "Livingstone-I-Presume," functions as the explorer's uncanny double. In one encounter, the two of them sit together as they eat a meal, drink coffee, and sip cognac. As they sit together, during which time one hundred years passes, The Traveller and Livingstone-I-Presume share stories about their respective adventures: "One hundred years later, there we were—still sitting before the fire—Livingstone and I and Silence. I stretched out my hand and touched him—he seemed asleep; I shook him gently by the shoulder."[17] Livingstone-I-Presume represents David Livingstone's colonial legacy, which continues to haunt the African continent through the names of places, supplanted language, and lost tribal culture. Contrary to the colonial belief that Livingstone established order on the African continent, Philip's text reveals that he disrupted the order of the various cultures he encountered, which resulted in the confused jumble of their original name, Silence. Colonization has shattered the once "whole, indivisible, complete" Silence into anagrams.[18] Anagrams for silence include place names such as LENSECI, SCNELIS, SCENILE, ECNELIS, and SINCEEL. The Traveller's encounter with the evanescent Livingstone and his colonial legacy suggests an experience of the uncanny: as a ghost Livingstone is evanescent but his colonial legacy is ever-present.

The literary critics David Mikics and Lois Parkinson Zamora note the underlying historical significance of the uncanny and the appearance of ghosts in magical realist works of literature. David Mikics argues that "magical realism is a mode or subset of the uncanny in which the uncanny exposes itself as a historical and cultural phenomenon." As with the cohesion of the realistic and the supernatural in magical realism, in the uncanny "ordinary life may also be the scene of the extraordinary" and the "dreamlike suspension on the border between the fantastic and the mundane offers a utopian, if evanescent, promise of transfigured perception, the hypnotic renewing of everyday existence." As such, the uncanny "realizes the conjunction" between the realistic and the imaginative "by focusing on a particular historical moment afflicted or graced by this doubleness." Given the cross-stitching between the uncanny and magical realism, particularly because "magical realism surrounds with its fabulous aura a particular, historically resonant time and place," Mikics argues that "the theory of magical realism must supply an approach to history, not merely literary genre."[19] As for Zamora, she sees a connection also between magical realism and history. She notes the ability of ghosts in magical realist texts to "unsettle modernity's (and the novel's) basis in progressive, linear history." She argues that because ghosts "float free in time, not just here and now but then and there, eternal everywhere," they "embody the fundamental magical realist sense that reality always exceeds our capacities to describe or understand or prove." In places that were colonized, sublimity as the challenge to representation is often a crucial issue in finding an appropriate vehicle for conveying the extreme and excessive—the limit-breaking realities of the colonial condition. The purpose of literature, then, as Zamora sees it, is to "engage this excessive reality, to honor that which we may grasp intuitively but never fully define." By engaging the "excessive reality," literary works embodying the magical realist aesthetic "ask us to look beyond the limits of the knowable" to identify that which exists "in/between/on modernity's boundaries."[20] The appearance of Livingstone's ghost points both to the figural and yet the literal aspect of imperial history as a nightmare that perpetually haunts, a representation that also goes far beyond the capabilities of literary realism and which borders on the sublime, given the magnitude of the multitudinous colonial ruptures brought about by the forces of modernity.

For Philip, *Looking for Livingstone* serves as a palimpsest text, a text in which her insertion of magical realism into the travel narrative genre allows her to unsettle history by writing over the official story of British colonial explorations in Africa, her ancestral homeland. Trouillot explains that "any historical narrative is a particular bundle of silences, the result of a unique process, and the operation required to deconstruct these silences will vary accordingly."[21]

Likewise, in the essay "In a Spirit of Calm Violence," Homi Bhabha states that "The grand narratives of nineteenth-century historicism on which its claims to universalism were founded—Evolutionism, Utilitarianism, Evangelism—were also, in another textual and territorial time-space, the technologies of colonial and imperialist governance." He argues further that it is the "rationalism" of these ideologies of progress that increasingly come to be eroded in the encounter with the "contingency of cultural difference . . . [H]istory in that era [is] most renowned for its historicizing (and colonizing) of the world and the word."[22] Philip challenges the representation of Africans as ahistorical, silent beings, and, as the text suggests, history is "not a thing to be discovered, so much as recovered."[23]

As a (re)presentation of history, in the passage below Philip offers "Silence" symbolically as the erasure of indigenous African culture that resulted from British colonization. As agents of colonization—and using the euphemistic term of "discovery" as a paradigmatic tactic of erasure (as in the production of myth) through linguistic substitution—Livingstone and Stanley have also created silences by erasing the already existing cultures and histories: Livingstone was "one of the first Europeans to cross the Kalahari—*with* the help of Bushmen; was shown the Zambezi by the indigenous African and 'discovered' it; was shown the falls of Mosioatunya—the smoke that thunders—by the indigenous African, 'discovered' it and renamed it. Victoria Falls. Then he set out to 'discover' the source of the Nile and was himself 'discovered' by Stanley—'Dr. Livingstone, I presume?' And History. Stanley and Livingstone—white fathers of the continent. Of silence."[24] Colonist history often omits, thereby silencing, the physical and sexual violence that accompanies the voyages of colonization. As suggested also in the passage above, there is a symbolic link between the land and the African woman's body, as both were raped during colonial encounters. That is to say, an unspoken sexual violence is implied in both cases, specifically the sexual violence that accompanied the act of "discovery" because the narrator refers to Stanley and Livingstone as the "white fathers of the continent. Of silence." In one episode The Traveller talks about a recurring dream in which she and Livingstone "COPULATE LIKE TWO BEASTS—HE RIDES ME—HIS WORD SLIPPING IN AND OUT OF THE WET MOIST SPACES OF MY SILENCE." After trying to fill every crevice of The Traveller's silence, Livingstone withdraws to the forest to weep, and there he tells Stanley that his "WORD IS IMPOTENT." He is distraught because, as he explains, "WITHOUT MY WORD, THE CONTINENT IS BEYOND ME—BEYOND US."[25] Written in all caps, this episode calls attention to the mythic discourses and sexual violence that are central to conquest. "The Word" has the masculine function of violating silence: silence is feminized and functions as a sliding metaphor for the female body and the African continent as a whole, while the "the Word" represents the phallus and colonial discourses. As Philip demonstrates, without discourse as a tool of domination, colonial rhetoric is impotent.

Philip portrays other instances when the masculine, colonialist discourse has a dominating and virile power, having the ability to impregnate and silence. When Chareem the youngest pubescent girl among the ECNELIS speaks about the power of words, The Traveller describes the onerous effects of words on this precocious orator: "The words were too heavy and ponderous for a child of her years, but she was at home with them, as if her body, her bones had stretched with them as companions, her flesh rounding out around the ideas they contained."[26] This passage demonstrates the impregnating force of words because the words have "stretched" and have made Chareem's body "round." Chareem's pregnancy is suggested also because she has to pause—becoming silent—in order to "still her words" for "days and days" before continuing the story.[27] At this point in the narrative Chareem takes on the qualities of the Madonna and her Immaculate Conception, but the analogous depiction of Chareem's pregnancy as being immaculate "silences" the sexual violence of rape, both physical and cultural. Similar to the Madonna, Chareem gives birth to "the Word," the "Offspring of God."[28] As the ECNELIS explain, "God laughed, believed himself vindicated, and rewarded the earth with words and more words" and "their ancestors, so their stories tell, mounted armies of words to colonise the many and various silences of people round about."[29] Despite the apparent circular chronology in the story, Chareem's pregnancy suggests the indoctrination of a new religious dogma, while giving birth to an alien dogma ("the Word") implies a great degree of epistemological violence, which is further exacerbated when one belief systems is supplanted by another through the violence of colonization and the evangelical mission involving "word" wars.

The narrator had visited the ECNELIS during a time when they were preparing to go to war with the SINCEEL. It was a war to be fought over the supremacy of culturally specific belief systems. A man tells her that "Every hundred years by our calendar, during the month of Cassiopeia, we go to war with the SINCEEL—those whose beliefs differ from ours, about the primacy of word or silence in the beginning of the world." He continues to say that the loser of the war is "condemned to follow the beliefs of the winner" for "the next hundred years" and that the victor "imposes" their own conflicting discourse: "Where there was silence, the winner imposes the word; where the word, silence."[30] The contending belief systems are apparent between those who value silence and those who "believe in the power of words."[31] Trouillot argues that history is a story that silences or excludes the perspective of the conquered.[32] All in all, this episode challenges the Western Christian doctrine ("the Word") by parodying the fixation on the word itself and the processes of silencing that are integral to its dissemination during colonial, evangelical missions. As The Traveller takes her leave, her "last image of the ECNELIS is of them sitting around a fire sharpening their tools of war—words—for the battle of the cosmonogies."[33] This impending word war is to be fought over the theoretical beliefs supporting the origin of the universe, as the word cosmogony suggests. It denotes the struggle between two incompatible or paradoxical notions of self that relates to one's ontological and epistemological sense of orientation in the universe.

As given in the New Testament's *The Gospel According to John*, "the Word" is a symbol for the Christian God: "In the beginning was the Word, and the Word was with God, and the Word was God."[34] In this biblical version, "the Word" has a triple function, as it precedes the beginning of beginnings, is sanctioned by God, and functions also as a symbol for God.[35] *The Gospel According to John* also gives context to David Livingstone's appellation as "foe of darkness." In a reference to Christ, this Gospel explains that "All things came into being through him, and without him not one thing came into being. What has come into being in him was life, and the life was the light of all people. The light shines in the darkness, and the darkness did not overcome it."[36] As this biblical text reveals, "the light" overcomes darkness, even though it is posed in the passive voice, as in the domination of darkness by light. Frank Kermode explains that the word "darkness" denotes the "darkness of that primitive chaos which, as later thinkers remarked, had only the potentiality of becoming."[37] This notion is also symbolic of the domination of Europeans over Africans on the basis of the latter's presumed evil, barbaric, and nonhuman identity—the notion that their humanity was inchoate, as I discussed in chapter 1. It is in this regard that Livingstone and other colonial adventurers thought it their duty to bring Africa and Africans out of "primitive chaos" and to transform potentiality into actuality through Christian *enlightenment*. Thus Livingstone's appellation as "foe of darkness" has a double meaning: first, as the racial distinction between himself and native Africans and, second, as his role of bringing light—"the Word"—or civilization to African peoples. Since Livingstone is regarded as the "foe of darkness," it is imperative that we consider the complement to his identity as the bearer of light, his representative role as a missionary representing Christ. As Christ commanded miracles, Livingstone, too, simulates the same ability while in Africa, but he is armed with modern supplies: guns, the "good book—the Holy Bible—the word of God," and a "magic lantern to frighten and impress the 'savage heathen.'"[38] The guns, no doubt, easily facilitated a religious conversion, not because of the natives' passive acceptance of "the Word" but because of their mortal fear.

During colonization, the materialist project coupled with the "enlightenment" or the evangelical mission of spreading Christianity to Africans was a double-edged sword in the fight for racial/cultural preeminence. It was a fight in which one culture supplanted the ontological and epistemological theories of the other. According to Paget Henry, a culture's religious beliefs or creation myths are integrally tied to its linguistic/discursive infrastructure and are also complementary to the physiological makeup of that culture.[39] While Western philosophy is coded in the "impersonal language of being and non-being, in-itself and for-itself," African philosophy is concerned with a "more personal language of gods and spirits who were in charge of various aspects of creation, including the process of ego genesis and hence ego performance."[40] African theogonies are not structured according to a binary system either, unlike the Western thought system in which the transcendental signifier is God—a male, white figure associated with light and transcendence. Moreover, for Christians, the Bible represents a linear, genealogical, and historical narrative from the beginning to the end of time. By employing the genre of magical realism, Philip offers a counter-narrative about what happened "in the beginning" in order to destabilize the mythic biblical representation. Bellune, the oldest women of the ECNELIS, explains the following in which the reference to *God as female* opposes the masculine, Western representation: "God first created silence: whole, indivisible, complete. All creatures—man, woman, beast, insect, bird and fish—lived happily together within this silence, until one day man and woman lay down together and between them created the first word. This displeased the God deeply and in anger she shook out her bag of words over the world, sprinkling and showering her creation with them."[41] Philip's counter-representations suggest that the meanings of words are arbitrary (yet relevant) in a closed system of signification such as culture rather than as a universal matrix. Thus the parable points to the discursive power of creating myths, of creating socially constructed meanings through language. Philip challenges also Christian hegemony, particularly the patriarchal idea that God is male. In this version of creationism, silence is God's first creation and the sexual union between man and woman produces "the first word." The implication is that humans invented the "first word" out of desire—which, in this case, literally comes between them or inhabits the difference between them. In this same episode about creation, not quoted here, Philip uncovers the violence of belief systems in order to dispel the authority of "the word," which, in addition to its burdensome nature, seems to have the contagious qualities of a disease: it can "spread" and "infect." In so doing, Philip extends her critique to Christianity as a whole because it is a culturally specific system of myth, which has a hegemonic potential for social death when forced upon another culture that has its own culturally/racially relevant beliefs and value systems.

Philip's travel narrative departs from the masculine discourses of "the Word," which dominates, feminizes, and silences indigenous African cultures. Her work discredits the assumed passivity and mental inferiority of the silent native, and, as such, challenges the colonist view that renders the African as a "speechless, denuded, biologized body."[42] Abena Busia points out that "one of the primary characteristics in the representation of the African woman is the construction of her inactive silence." She notes that "The African woman is conjured up out of a void, a fissure or space out of which there can be for her no coherent or comprehensible language: not because it cannot be uttered, but because . . . her language either cannot be heard or cannot be understood."[43] In her well-known essay "Can the Subaltern Speak?" Gayatri Spivak addresses the issue of gender-specific silences within the postcolonial/colonial context when the masculine Christian imperatives clash with native cultures. The kind of silences that Spivak uncovers in her native India are no different from the African context that Philip presents, especially because in both situations the colonizer is British and the silencing occurs in terms of race and gender since race is oftentimes articulated in gendered terms. Spivak points also to the "silenced areas" of academic disciplines, which include history, arguing that the imperialist "mingle[s] epistemic violence with the advancement of learning and civilization. And the subaltern woman will be as mute as ever."[44] The postcolonialist project, then, according to Spivak, is to critique or "unlearn" without simply resorting to a substitution of the "lost figure of the colonized."[45] Thus, for Spivak, part of the "unlearning" process involves the negation of masculine discourse.[46] However, as Spivak argues, rendering the subaltern a voice in history is problematic because, as she concludes her essay, the "subaltern cannot speak."[47] In a way, Philip, too, values the underlying significance of the subaltern's silence.

At the end of each episode the text lapses into poetry at key moments when the prose narration "cannot speak" or represent the extreme violence that the narrator/speaker has either witnessed or endured. It brings to the fore an element of the slave sublime aesthetic in which representation is achieved through boundary crossing. In *Looking for Livingstone* the poetic intrusion into the prose narration is an aspect of magical realist border crossing in which poetry allows for gaps and fissures in the narrative, Philip's way of symbolizing the gaps or silences in Western renderings of African history before and after colonization. The gaps and fissures in poetic narration suggest also psychological trauma, as represented below as the violent impact of word wars:

> it bound the foot
> sealed the vagina
> excised the clitoris
> set fire to the bride
> the temple dance
> > no more
> in the banish of magic[48]

Words have impeded movement, reproduction, and sexual gratification as well as the sanctity of sacred indigenous beliefs. The violence stemming from word wars is suggested also in a poem from the previous episode, but this poem differs because it involves racial epithets that serve as forms of epistemic/ psychic violence. The racial epithets include bifurcated words such as "nigger-woman," "Queen or Jemimah," "whore-wife," and "virgin-slut."[49] The implication is that these epithets symbolize the birth of a new, disruptive self as the result of word wars. In the linguistic sense, these horizontal, metonymic juxtapositions of the bifurcated epithets that occur on the combinative axis of representation suggest that Philip identifies psychic violence within language itself as social death and linguistic rape, a metaphor for the horizontal violence of rape that accompanied conquest.[50]

In yet another poem, the prevailing motif of "silence" suggests that the tongue—a metonym for language—becomes "bruised by tongue under teeth." The word "teeth" represents tools of war in the battle over words or ideology. Lured in by the seduction of words, "lips caress / before / the cruel between of teeth / crush / grind / the hard kernel / of silence."[51] The speaker's active resistance rather than passivity is suggested by her reference to the "words" as "bile" which she has "retched" up. Her resistance is marked also by her attempts to "kick," "shove," and "push." Despite the initial self-defense attempts during the implied colonial encounter, the speaker nonetheless gives into the seduction. She "stroked the kin" who, paradoxically, is also "the stranger" (an implicit reference to the notion of Stanley and Livingstone as the "white fathers of the continent. Of Silence") and has taken him within the intimate areas of her body, the interior of the African continent: "I have— / stroked the kin / the stranger / within it / taken it to places secret / with within / from between the thighs."[52] Colonization as cultural and linguistic rape has resulted in the birthing of a new self and simultaneously a lost identity: the speaker has "expelled . . . with the force of full / driven it / —a giant birthing—."[53] Having to face this new self is fraught with paradoxes and contradictions: the "smell of birth / sweet / clean / clings" but "some days / its odour / rank / upon me." Because of the disjunction between the old and the new self, the process of recovery from such psychic trauma involves an endless journey of self-recovery or, as the speakers puts it, "re / cognition": "I re / cognize it / in its belonging / know it again."[54] The prefix "re" in the word "re / cognition" indicates the return to a previous condition of knowing, as a cognitive restoration to a former state of knowing and a withdrawal from the present one. The prefix connects metonymically to words such as renew, retrace, reunite, which indicate the physical acts of repetition and return that are central elements of the slave sublime aesthetic. These contiguous relations on the combinatory axis of language suggest why The Traveller undertakes a circular, Sankofan journey through history: it involves both a psychological and physical return to the past in order to reclaim what is lost, so as to be able to move forward.

By depicting history as a circular narrative, Philip subverts the Western linear view of history. In direct contrast to linearity, the speaker/narrator of *Looking for Livingstone* reveals, "I have been travelling in circles these past hundred years—circle upon circle—ever widening; as I went I questioned, with very little success, everyone I met about what I was searching for. And what was I searching for? I was not at all sure—had only the barest of intimations of what it might be."[55] In efforts to indicate a break from Western reason, its scientific and historical theories, Philip, through her speaker/narrator, depicts the "the ever widening" circles to indicate the progression of time. Philip demonstrates the incompatibility between the Western and the African formulations about the progression of history and time. In terms of the African timeframe, The Traveller has visited the ECNELIS who were preparing for war during "THE FOUR HUNDREDTH DAY IN THE SIXTEENTH MONTH OF THE TEN THOUSANDTH YEAR OF OUR WORD." After her conversation with the women, they "withdrew to their huts; they remained there for a long time."[56] By The Traveller's calculation "they were gone for three months" but the women pointed out that they had been gone for only "half a day."[57] Here, Philip critiques Western positivism,

particularly its defense of linear historical narratives and its tautological assertion of truth. She is also critical of "the Word," which functions as the basis of
truth, itself a system of myth.

In a counter-hegemonic rendering of Western history, Philip uses the ancient Egyptian cyclical concept of time.[58] For these indigenous Africans, the
concept of cyclical time "remained in the framework of perpetual return":
"This is because on the historical level, as on the cosmic level, of which the
historical was undoubtedly only the projection in the real world, the only
thing that counted was the perpetuation of continuity . . . This cyclical functioning played a fundamental role in cosmic time, of which historical time
was only an application or an avatar on the human level."[59] With the narrator's circular journey, Philip employs an African cosmic notion of time in her
text, and using the genre of magical realism she fuses together seamlessly different historical time periods that become transhistorical. In a face-to-face
encounter, The Traveller asks a ghostly figure resembling Livingstone, "did you
know those bloody South Africans bombed your town, the one named after
you—Livingstone, foe of darkness—let's see, it was in nineteen hundred and
eighty seven, I believe, in April to be exact—by the old calendar."[60] The Traveller encounters (what the reader knows to be a deceased) Livingstone and
asks about an actual historical event that happened more than a century after
his death. David Livingstone died in 1873, but the event in South Africa happened in 1987. The mention of an actual historical event points to the text's
frequent magical realist intermingling of the imaginary and the realistic. As
Zamora explains, magical realist texts "question the nature of reality *and* the
nature of its representation."[61] As such, Philip's text seems to suggest that the
current cycle of violence that permeates the (post)colonial world of Africa
has to do with the experienced reality of the initial violence of colonization
and its perpetuation, its *changing same* that extends the practices of colonialism in forms of state-sanctioned violence, specifically the repressive violence
of the apartheid state. By revisiting the initial moment of conquest, The Traveller exposes the potential problems of state-approved discourses that are
based on "the Word" and its foundation in Christian dogma.

In contrast to Livingstone, The Traveller only carries maps, her body, and
her silence. Her silent thoughts are expressed in poetic form rather than
prose. In poetic representation, the Traveller describes the contact between
colonial adventurers, such as Livingstone, and native Africans as the meeting
between the "Alpha and the Omega / in one beginning."[62] She equates the explorer with a "wanderer," "adventurer," and "expert" who is "certified / in silence
/ in ancient schools / their mysteries / secrets / sciences / studied / —their

silences—."[63] The text points to the irony of silence's supposed inferiority to "the Word," especially because of the mystery, secrecy, and silence that shrouds and protects these systems of knowledge.[64] In a coded manner, Philip critiques the range of knowledge that Christian mysticism and science have produced, from the notion of the "fall" or "original . . . sin," "flat-earth," the big "bang" theory, to the historical discourses that are based on a "straight line." But the poem ends with "circles / widening / into ever / from the silence of / stone / dropped"[65] to suggest a contrast to the previous linear perspectives. Silence is "sacred" and "secret," while words are "profane" in "[their] uttered-ness."[66] In the figurative sense, The Traveller's voyage in search of Silence is an attempt to travel to a time before the fall, before colonial discourse "spread" and "infect[ed]" native African cultures. The simultaneous search for Livingstone, in this regard, represents the importance of uncovering and demasking Western discourses in their attempts to "dance with the shadows," to disguise their actions while engaging in physical and social death.[67]

In a sense, Philip's work can be regarded as revisionist, which implies also the cyclical act of return. In revisionist work, writers return "to the scenes of domination and oppression . . . to reactivate attempts at speaking that other forces tried to obliterate and keep from having effects."[68] As Steven Slemon puts it, the "'re-visioning' of history, then . . . come[s] into dialectical play with the inherited, dominant modes of discourse and cognition in colonialism's 'phenomenal legacy' and work[s] toward transmuting perception into new 'codes of recognition.'"[69] In direct opposition to European masculine imperatives and beliefs recorded during the British colonial era, Philip's Afrocentric and feminist perspective offers a counter-narrative to the purported historical and factual claims of colonial narratives. Moreover, her work challenges the discourses of the travel narrative genre by using the magical realism genre in order to question the validity of historical narratives that, by the mere nature of their form, are supposed to impart truth, as Behdad, JanMohamed, and Pratt have argued. Philip cements magical realism to the architectural structure of the travel narrative genre in order to critique the colonialist discourses that this literary convention fosters. As such, her text belongs to the genre without actually belonging; in other words, it breaks the form though it is subversively parasitic on its discourse.

Philip attempts to fill the blanks of those silences for Africans, women in particular, and, heeding Spivak's warnings against essentializing the subaltern, she focuses mainly on the issue of silence without presenting the African continent as an undifferentiated or singular culture. In direct opposition to the masculine imperatives and beliefs recorded during the British colonial era, Philip's Afrocentric and feminist perspective offers a counter-narrative to the purported historical and factual claims of colonial narratives. When The Traveller encounters the various African cultures, the contact does not depict the commonplace domination of indigenous African peoples; rather, it is The Traveller who must adapt to those cultures' way of life. In other words, The Traveller is subsumed by the cultures with which she comes into contact. She even has to undergo many trials or tests or simply has to work for room and board, suggesting that she does not assume a colonist role. The magical realist aspect of the text allows Philip to subvert further Western rationalistic discourses such as scientific or historical thought, which render Africans as inferior and primitive.

Part of Philip's project in *Looking for Livingstone* is to show the failure of Western models to represent the African way of life. For postcolonial writers such as Philip, the tools of the master, the travel narrative genre for example, must be reconfigured in the same way that the colonial language is transformed to the demotic or creolized language. There are limits to *Looking for Livingstone* given the revisionist project that Philip undertakes while being parasitic on its discourse at the same time as she challenges the formal and generic limits of the travelogue. Her collection of poems in *She Tries Her Tongue* exceeds those limits, as it extends the kind of problematic of deconstructing the colonial genre into a deconstruction of language itself, and by using creolized language she is able to extend her reflections of language and social death. Philip has extensive knowledge of European myth, language, theory, and narrative form and she uses it against its own grain. By raising the tradition of form to total self-consciousness, in a manner that demands that she uses the same form she is attempting to deconstruct, she brings attention to the ways in which form itself does violence to (post)colonial identity. For Philip, colonial violence and sexual assault, linguistic violation and rape, tongue and phallus alternate as metaphors for one another and as social death.

In *She Tries Her Tongue*, Philip offers a feminist perspective on Caribbean discourse, specifically the function of language in literary production. In doing so, she engages with and challenges the theoretical ideas of Edouard Glissant and Kamau Brathwaite, who both write from a male-centered Caribbean perspective. Using the masculine pronoun for the Caribbean subject, Glissant critiques and demystifies Western historical discourses, which offer a totalizing perception of the non-European world through a kind of "ethno-cultural hierarchy."[70] For Glissant, History (with a capital H) is a system of signs that is embedded in the discourse of domination, and, as he sees it, literature has an "equally pernicious" potential. He points to Hegel's ethnocentric and discriminatory classification of Africa as ahistorical, and, suggesting a collusion between historical and literary ideologies, he states that the "hierarchical system instituted by Hegel (ahistory, prehistory, History) corresponds clearly with the literary ideology of his time." As such, "Literature attains a metaexistence, the all-powerfulness of a sacred sign, which will allow people with writing to think it justified to dominate and rule peoples with oral civilization."[71] Glissant argues also that there is a "parallel between the pretension to objective interpretation on the part of the historian and the belief in the power of the realist narrative" and that "The surface effects of literary realism are the precise equivalent of the historian's claim to pure objectivity."[72] What Glissant is outlining is the kind of epistemic violence that is rendered as objective truth by these supposedly, disinterested colonial perspectives, not to mention the ways in which the legacy remains pernicious today. It is a process that adduces social death in the native's object position as naturally different from the subject position of the historian/literary writer.

Glissant argues that, given the logocentric assumptions of the colonial powers in the Caribbean, creole languages emerged out of the colonial context in which the necessity of hiding meanings through "public and open expression" occurs as a display of agency.[73] This is similar to chapter 1's discussion about the Anancy strategy in which Andrew Salkey engages as an element of the slave sublime's counter-hegemonic aesthetic. Such strategies of "public utterances" call attention to the degree to which Caribbean people felt "circumscribed by imperial laws and their attendant codes of conduct," such that "these subjects were obliged to seek expression through opaque, surreptitious, and resourceful means."[74] Glissant calls for a national literature by highlighting the need for a revisionist process, one which demystifies and "expose[s] the hidden workings" of a system and which reunites a community around its own myths and ideologies.[75] He critiques the use of realism in such a revisionist process in the Caribbean and other parts of the Americas, arguing that it "is not inscribed in the cultural reflex of African or American peoples."[76] Pointing to Gabriel García Márquez's *One Hundred Years of Solitude*, in which circularity deeply defies the linear notion of Western history, he argues against using linear narratives, contending that "our quest for the dimension of time will therefore be neither harmonious nor linear" and that its "advance will be marked by a polyphony of dramatic shocks, at the level of the conscious as well as the unconscious, between incongruous phenomena or 'episodes' so disparate that no link can be discerned."[77]

On some level, Glissant engages with Kantian sublime and the notion of its unrepresentability. As he suggests, speech or orality plays an important role in the construction of a national literature, but he points out that there is a challenge to literary expression given the legacy of the colonial language, which, to some degree, binds the tongue of free expression and produces "an unsuspected source of anguish."[78] Nonetheless, by focusing on the bodily element that attempts to find expression, Glissant proposes the embodiment of violence and terror, in the vein of the slave sublime. Glissant groups these kinds of poetic expression into two categories: natural (free) poetics and forced (constrained) poetics. Free or natural poetics he defines as "any collective yearning for expression that is not opposed to itself either at the level of what it wishes to express or at the level of the language that it puts into practice." He argues further that the "most violent challenge to an established order can emerge from a natural poetics, when there is continuity between the challenged order and the disorder that negates it."[79] Contrastingly, forced or constrained poetics "exist[s] where a need for expression confronts an inability to achieve expression," in other words, a "confrontation . . . between the content to be expressed and the language suggested or imposed."[80] Glissant argues that "Counterpoetics carried out by Martinicans therefore records simultaneously both a need for collective expression and a present inability to attain true expression."[81] For Glissant, the logocentrism inherited from Western culture, the importance of writing, in particular, in addition to the imposed colonial language, presents this challenge to expression that maintains silences.

Kamau Brathwaite references Glissant's notion of "free and forced poetics" in his discussion of "nation language" in the essay "The History of Voice." According to Brathwaite, Glissant characterizes "forced poetics" as "a kind of prison language,"[82] given the existence of linguistic plurality in the Caribbean where the colonial language functions as an "imposed language" in contrast to creole language.[83] Brathwaite refers to the creole language spoken in the Caribbean as "nation language" rather than using the word dialect, which, as he argues, has "pejorative overtones."[84] For him, "nation language" is "the kind of English spoken by the people who were brought to the Caribbean . . . the language of the slaves and laborers, the servants who were brought in."[85] As he explains, "nation language" is highly influenced by the oral African tradition and it may be considered as English in regard to its lexicon but not in "terms of its syntax, rhythm and timbre, its sound explosion" and "contours."[86] Although the Jamaican poet Claude McKay is mostly known for his work during the Harlem Renaissance and for his use of standard English and verse form, Brathwaite notes that his earlier work that reveals his "Clarendon syllables" erodes the formal structures of pentameter in a poem.[87] More notable is Louise Bennett's poetic oeuvre, even though, because of her use of Jamaican patois, she had been largely ignored by the Jamaican newspapers and national media until the advent of a cultural revolution in the late 1960s.[88] Brathwaite quotes her as saying, "I have been set apart by other creative writers a long time ago because of the language I speak and work in . . . From the beginning nobody recognized me as a writer."[89] While Bennett brought attention to the political challenges to using Jamaican patois in her writing, Philip's use of the Trinidadian demotic extends Bennett's concerns by calling attention to the psychic problems that arise when one attempts to use the master's tongue. Like Glissant, part of what Philip is doing is to dislodge language from signifying processes by reducing it to noise through plays on language and violence, and what matters to her also is the dissonant sound of the word in the enactment of creolization as a process. And unlike Brathwaite, for whom "nation language" is a body of language material to be deployed and used, Philip seems more interested in the idea of creolization as a process of deformation and distortion; thus she enacts that process rather than miming a given language, a strategy that highlights why *She Tries Her Tongue* is a step beyond revisionism.

To some degree, Philip's work and her engagement with the sublime and the issue of articulation sets her apart from Glissant's perspectives on orality. Although suggesting the "anguish" that arises from using the colonial language, her work disavows Glissant's notion of the "inability to find expression" as *she tries her tongue* to display agency. Thus, for Philip, the oral is not about presence but rather an effort to speak. Her focus is on the literal mechanics of utterance; the idea that the tongue functions as a site of punishment, for instance, suggests that the sublime has a physiological element for Caribbean people and their African heritage. Philip calls attention implicitly to the African practices of signifying in Thoth, the Egyptian god of writing, who takes messages like a trickster figure (similar to Eshu in West Africa and his figuration as Anancy in the Caribbean) and confuses them. Arguably, in this sense, Thoth functions as the original "signifying monkey" given his iconography and his effects and because he serves the function of mediating language, both as speech and writing that involves trickery, which John C. Rowe defines "as some combination of 'critical' and 'poetic' powers."[90] Signifying for Philip emphasizes the materiality and presence of language in speech.

Giving specific context to the dual histories of slavery and colonialism in the Caribbean, Frantz Fanon argues in *Black Skin, White Masks* that speaking the colonial language means that a Black subject inherits the collective consciousness of the colonizer and that doing so creates a fundamental disjuncture between one's consciousness and body.[91] Fanon asserts that "To speak means to be in a position to use a certain syntax, to grasp the morphology of this or that language, but it means above all to assume a culture, to support the weight of a civilization" because the person "who has a language consequently possesses the world expressed and implied by that language."[92] Fanon's argument that the internalization of racial inferiority results from the coming into being as the Other, through the colonizer's racialized and linguistic universe, exhibits Lacanian strains regarding the foundational role of language in subject formation. Within a (post)colonial framework, the English language poses a crisis of identity because of the *distorted* mirror image that ensues from Black subjects' coming into being through a racialized Eurocentric structure, a possibility Lacan does not explore. If, as Lacan argues in "The Mirror Stage,"[93] subject formation occurs through language, which is transmitted from the father to the child (the master and slave), then the transmission fails to promote a coherent self-image because of the negating aspect of the colonial language and its role in barring access to full personhood within the framework of European discourses about who qualifies as the *human*. For Lacan, the mirror stage produces a split in the subject, but as Fanon argues a double split occurs for the colonial subject, not only between "having" and "being" (that is, between the entry into language and self-consciousness that "bars" the imaginary wholeness of the narcissistic infant), but also in the assumption of a "body imago."[94] When the colonial master assumes the symbolic role of the father, the transference of language is problematic because of the negative images that are endemic to the representation in colonial languages. Representation occurs within language in the sense that meanings are derived and constructed through language as discourse, which can be characterized as a form of myth-making in which the ideological gaze becomes naturalized as inherent knowledge. Such ideation depends upon the cultural imagination that structures how we interpret signs in relation to our socialized worldview and demonstrates how the subject is formed in and through language.[95] This is why Fanon calls attention to the displacement of Black identity through colonial language structures.

Demonstrating the function of the English language as a vehicle of colonial oppression, Philip addresses the problem of losing touch with the self-valuating power of her ancestral language and the challenge of finding a proper language for poetic expression. Philip thus echoes Fanon's argument that a Black person participates in the collective unconscious—a culture's prejudices, myths, and collective attitudes—when s/he adopts a colonial language. In *She Tries Her Tongue*, Philip views language as a structural system of representation similar to a system of myth. For her, English, as a colonial language, is a dominating force that replicates the violence between masters and slaves. Philip condenses the positions of woman and slave/colonized in recognition of the fact that there is a doubling of oppression for Black women, a double loss of the mother tongue to patriarchy and colonialism. Unlike other British colonies, such as India or West and East Africa, where the native languages were largely untouched beyond the intellectual classes, the Caribbean islands were sites of an almost total linguistic replacement. Quite striking, then, is Philip's vocabulary in which tongue and wound function as recurring tropes and her feminist representation of the forced insertion of the patriarchal colonial language as violence against the female body and psyche. Philip not only suggests the embodiment of the sublime as a linguistic violence to the tongue, but also demonstrates the ways in which the English language fails as the appropriate linguistic medium for representing her postcolonial experiences. As Philip suggests in her work(s), linguistic colonization greatly impacts the form and content of postcolonial writing and one's consciousness. English, as a colonial language, not only operates as an unconscious power system that is structurally and semiotically opposed to Trinidadian identity, but also as a power system that renders the Caribbean identity as inferior because of the unequal balance of power created by that colonialist knowledge system. Given the conflict and self-negation the patriarchal and colonial English language poses, Philip argues that it is "etymologically hostile."[96]

Many of Philip's poems in *She Tries Her Tongue* search for and hover between the possibilities involved in choosing a proper language for poetic and self-expression. She mimes the effects of being torn (apart) by the incoherence of language, which can be seen in her (re)rendering of classical myths recast with Black Atlantic subjects. At the core of her poems is the critique of the English language as an imposed racial and patriarchal system that is able to negate and "strip" the identity of Caribbean people. For Philip, the English language is a power structure that goes beyond the linguistic function of a sign because signs convey cultural values beyond the mere lexical meanings of the sound or visual image. Essentially, Philip's poetic representation points to the operations of language that repeat and structure relations of domination, both syntagmatically and paradigmatically. Highlighting the different valences of demotic and standard English as literary language and the attempt to mime creolization itself are more important for her than using a given lexicon. Heeding Fanon's concerns and using what Philip calls the Trinidadian demotic (a creolized version of English), which destructures the very syntax of the English language, Philip disavows its power structures, cultural implications, ideologies, and myths. Such destructuring conveys the aesthetics of the slave sublime and its subversive principles of distortion, a repetition of colonial violence as embedded within the structure of myths. The (post) colonial Trinidadian identity must, for Philip, be linked to the ancestral mother tongue, which has left traces in creolized demotic language.

As noted in the introduction of *She Tries Her Tongue*, Philip also draws upon Rastafari demotic language that privileges "I" so as translate Black identity from social death, from an object to a subject position. This reimaging proposes an alternative epistemology through an insurgent language that seeks to change the signification of Black identity in Western settings, specifically in the relationship between the sign and what it signifies. As Ennis Edmonds puts it, the Rastafari language "reflects the specificities of their experience and perception of self, life, and the world."[97] He explains that "Rastas use 'I-an-I' as subject (even when the sentence calls for an object) to indicate that all people are active, creative agents and not passive objects" in a manner that conveys a "commitment to the struggle for selfhood and dignity."[98] Rastafari language, as Philip utilizes it, emanates from a Black subject position that highlights the possibilities of enunciations (by trying the tongue) whereby symbol-indices that underlie the personal pronoun "I" regrammaticalize, reencode, and reregulate attitudes about the Black self-image. Adrian Anthony McFarlane explains that the emphasis on "I-words" is an "informed utterance" that connects to their "self-affirmation" and a "language medium" for "self-liberation" that is fostered by creating a "new vision of values" in order to "create a new identity and meaning for the speaker."[99] This re-identification is made possible by a metaphoric mirror, as Dennis Forsythe argues, in which they can see themselves and "return home" to self-consciousness.[100] In Philip's *She Tries Her Tongue*, this return is no longer a Sankofan journey back to Africa but a return, so to speak, to self-awareness to counter the social death stemming from coming into being through a European worldview and language.

The demotic also refashions the master's tool of language to reflect an undistorted image of the self by bending the formalized syntax and rhythm of the English language. It chops and inserts African and locally derived phraseologies so as to remake the master's language as a "living language [that] continually encapsulates, reflects and refines the entire experiential life and world view" of New World Africans.[101] As Philip also explains in the introduction of *She Tries Her Tongue*, the "formal standard language" is "subverted, turned upside down, inside out, and even sometimes erased. Nouns be[come] strangers to verbs and vice versa."[102] Philip refers to these changes as the "havoc that the African wreaked upon the English language"—which, for her, is both "the metaphorical equivalent of the havoc that coming to the New World represented for the African" and "the truest representation, the mirror i-mage[103] of the experience."[104] In order to combat the distorted image, Philip asserts that "an attack must be made at the only place where true change is ever possible: at the heart of language."[105] Accordingly, Philip represents classical myths metaphorically as the cultural equivalent of the English language, and, consequently, she chops, splices, and turns them upside down as she mimes the demotic process.

Philip undertakes the mission of choosing a proper poetic language by taking the processes of the Trinidadian Creole language and using it as a poetic language structure; for her, this poetic language is a formalization of the demotic. In the following lines from "Sightings" a mother searching frantically for her daughter is confused by the distortion of sound and visual images:

> was it a trompe d'oeil[106]—
> the voice of her sound, or didn't I once
> see her song, hear her image call
> me by name—my name—another sound, a song,
> the name of me we knew she named
> the sound of song sung long past time[107]

Although Philip occasionally uses Creole, here she enacts a kind of creolization by twisting its syntax and bending individual words and their meanings. It is a poetic that *learns* its structure from creolization rather than mimicking it. In the example under consideration, the speaker transposes her words when she states "voice of her sound" and "see her song, and hear her image call." At the same time the speaker laments her lost name, a lost language, if you will, that denotes who she is. Philip makes clear the problematic of the mirror image, one's visual conception of self, where self-recognition is impossible in a language that is not one's own. And, indeed, in Lacan's account of it, the mirror stage is a kind of summoning or "calling forth" of the subject by its appearance to itself as an image in the mirror. Philip's extension of Rastafari linguistic reimaging to the Trinidadian demotic is one of many approaches to creating a racially and culturally relevant semantic universe,[108] since the demotic variant of colonial language has its origins within slave culture as "living language."[109]

In a metaphoric search for the lost mother tongue and the demotic's destructuring potential in "Adoption Bureau," Philip alludes to the mythological tale in which Ceres/Demeter searches for her estranged daughter

Proserpine/Persephone. However, the poet turns the myth upside down when she depicts the daughter searching for her estranged mother: "She whom they call mother, I seek."[110] The theme of estrangement is even more pronounced in the following lines in which proper modifiers are estranged from their objects: "Watch my talk-words stride, / like her smile the listening / breadth of my walk—on mine / her skin of lime casts a glow / of green, around my head indigo / of halo—tell me, do / I smell like her?"[111] The very first line presents what seems like a mixed metaphor when the daughter invites the reader to "watch" her "words" as they "stride." In the above quotation Philip plays upon the classical notion of poetic meter as composed of feet and African rhythms as based on dance steps to signal the importance of performance, and she continues to play upon words when her speaker ends with the question, "do I smell like her?" There is a slippage between the words "smile" and "smell," and since the subject of this sentence is "talk-words," then the question about whether she smells like her mother is really a question about whether her language is similar to that of her mother.

In his discussion of Korean American writer Theresa Hak Kyung Cha's *Dictee*, Naoki Sakai presents a similar argument about the difficulty of learning a foreign language and the resulting lack of correspondence between what is uttered and what is intended. He labels this lack of correspondence "intentional mimicry," a misrepresentation that is linked to the "speaker's corporeality" as a concerted effort to disassociate the self from the "host nation." Sakai thus redefines mimicry to denote both resistance and what he calls "a paean to the social." For him, the disconnection between the thought and that which is uttered is a tactic deployed to create "opacity" that prevents the speaker from internalizing the language. The space between the uttered and the system of language is a "space for 'community' for subjects in transit."[112] By referring to a "space" for "subjects in transit" Sakai implicitly identifies a kind of liminal subjectivity that is indeterminate, in other words, suspended in an in-between state and marginalized in relation to social structures. Such a subject, therefore, is not governed by structural codes or regulations to which language belongs. This subversive strategy as Philip uses it announces its lawlessness as the slave sublime aesthetic defies boundaries by its situatedness in the in-between to destabilize myths within language that masquerade as signifiers of truth. To undermine the English language and to create opacity in her poems, Philip uses metonymy as a dominant trope because of its rhetorical function of signifying a referent indirectly, as it neither implies nor states the connections between concepts. Is Philip's opaque language a similar attempt at "mimicry" and therefore a resistance to Western culture in order to create an "in-between"[113] space for the postcolonial subject, where the demotic functions as a *bricolage*, filling the gap between the utterance and the thought? Even if so, as Philip suggests in her representation of the separation between a mother and daughter (symbolized as the loss of the mother tongue), there will be an ongoing search and nostalgia for what has been lost, despite the demotic language's function as a *bricolage*.[114]

The unrelenting desire for what is lost supports the notion that Philip's use of Trinidadian demotic language destructures the English language by challenging the semiotic codes. At the same time its liminal status suggests a yearning for reassimilation. In *The Rites of Passage*, Arnold van Gennep explains that a person undergoing initiation passes through three physical/psychological phases: first, s/he is separated from and is stripped of native culture; second, s/he undergoes a liminal period in which there is social and structural ambiguity; and third, s/he is ultimately reassimilated to the native culture.[115] The demotic language's liminal status as occupying an in-between space suggests a yearning for reassimilation, which is only possible during the tertiary stage. Postcoloniality in Trinidad, however, poses a challenge linguistically, given that its liminal condition is one that lacks any point of return due to the history of slavery and the loss of ancestral language. That is to say, due to its liminal status, the demotic language by nature engages in a process of destructuring that lacks either a stable terminus or a point of departure to which to return. It accordingly subverts the English language's standard codes and value system through which knowledge is disseminated rather than "reterritorializing" in the language of the new colonial culture. On the whole, van Gennep theorizes the mirror stage from a new direction, but one that is quite comparable with Fanon's *Black Skin, White Masks*. Van Gennep's theory assumes a return or reassimilation to a new relation to the old/native culture, given his description of a kind of upward spiral and reintegration. The colonial culture, as Fanon points out, demands instead an acculturation that negates the original one, hence breaking the cycle of return.

By representing the daughter's nostalgia for the mother tongue in "Discourse on the Logic of Language," Philip unmasks the ideological nature of empirical knowledge and challenges the basis of truth and its signifying properties. The boundary crossing of genre in this poem containing a narrative, a historical edict, and a multiple-choice quiz points to the many colliding and competing systems of truth, value, and representation. Philip employs boundary crossing in order to point out the referential problematic and competing truth systems that are endemic to an imposed father tongue. Because English occupies an ambiguous and incompatible position as both mother and father tongue, it induces the speaker's painful experience of being torn apart, disciplined, and silenced by language. A side-bar prose narrative, appearing vertically in relation to the central poem, conveys the trauma that a new-born baby experiences when the "mother's tongue" "lick[s]" and silences her. Here, if the mother's "licking" is taken as corporal punishment, the mother's tongue functions as the agent of formative discipline that replicates the system of domination between masters and slaves. This paradox of the slave sublime in the reenactment of plantation violence is apparent. As an expressive act of love, licking is part of the anguish that comes from using an imposed language, given its referential power to transform even loving (pleasure) into a modality of domination (pain). In a sense, Philip highlights the split position of the mother, as agent of (post)colonial discipline and site of a possible alternative (relation to) language. One of the strengths of *She Tries Her Tongue* is that Philip avoids the temptation, unlike some versions of mythic/essentialist feminism, to idealize the mother. The fact that the mother and daughter do not reunite, as revealed in "Adoption Bureau Revisited," highlights the irresolvable linguistic trauma that results from losing the mother tongue. To convey the slave sublime, there is no resolution in the transformation of displeasure to pleasure in Philip's representation of linguistic violence in her revision of the original myth.

Philip compares the linguistic trauma of losing the mother tongue to aphasia, a disease that impedes normal linguistic abilities by creating an exclusive preference for metonymic or metaphoric language. Both the metaphoric and metonymic capacities are usually operative in normal verbal behavior; however, aphasia can affect "the faculty for selection and substitution or for combination and contexture."[116] According to Roman Jakobson, the first affliction deals with a "deterioration of metalinguistic operations, while the latter damages the capacity for maintaining the hierarchy of linguistic units."[117] In other words, a person with the similarity disorder cannot use metaphor, while a person with contiguity disorder cannot use metonymy. Metonymy is a linguistic trope that works by associating things according to contiguity (adjoining words or things) and syntax, unlike metaphor which requires similarity by means of substitution on the basis of semantics. While metaphor maps onto the paradigmatic axis, metonym maps onto the syntagmatic axis by setting up chains of words next to one another. However, the principle of that organization is not mere contiguity, as both sets of chains can have an effect of displacement.

There are fundamental disturbances on the axis of contiguity, too, specifically the classical myth about Proserpine/Persephone and Ceres/Demeter in which the mother and daughter are estranged, but with Philip's revision the myth becomes centered on the search, which the daughter takes upon herself as well. Both the original myth and Philip's revision disturb both the syntagmatic and the paradigmatic axis: the syntagm noun-verb-object is disturbed if the paradigmatic function of verb is improperly applied, and the paradigmatic series is also disturbed if the syntagmatic relation to mother-daughter is affected. This destructuring, in turn, undermines normal syntagmatic processes in which the grammatical forms determine the proper placing and usage of words. In this miming of the demotic process—in which classical myths represent the colonial language—the colonial language becomes destructured and no longer means what it originally meant. On the metaphoric axis, she takes the chains of association, a principle of the associative imagination underlying the slave sublime, which connect the Proserpine/Persephone myth with Western systems and reconnects them with African myths in another form of destructuring.

Philip mimes the demotic process most of all by disturbing the paradigmatic function of metaphor as represented below in "The Search," where nouns function as verbs and vice versa, or each as an adjective:

all day long she dreaming about wide black nights,
how lose stay, what find look like.
A four-day night of walk bring me
to where never see she:
is "come child, come," and "welcome" I looking—
the how in lost between She
and I, call and response in tongue and
word that buck up in strange;[118]

Philip omits words and fuses others together in a linear sequence without observing grammatical rules, including tenses and parts of speech, for example, when the speaker uses the verb "lose" as a noun and another verb "stay" as its modifier. In this same line the speaker imagines her daughter "dreaming" about how to conceptualize the abstract notions of loss and discovery, which explains why verbs function as nouns because dreams typically represent abstract nouns as concrete metaphors, and evoke resemblance or similarity on the paradigmatic axis. Philip disturbs the metaphoric function by an almost exclusive use of metonyms, even though both metaphors and metonyms are necessary for normal linguistic comprehension, much in the same way that dreams require both displacement and condensation for interpretation. Sigmund Freud explains in *The Interpretation of Dreams* that "dream-thoughts and dream-contents are presented to us as two versions of the same subject-matter in two different languages" as displacement and condensation.[119] Furthermore, as Freud asserts, "condensation in dreams is seen at its clearest when it handles words and names [and] . . . words are treated in dreams as though they were concrete things, and for that reason they are apt to be combined in just the same way as presentations of concrete things. Dreams of this sort offer the most amusing and curious neologisms."[120]

Although condensation is usually understood as equivalent to metaphor, Philip treats condensation as a correlative to metonymy. In the fourth line of the poem quoted above, "where never see she" is a neologism and a metonymic representation of loss as a place name. The substitutive property of metaphor is displaced, thus rendering it a concrete object by combining words that have a linear relationship. The normal mapping from the abstract to the concrete is displaced, however, and is rendered instead as a mapping from one abstract term to another, whereas metaphors would have mitigated the somewhat strange texture of the poem. The line that follows presents a literal (concrete) yearning for linguistic expression but the expression becomes a figurative abstraction, in other words, a metonym that represents the loss of the mother tongue. Even though the speaker uses demotic English, signification is occluded in "The Search" because of Philip's profuse use of metonyms. The speaker's abducted daughter has been brought to a new place, and the linguistic system breaks down as it comes into contact with another semiotic system: "She / and I, call and response in tongue and / word buck up in strange; / all that leave is seven dream-skin."[121] Along with the word "tongue," "call and response" functions as a metonym for language, in the sense that the tongue is a component of speech within the call-and-response tradition of Afro-diasporic culture. Because the colonial language and the mother tongue belong to two different linguistic systems with incongruous signifying codes, signification is opaque in the conversation between mother and daughter, as "words buck up in strange." Demonstrating further this opaque signification, Philip presents "seven dream-skins" in which the speaker's aphasic preference for metonyms prevents a metaphorical reading of the text.[122]

"Dream-skins" follows a line of metonymic representation, and the opening lines suggest that the speaker is torn between two linguistic systems: "Dream-skins dream the dream dreaming: / (*in two languages*)."[123] Since aphasia imposes a dividing line between metaphor and metonym, quite appropriately Philip divides the poem into two columns: on the left is a list of the seven "dream-skins" given as metonyms and on the right is a metaphorical narrative explanation. Because of the dividing line between metaphors and metonyms, the metaphoric and metonymic chains must be analyzed discretely:

> six-limbed
> my body dances
> > flight
> from her giant promises
> she reaches down
> > gently
> snaps my head
> a blooded hibiscus
> from its body
> crooning
> she cradles the broken parts[124]

Words such as "flight" work at the nexus of possible metaphoric chains, thereby introducing displacement into the axis of metaphor. "Flight" as a metaphor produces words that are related by comparison and, in this sense, represents journey, the act of fleeing, bird, and butterfly. These are images and movements related to metamorphosis as suggested by Philip's revision of Ovid's tales. Moreover, the reference to "butterfly" (given in the "Foreskin" stanza) evokes metaphorically a symbol that actually epitomizes metamorphosis. In the metonymic representation, on the other hand, the word "head" serves as a substitutive symbol for the "body" and "flower." "Head" serves as a synecdoche for the body, while "flower" stands for the metamorphosis of the body, as in the Egyptian tale about Osiris's transformation to a tree. The flower is also a reference to Proserpine/Persephone whom Jupiter/Hades captured while she was making a bouquet. This representation also works as a metaphoric frame to symbolize African women whom slave catchers abducted and brought to the New World in a state of social death through natal alienation. Since Philip equates the ancestral African past with the mythic classical age, the Black women's (Proserpine's/Persephone's) encounter with slave catchers (Jupiter/Hades) is a traumatic déjà vu. Furthermore, this comparison also allows Philip to elevate the status of the African women who were ravished, showing both their social value and aesthetic desirability, thereby challenging the devalued image of Blackness as refracted through the colonial English language.

As revealed by the metonymic and metaphoric chains, Ovid's *Metamorphoses* represents the colonial English language, which Philip destructures by splicing in African/Egyptian myths in order to mime the demotic process, a form of syncretism that is recognized as one of the principal operations in Caribbean culture. Metaphors thus act as metonyms conveying relations of contiguity in which not only the connections among meanings of terms are relevant but also the syntactic relation. In another stanza of "Dream-skins," metonymic and metaphorical signifying chains reveal that Philip compares language ("voice") to menstruation, in which the shedding of blood represents the shedding of colonial language:

> the wide open of mouth
> blood of rush
> hieroglyphs
> her red
> inscriptions
> [...]
> wounded mouth
> [...]
> "the voice, the voice, the voice"[125]

The words "wounded mouth" trigger a chain of meanings when we assume that "mouth" represents the vagina: the "blood" of menstruation, thus, represents the violence of "linguistic rape" or the rupture from the mother tongue. One would also consider the idea of utterances as literally "periodic," a flow that intermittently punctuates the silence of oppression. Also, one of the many linguistic ruptures is the tearing apart of the Greek from its original African/Egyptian source.

Despite her allusions to Western reformulations of African myths, Philip challenges the imperialist ideology of Western civilization. Her use of the Isis myth, often considered the mythic hinge between African and European cultural models, is a deliberate effort to challenge the dominance of the Greco-Roman/Western civilization model. Isis moves toward Venus/Mary in the West and toward Erzulie in the Caribbean, via West Africa. As Martin Bernal's *Black Athena* shows, Greek (European) and Egyptian (African) cultures were closely tied until the racist scholarship of the late Enlightenment that promoted the notion of Greece as the pure origin of the West.[126] Referencing the ancient writer Herodotos, Bernal contends that "the majority of names found in Greek mythology are primarily Egyptian"[127] and that "Herodotos and other ancient writers paired Egyptian with Greek deities."[128] Bernal suggests that there was a splitting, matching the racial ideologies of the West.

Thus, in a regained mythology African myths would rightfully serve as the foundational source of Western mythology.

In *She Tries Her Tongue* Philip portrays the violence of British colonization and the impact of "linguistic rape" as social death.[129] The elements of boundary crossing and distortion of signifiers convey the aesthetics of the slave sublime as Philip repeats through mimicry in order to critique the very linguistic and onto-epistemological violence that African and Caribbean subjects have continued to endure since colonialism and slavery. Repeating this violence is Philip's strategy of calling attention to the roots of violence in the postcolonial world, which result from the ratiocentric discourses of modernity. Her use of the Trinidadian demotic alongside Rastafari "I-an-I" reimaging of self is one possible way to disrupt the standard linguistic codes of the patriarchal, colonial language. Given the underlying masculine imperatives of colonization that reproduce themselves in nationalist modes of decolonization, it is no wonder that Philip shies away from using Barbadian poet Kamau Brathwaite's term "nation language." Instead, she destructures both the paradigmatic and the syntagmatic axes of language as she tries to shift the paradigms. Philip highlights a common-sense, urgent need to free the silenced, colonized tongue. Nonetheless, she displays her entrapment within the language of the colonizer, despite her efforts to subvert the language model from within. She admits that Caribbean musical traditions have been more successful in generating "indigenously created i-mages" given that they are not dependent upon textuality because of their emphasis on the vernacular as "living language" and sound as text.[130] All in all, Philip's works show the ways in which, across the Caribbean, the violent rupture from and loss of African culture intersect with a feminist desire for its recuperation and to change the "way a society perceives itself and, eventually, its collective consciousness."[131]

CHAPTER THREE

The Changing Same for I-an-I in Babylon

*Bob Marley's Representations of the Slave Sublime
in Postcolonial Jamaica*

Yeah, we've been trodding on the winepress much too long
Rebel, rebel
[...]
Babylon system is the vampire, yeah
Suckin' the children day by day, yeah
Me say de Babylon system is the vampire, falling empire
Suckin' the blood of the sufferah, yeah
—Bob Marley, "Babylon System"

Despite the legal proclamation ending Jamaican slavery in 1834, freedom
has been continually forestalled as the substituted forms of governance—
apprenticeship, colonialism, and globalization—have deliberately masked their
biopolitics of power, structural violence, and hegemonic discourses. These
recurring forms of oppression are what I refer to as the changing same, what
Rastas identify as Babylon systems of oppression, which restrict social, economic, and political agency across historical spaces and time as forms of governance change but remain the same in their practices. This idea of Babylon
as the changing same suggests a self-constancy as unchanging sameness, which
philosopher Paul Ricoeur calls *idem* identity in his book *Oneself as Another.*[1]
It is the recognition of the *self* as *self* despite change or mutability to suggest
permanence throughout time. Another philosopher, Achille Mbembe, talks
about the "spectral" nature of similarity and difference in his discussion of
power in a manner that fuses the ideas from Ricoeur: "Power is being simultaneously present in different worlds, under different modalities . . . And
power is what was able to escape death and return from among the dead. For
it is only in escaping death and returning from the dead that one acquires
the capacity to make oneself into the other side of the absolute. There is,
therefore, in power as in life itself, a share that depends on the ghost—
a spectral share."[2] According to Mbembe, power achieves its dominion through
mutability—that is, metamorphosis while maintaining the presence or trace
of its former identity. As I argue, imperial nations maintain power over for-

merly colonized nations, such as Jamaica, where there is a phantasmagoric refiguration of plantation structures to suggest that postcoloniality is itself a myth. The metamorphic substitution of one economic order for another denotes equivalences, especially given the exploitation of labor and reliance upon violence as a kind of grammatical structure. The continued deferral of freedom, therefore, connects to the materiality of a Caribbean subject's entrance and embeddedness into a language of violence—the violence of the slave plantation in its transition to the (neo)colonial order wherein ideological conventions about capitalism, along with European and American hegemonic systems such as the IMF and World Bank, maintain the sublime presence of slavery as the Real of freedom.

In its ever-changing sameness, Babylon has a dialectic impact on the postcolonial self, the "I-an-I" first-person speaker that Bob Marley represents in his musical poetics. This speaker maintains the historical identity of a "bounded" slave during the postcolonial era to suggest a transhistorical self-constancy since slavery. In *The Problem of Freedom*, Thomas C. Holt argues that the kind of emancipation that was conceived of in Jamaica had little to do with personal liberty because it was caught up with the abuses of capitalist labor that needed their own kind of coercion and discipline, quite akin to a slave economy.[3] Saidiya Hartman puts it in a broader Atlantic slave society context and argues that "the texture of freedom is laden with the vestiges of slavery" because the "plantation system" is reorganized "through contiguous forms of subjection."[4] This restructuring of plantation systems in the postcolonial era is what Fred Moten would call the "semiotic structuration of a system of likeness that subsumes questions of difference and absence."[5]

I argue that this "semiotic structuration" of "likeness" and "difference" can be read as a language that operates on the paradigmatic axis of language that privileges metaphoric substitution and similarity as the changing same, an underlying element of the slave sublime. Slavery, apprenticeship, and colonialism in the Jamaican social context are structural or linguistic signs that operate on the paradigmatic, vertical axis of language in which metaphoric substitutions reveal resemblance or similarity. In language, metaphorical substitution occurs between two semantically similar terms, but the similarity is not always evident without the aid of associative properties. Consider, for example, violence or oppression as the associative property that existed in Jamaica in the forms of slavery, apprenticeship, and colonialism—each semantically similar and each revealing the substitution of an endless signifying chain of symbols for domination, which is communicated metaphorically as a language of power and violence to denote the unfaded echoes of slavery.

Offering a nominal definition of metaphor, Paul Ricoeur states that in "the tropology of classical rhetoric, the place assigned to metaphor among the figures of signification is defined specifically by the role that the relationship of resemblance has in the transference from initial idea to new idea" and resemblance is "the foundation of the substitution that is set in motion in the metaphorical transposition of names and, more generally, of words."[6] The metaphorical structure of governance throughout Jamaican history highlights the transposition of meanings and the practice of violence from one institution to another in which the slave, apprentice, and post/colonial subject function as the objects of violence. In essence, the violence of post/colonialism follows the paradigmatic structures of substituting violence from the slave plantation to the colonial order. These structural practices of power and violence resemble one another, not casually but in their deep historical identity, given the continuity across the plantation and post-emancipation eras. This latter point highlights the semantic and substitutive aspect of the exploitative violence that has occurred throughout Jamaican history; in essence, each power structure has been semantically related, despite the ideological strategies that have been employed as a tactic to camouflage the exploitation of labor.

I use the term slave sublime to characterize the ever-present and immeasurable magnitude of psychic violence stemming from the stark realization that plantation structures continue in a paradigmatic fashion through new mechanisms of economic tyranny. The slave sublime foregrounds the overwhelming awe stemming from this unrelenting violence, which, nonetheless, does not override the imagination's ability for representation. While Kant imprisons the imagination through reason as it advances from the beautiful to the sublime, the slave sublime diverts this directionality, progressing from the sublime to the beautiful as it liberates the imagination. It is the associative power of the imagination that perceives time as transhistorical to identify the changing same, despite power's amorphous quality and uncanny ability to hide its presence. Thus the associative imagination has three key aspects: (1) its empirical character, which is informed both by the sensible and intangible worlds; (2) its power, which relies upon observations, intuitions, senses, and feelings so as to form images and perceptions; and (3) its cognitive ability, which forms patterns and associations and seeks to break down existing systems of representation or aesthetic boundaries. Overall, the slave sublime is a reformulation of the Kantian sublime to suggest not only a merging of the beautiful and the sublime, but also the notion that the sublime is a bodily experience in which the imagination interiorizes terror—wherein the terror associated with the sublime remains ever-present without transcendence through reason. In contrast, the metaphysical interiority of Kant's sublime privileges the Cartesian dualism, which nullifies and thereby transcends a somatogenic notion of phenomenology that overlook the body's importance, which is so central to African and African-diasporic experiences and worldview.

As I contend, certain aesthetic forms inherited from the West, for instance the reliance on textuality and third-person omniscient narration, demand a certain kind of representativity for conveying the slave sublime. Key differences between Western and African societies lie in their contradistinctive systems of representation, the significance between writing and performance and between logos and speech. Therefore, I explore orality, sonic elements, and the counter-hegemonic potential of the first-person bodily discourse in Bob Marley's reggae music and the ways in which this genre offers an alternative to the static nature of scribal language for representing the deeply felt terrors of the violence that stem from plantation structures. I argue that Marley's musical prowess lies in his defiance of Western aesthetic boundaries by communicating somatically to convey a cognitive basis of knowledge that relies on the imagination and the body. In doing so, his slave sublime aesthetic announces a subaltern agency that seizes the powers of representation. Marley's focus on the imagination provides agency as a means of transcending boundedness, symbolically violating the limitations imposed by reason, as conveyed by the aesthetics associated with the Kantian sublime.

In the Western tradition there is an emphasis on textuality, the privileging of logocentric over somatogenic knowledge (as derived by the body and senses) because of an ideological assumption about the superiority of written cultures over oral ones. This tradition also privileges the importance of reason/logic (the mind) over knowledge derived from other mediums, such as bodily sensation, as the arbiter of transcendental truth and the presence of the hierarchical principle in discourse and meaning. For this reason, I employ the term slave sublime to convey the significance of the body to affect, empirical knowledge, and language. In his book *The Black Atlantic*, Paul Gilroy also draws a connection between the body and language and notes that the Western emphasis on textuality precludes the possibility of a vast range of meanings for which language cannot account, especially because the philosophy dismisses "sensuous" knowledge in favor of rationality. He explains that, because African slaves were barred from literacy, they consequently relied on polyphonic modes of communication. As Gilroy insists, the terrors of slavery could not be silenced by denying language because even though it was "unspeakable" it was not "inexpressible."[7] As I argue, even if slavery was a form of social death, such a condition need not entail that slaves lacked a complex and profound ability for forging creative responses to their peculiar circumstances. In fact, the Jamaican plantocracy segregated slaves along ethnic lines so as to deter communication and thereby thwart revolts, which, in effect, necessarily led the slaves to rely on nonverbal means of communication. For instance, the sound of the *abeng* (a hollowed-out cow horn) signaled to the slaves the start of the workday in the cane fields, but a tonal variation suggested also the start of a rebellion.[8]

Jamaican phonocentric forms that are rooted in slavery, including the drum and base riddim and dub aesthetics underlying reggae, are connected to tonal patterns of meaning that are present in African languages and music—thereby revealing their potential for transcending the limitations of the Western sublime in their ability to convey the ineffable. In a discussion about the linguistic aspect of Yoruba music, Wole Soyinka makes a connection between music and sensibility in relation to the symbolic realm. Although attention has been given to the tonal elements of African music that transmit "meaning and allusion," he notes that the "aesthetic and emotional significance of this relationship has not been truly absorbed." African music, he asserts, comes from a "culture of total awareness and phenomenal involvement." His choice of the word "phenomenal" suggests the aesthetic connection of music to the emotions—the sensible—rather than to logical thought. Because of this "phenomenal involvement," he goes on to argue that "Language therefore is not a barrier to the profound universality of music but a cohesive dimension and clarification of that willfully independent art-form."[9] Here we see a contrast to Western notions of the sublime in which there is a linguistic barrier to expression.

To convey the overwhelming awe associated with the slave sublime, Jamaican musical forms challenge Western notions about the hierarchy of rational thought and written texts as the preeminent modes of expression, precisely because the Western perspective does not account for the structures of feelings that profoundly impact meaning. Long after slavery, as a number of scholars have noted, the tradition of using sound as a language continued in Jamaica, suggesting a deep connection to African roots. Louis Chude-Sokei notes that "For the Rastafari, 'word sound' had immense power, and that power was in the sound itself, not just in the syntactic or logocentric properties of meaning," especially in the Rastafari use of "African 'Burru' percussion, [which] produced a vocabulary of meanings."[10] Early Jamaican reggae, heavily influenced by Rasta music and grounded to its roots not only in Kumina but also in Burru drumming from the (post-)slavery eras functioned as reappropriation of African-derived culture that speak about the debased social conditions.[11] The Rastafari movement emerged in colonial Jamaica during the 1930s, a period of depressed economic conditions that contributed to latent sociohistorical factors stemming from slavery. Out of this context, the Rastafari concept of Babylon emerged to signify the notion that Jamaica was a land of oppression that was "shaped by the history of plantation slavery and organized around European-derived values and institutions."[12] Rastas identify the post-slavery emergence of capitalism as the transhistorical perpetuation of Babylon, given its metamorphic power to remake itself across different historical periods, thereby disguising its *idem* identity, the changing same, and denying the freedoms that emancipation supposedly promised.

In Bob Marley's song "Babylon System" two central lines in the first verse, "Talkin' 'bout my freedom / People freedom and liberty," speak to the continued deferral of freedom since the formal end of Jamaican slavery and the substitution of apprenticeship and later (neo)colonialism to transform (ex-) slaves to the proletariat of an emerging capitalist system.[13] The aforementioned lines are followed up with a call to action: "Yeah, we've been trodding on the winepress much too long / Rebel, rebel." Grammatically speaking, Marley's use of the word "trodding" reveals the commingling of the past and present. To put it differently, the word trod is not simply the past tense of tread but more so a revelation of Marley's underlying apocalyptic, Rastafari imagery in which the present perfect continuous tense in the word "trodding" draws from biblical language to denote the transhistoricity of plantation structures—the omnipresence of systemic oppression under Babylon's capitalist system as *sufferahs* continue trodding on the treadmill.[14] This notion of Babylon is akin to Aníbal Quijano's argument that once the formal practice of colonialism ended, it transformed into the "cornerstone" of the "capitalist colonial /modern world power."[15] Under this lens, a more full-fledged definition of Babylon in the Jamaican "sociopolitical" context is the "complex of economic, political, religious, and educational institutions and values that evolved" from colonialism and is now forged by an American and European alliance through global capitalism.[16] Given the perseverance of coloniality on a global scale, as Bob Marley suggests in an interview, "Babylon is everywhere."[17] Because of its transhistorical and transnational power of exploitation in the face of continued unfreedom in the postcolonial era, in the song Bob Marley characterizes Babylon as a "vampire" that is not only "suckin' the blood of the sufferahs" but also "the children day by day."[18] As a vampire, Babylon has no care for whom it exploits as its existence depends on draining the life force of the living.

Significant for understanding the exploitative power underlying Western economic systems, Marley's vampire trope for capitalism (Babylon) echoes Karl Marx's ideas. In *Capital*, Marx characterizes capital as "dead labour which, vampire-like, lives only by sucking living labour, and lives the more, the more labour it sucks." Thus, the power underlying capitalism and its extraction of labor can be read as vampiric in nature; it does not die but sucks the life force out of others perpetually. Along the lines of this notion of the changing same, Marx's vampiric metaphor for capital harnesses metamorphic power by constantly remaking itself; according to Marx, capital "posits the permanence of value by incarnating itself in fleeting commodities and taking on their form, but at the same time changing them just as constantly."[19] The vampire is therefore an apt metaphor for the Babylon system: its transhistorical perseverance is akin to the perpetuation of plantation structures and its death campaign to preserve its own existence transcends historical time, given its immortal power. Babylon, similar to the vampiric nature of capitalist systems, escapes death by remaking itself across historical periods with an ethic and practice that refuses to die, even as it engages perpetually in death and destruction.

In "Babylon System," Marley also symbolizes Babylon's incessant exploitation of labor through the imagery of a winepress that drains lifeforce. It is as if the *sufferahs* are the wine grapes that have been "trodding on the winepress" and have "been trampled on" and "oppressed."[20] As listeners, through the associative imagination, we envision a series of sliding metaphors (grape/wine and body/labor) in which the grapes become a signifier for the *sufferahs'* bodies, as both are macerated and broken down, as the life force (juice and blood) is extracted and transformed into a commodity. The proto-capitalist plantation system of the long sixteenth century inaugurated a world ecology connected by cheap nature such that the labor of humans was collapsed into the nonhuman landscape and both could be rendered somehow inhuman—and, therefore, fungible because of their alienation from lifeforce. Furthermore, as commodities, wine and labor have a paradigmatic, metaphoric relationship of similarity, made possible by Bob Marley's winepress imagery, which we can equate with the treadmill from the apprenticeship era in Jamaica.

The treadmill was a horrific instrument of torture used to impel labor during the apprenticeship period that began in 1834 and maintained the practices of slavery despite its supposed end through judicial decree (see figure 1).

FIGURE 1 The Treadmill, Jamaica, 1837. Courtesy of *Slavery Images: A Visual Record of the African Slave Trade and Slave Life in the Early African Diaspora.* http://www.slaveryimages .org/s/slaveryimages/item/1297.

While children under the age of six were freed automatically, older slaves had to continue working on their masters' estates (plantations) for a period of four to six years before gaining their freedom. Planters (estate/plantation owners) would supposedly teach their ex-slaves a trade and the ex-slaves, in turn, would supposedly learn how to be free. Needless to say, apprenticeship was little more than a different form of slavery. In *A Narrative of Events,* James Williams gives an account of the forced labor and degree of torture apprentices experienced on the treadmill, highlighting the fact that apprenticeship was basically slavery in a different form and, on some occasions, was even more brutal:

> Almost every apprentice that sent to the workhouse by magistrate, have to dance treadmill, except the sick in the hospital. It was miserable to see when the mill going, the people bawling and crying most dreadful—so they can't dance, so the driver keep on flogging; them holla out, "massa me no able! My 'tomach, oh, me da dead, oh!!"—but no use, the driver never stop—the bawling make it rather worse, them make the mill go fast—the more you holla the more the mill go, and the driver keep on

flogging away at all them not able to keep up; them flog the people as if them was flogging Cow.[21]

There was one old woman with grey head, belonging to Mr. Wallace, of Farm, and she could not dance the mill at all: she hang by the two wrists, which was strapped to the bar, and the driver kept on flogging her;—she get more than all the rest, her clothes cut off with the cat—the shoulder strap cut with it, and her shift hang down over that side—then they flog upon that shoulder and cut it up very bad; but all that flogging couldn't make she dance the mill, and when she come down all her back covered with blood.[22]

Now we can more clearly understand the significance of Marley's use of the word "trodding" as the present perfect continuous tense of the word "tread" to signify through metonymic association the torture of the treadmill and the ever-present trauma associated with the slave sublime. Williams's narrative also references Amelia Lawrence's testimony about the overwhelming and unforgettable pain she experienced from being tortured on the treadmill: "I have never recovered up to the present moment from the punishment of the treadmill; I have pains all over my body since then, which I cannot get over."[23] Diana Paton notes in *No Bond but the Law* that the treadmill was praised as a "non-brutalizing" form of punishment during the early stages of apprenticeship.[24] However, as I argue, Lawrence's testimony reveals that the Western notion of the sublime is false in its denial of the body, and, as Paton suggests in her commentary on this apprentice's testimony, "The treadmill, then, is a clear illustration of the inextricability of the body, the mind, and the labor performed by the body."[25] The Enlightenment-inflected notion of reason that undergirds the Kantian sublime is inapplicable to this context owing to its transcendentalist logic that privileges the mind over bodily sensations.

Similar to the treadmill torture, when Bob Marley states in "Babylon System" that the *sufferahs* have been on the "winepress" for "much too long" and have "been taken for granted much too long," he calls attention to the embodiment of pain and the denial that comes with the torture from hard labor. One of the key elements of torture that Elaine Scarry discusses in *The Body in Pain* is the notion that the victim's pain is often denied by those in power.[26] I connect this denial to the Kantian tradition of the sublime in which this philosopher links the overwhelming affect of the sublime to the mind alone as a transitory experience, thereby denying the corporeal effect. As a contrast to Western philosophy, the slave sublime not only calls attention to the limitations of the Cartesian dualism that underlies the Kantian sublime in its privileging of the mind over bodily sensations, but also challenges the ephemeral conditions of this concept. Instead, Marley suggests the longevity of this torturous experience that has been happening "From the very day we left the shores / Of our Father's land."[27] The pain is ever-present: it is a transhistorical experience of shared memory that has been occurring since the capture of Africans, the subsequent voyage to the New World during the Middle Passage, and the arrival on Jamaican slave plantations.

Also demonstrating transhistorical continuity, another underlying significance in Marley's metaphoric representation of capitalism is the notion that it not only drains in a vampiric fashion the labor of its victims but also instills ideologies that distort Black selfhood and worldview "continually." For Marley, this continual drainage and erasure of dignity are the necessary corollary to maintaining the colonialist-imperialist Babylon system, as is signified by the internal and end rhymes of "vampire" and "empire." Because of this, Bob Marley critiques the two hegemonic institutions—"the church and university"— that have played key roles in disseminating colonialist ideologies to maintain imperialistic practices. As Kwame Dawes rightly argues, "The greatest tool of the Babylon system, the colonial system and the imperialist system is to try and force the people of the world to conform to their ideas and views."[28] Eight times Marley repeats the refrain "Tell the children the truth" in elevated pitch, even imploring them with the phrase "Come on, and tell the children the truth."[29]

In the song "Rastaman Chant," Bob Marley sings about the coming of redemption from colonial abuse when the Babylon system is dethroned after the apocalypse. As Bob Marley takes the lead in this Wailers song, Peter Tosh and Bunny Wailer provide the choral elements in a morose manner, chanting the key phrase, "gone down, gone down; Babylon, you throne gone down." The off-tempo fashion of their choral rendition elevates the song's dissonance as they chant down Babylon, so to speak. The song alludes implicitly to the book of Revelation in which three angels announce the imminent apocalypse (made possible by the fall of Babylon) and the promise that the faithful will enter Mount Zion. In the last two verses Bob Marley sings about flying "home to Zion." The notion of flying home to Zion (Ethiopia for the Rastafari) connects a larger Afro-diasporic consciousness and belief that spiritually-awakened individuals will be able to fly back to Africa.[30] Bob Marley states: "One bright morning when man work is over / Man Will fly away home." The work to which he refers is the process of decolonization, which will awaken the spirit and African consciousness through loud syncopated drumming. The beating of syncopated drums symbolizes the act of arousing and reviving not only the socially dead, but also the negating of a nonhuman subject positioning (which comes from a colonialist worldview) so as to become ready and mentally empowered for revolutionary action and redemptive freedom. I use the term redemptive freedom to underscore the communal resistance to and subversion of mental slavery that Marley conveys in his well-known "Redemption Song." Redemption as a concept is significant in that it demands "respect and recognition." Mbembe argues that redemption is crucial because of the degree of violence and misrecognition that Blacks endured under slavery and colonialism. Redemption, therefore, highlights Fanon's notion that there needs to be an "obstinate search for the traces of life that survived this great destruction."[31] And as Marley suggests, through redemptive freedom, the spiritually awakened are able to regain racial dignity and to lessen the psychic traumas of their contemporary social condition. "Rastaman Chant," in this light, conveys the notion that the Rastafari can chant down the ideologies of Babylon, thereby fostering self-redemption and the possibility of an apocalyptic vision of and liminal passage to Zion.

With this slave sublime emphasis on the imagination, there is an attempt for the Rastafari subject to achieve consonance in the narrative or lyrical sense by envisioning an alternate existence outside Babylon, given the pronounced social dissonance in Jamaican society that the music replicates symbolically. David Roberts notes that "apocalyptic imagery and ideas" are linked with the "aesthetics of the sublime."[32] In philosophy, sublimity is a "*condition*" marked by "unease, of restlessness, of dissonance." Dissonance comes from a clash "between the imagination and reason which orientate themselves either to the faculty of cognition of the faculty of desire."[33] In the slave sublime, the dissonance points to the tension between an imaginative desire for freedom's fulfillment since slavery and the discord with rationalistic plantation structures and ideologies that prolong the experience of slavery. Leonard Barrett rightly links the dissonance in reggae music to the "social and cultural incongruities" in the Jamaican society that lead to the Rastafari's experience of "alienation whether real or imagined."[34] Jamaican reggae music's dissonance and stress of downbeats, in a manner that subverts the typical Western musical structure, create a musical signature that articulates the slave sublime discord between the imagination and reason in a worldwide musical discourse. To some extent the dissonance suggests that the musicians' focus on African-derived musical patterns and tonal expression is a means of signaling their departure from and contestations of Western systems. This is particularly evident in the language of Nyabinghi drumming, as suggested by the Rastafari belief that their drumming can beat down plantation-derived oppression.

In the song's function as a linguistic vehicle for tonal expression, poetic lyricisms are sparse and repetitive, a necessary strategy to suggest that the drums convey an even greater message about the apocalyptic death of the oppressive Babylon system.

The Nyabinghi is the Rastafari religious ceremony in which drums, influenced by the Burrus, function as both the medium for spiritual transcendence and the means by which violence against Babylon can be enacted—that is, symbolically. Through drumming, the Rastafari delivers violence to the Babylon systems of oppression by "stab[bing]" the "most vulnerable center of the drum."[35] There are three primary drums: the bass, the *fundeh*, and the repeater (peta). As the lead drum, the *fundeh* has the special task of maintaining the rhythm or what is commonly referred to as the "lifeline." It is this repetitive *fundeh* bassline of roots reggae that communicates "directly to the body"[36] in a syncopated bodily discourse that captures the heartbeat rhythm. The bass drum, on the other hand, which is usually low in pitch, picks up on the *fundeh*'s rhythmic pattern while providing a variation in both tone and rhythm. As for the repeater, it carries the melody as it maintains the *fundeh*'s tempo. Rastas refer to this three-drum set as the *akete* because of its complex system of tonal language.

"Rastaman Chant" captures not only the essence of sound as text through drum language, but also the significance of bodily discourse and paradigmatic spatial arrangements:

> When the drums speak, the pulsing thump of the bass dominates. The heavily padded drumstick effects a caress on the first beat of the bar, as the stick lies horizontal to the center of the drumhead. The third beat is an accented stab with the point of the stick, again in the most vulnerable center of the drum. This is the drum that really symbolizes the beating down of oppression, a principal objective of Rastafari . . . The repeater drum protests. It continually defies the rigid bass and *fundeh* patterns. This defiance could be regarded as symbolic of the hope to move out of and above oppression through creative application.[37]

There is also an underlying morphological structure to the language of drumming, and it involves operations of conceptualization, formulation, and articulation without verbal language, some of which are conveyed through the drummer's body language, mannerisms, or gestures, which correlate with visual cognition. Given the overlapping structural and morphological principles that underlie both drumming and violence, one can argue that, through drumming, violence can be communicated at the sublexical level. Violence functions similarly as an expressive medium in which its modes are rearticulated or resymbolized in Jamaican cultural forms. In this light, violence can be considered less as an inarticulate outburst resorted to when verbal means fail than itself an articulated system of representations, symbols, and structures, even having a certain syntax or set of organizing principles.

What can also be inferred from above is the notion that violence occurs on the paradigmatic/vertical aspect of language, in the sense that oppression can be beaten "down." The use of this particular signifier ("down"), rather than another preposition from the same paradigm set, relates to the preexisting lexicon about plantation violence. Discussions about power and violence often involve the binary oppositions up/down or above/below, which is indicated by Reckford's argument that Nyabinghi drumming symbolizes both the "beating down of oppression" and the Rastafari "hope to move above oppression."[38] The symbolic "stab[bing]" and "beating down" during drumming is a performance miming the violence that maintained the vertical power dynamic or spatial relations between masters and slaves. This spatiality can be considered as well in relation to the North/South divide in the global arena of neoliberal transactions that repeat or replicate colonial systems, as is evident in the Global North's political and economic domination over the Global South.

Bob Marley's metaphoric return to the plantation and its symbols of power, violence, and resistance suggest slavery's phantasmagoric presence as the changing same when colonial and postcolonial experiences of violence are continually associated with plantation structures. The significance of restaging plantation-derived violence is revealed in another song, "Slave Driver," in which Marley sings: "Slave driver / Your table is turned / Catch a fire / You're gonna get burned." This trope of "burnin'," utilized time and again by roots reggae and contemporary dancehall artists, is significant because it alludes both to the frequent means by which Jamaican slave masters burned slaves to death as punishment and the means by which the slaves, in turn, revolted against their oppressors by burning down plantations, thereby changing the violence from its original instantiation. When Marley states in "Slave Driver" that "today they say that we're free / only to be chained in poverty / Good God, I think it's illiteracy," the structural aspect of the plantation system becomes evident, with sliding signifiers highlighting the paradigmatic aspect: poverty and illiteracy are the chains that continue to hold the descendants of slavery captive. While the song functions as a historical memory of slavery ("Every time I hear the crack of a whip / My blood runs cold") and the Middle Passage ("I remember on the slave ship / How they brutalized our very souls"), it functions also as a personal outcry against the abuses of Marley's own time period.

Even though he is a subject of Jamaica's post-independence era, in "Slave Driver" Marley represents himself simultaneously as a slave and a colonial subject who is "chained." This identification undergirds the continuity of identity and functions as an anachronic constellation of history, a strategy of simultaneous identification of the self, which Paul Ricoeur calls "sameness." Suggesting its operation on the paradigmatic axis of language, Ricoeur notes that the qualitative aspect of identity involves "extreme resemblance" and also "corresponds to the operation of substitution without semantic loss."[39] As Bob Marley transcends historical time and space in his epistemological eyewitness account, he holds, to use Ricoeur's terms, "the material marks held to be the irrecusable traces of his connection to past/present and present/past to suggest the unbroken historical continuum."[40] He remains a "bounded" slave. This permanence of identity through time, according to Ricoeur, suggests an ontological "connectedness between events, whether these be of a physical or mental nature" and "any search for connections can be undertaken, whether this be on the physical or corporeal level or on the mental or psychic level."[41] Kim Atkins explains that Ricoeur's notion about the "uninterrupted continuity . . . pertain[s] to the complex phenomenon of personal identity. The difficulty for an account of personal identity is to find a model of permanence in time that can express each of the different temporal senses of 'same.'"[42] She notes also that Ricoeur coins the term *ipse* to annotate the first person and to signify self-constancy "by which the permanence of character is instituted as an inner, first-person self-referential activity in which one takes one's attributes *as* one's own and in doing so, carries those attributes forward in time, constituting the continuity (permanence in time) of *who* one is."[43] In this sense, the verses from "Slave Driver" work not by logic nor narrative sequences but by creating constellations of anachronic fragments that correspond to the layerings of violence: the historical chains, the paradigmatic substitution of various forms of bondage—the Middle Passage, slavery, apprenticeship, and (neo)colonialism—in essence, the changing same.

The Rastafari term "I-an-I" is a signifier of the self that demonstrates both a hermeneutical strategy and a semantic self-affirmation. By using the Rastafari personal pronoun "I-an-I" (the *ipse*) Bob Marley refers to the "permanence of character" or "self-constancy" in the first person in order to suggest the unbroken chains of violence in his contemporary era, the changing same, connecting him to the brutal experiences of slavery, thereby allowing him to forge an even more profound link to his predecessors. Take, for instance, the historical experience of the Middle Passage. The experience of captive Africans being chained so intimately together reduces individuality to the most fundamental degree: the bodily excrements and the shared capacity of such dehumanizing, psychic violence function as a key element of the collective, historical memory of depersonalization and objectification. Rather than the individualism underlying the Cartesian *cogito* "I think therefore I am," the Rastafari concept of "I-an-I" is a phenomenology that prioritizes collective or communal ties, quite in contrast to the Enlightenment legacy that celebrates Descartes's famous ratiocentric subject, who emanates principally from the mind. "I-an-I," therefore, not only signifies the plural self but also the ability to harness the power of self-representation that disavows Western formulations.[44] It is a method that destabilizes reason's supposed transcendent immateriality (as a locus for the cognitive abilities of a disinterested and egoistic European subject) while recuperating the spiritual dispossession and epistemo-ontological violence to Black subjectivity and imagination. Calling upon the imagination and its ability for free play, Marley achieves a form of redemptive freedom that challenges the positivist logic of linear time when he positions the imagination as an instrument of somatogenic cognition, as he "remembers" being on the "slave ship." In this expression of historical *(re)memory*, the imagination functions as a repository for transgenerational knowledge, forging a connection between Marley and his predecessors who experienced the soul-crushing violence of the Middle Passage—a violence to the imaginary, the spiritual and onto-epistemological basis of understanding one's humanity. "I-an-I" in this context of narrating oral history from a subaltern position allows for the display of discursive agency wherein a belief in this Rastafari notion of identity makes possible the "delinking" from Western spheres of knowledge by recuperating Black phenomenology and epistemology as collective embodiment rather than as detached individuality.[45]

Bob Marley, therefore, subverts the hierarchy of Western tradition's valuation of the written text by presenting himself as an oral historian. As such, his music functions well as a vehicle for historical fiction with a subaltern historiography that sublates the past and present as a speech act. Veena Das describes subaltern historiography as being able to displace "social action as defined by rational action."[46] It is a "form of discourse in which affective and iterative writing develops its own language. History as a writing that constructs the moment of defiance emerges in the 'magma of significations,' for the 'representational closure which presents itself when we encounter thought in objectified forms is now ripped open.'"[47] Here Das refers to history as a process of writing, but the kind of historiography that Bob Marley undertakes is an oral one that is "transgressive" because it splits "speech produced into state-ments of referential truth in the indicative present."[48] As Homi Bhabha ex-plains, the referential present that emphasizes the "disjunctive present of utterance" allows the historian not to define subaltern consciousness as bi-nary, whether as positive or negative, but rather to renegotiate subaltern agency so that it emerges as "relocation and reinscription."[49] By casting him-self into the narrative of slavery, Marley suggests that he is constrained nei-ther by the intersubjective/objective nor empirical/metaphysical factors of history and language. Furthermore, he subverts the hierarchy of Western tra-dition's valuation of the written text.

Bob Marley reinscribes history through speech and speech allows for a "temporal break" or intervention that takes on new meaning for the oral his-torian, giving him narrative agency. In her essay "Postcoloniality and Value" Gayatri Spivak describes this process of subaltern "renegotiation" as "revers-ing, displacing, and seizing the apparatus of value-coding."[50] In the context of oral history, the speech act suggests a radical linguistic intersubjectivity as the dynamic aspect of both social code and individual message that signifies a plethora of meanings beyond static representation, such as structures of feel-ing that arise from highly evocative and coded language from a first-person point of view—which illuminates an understanding of the slave sublime con-cept. For Kant, however, representation is linked to moral and social judg-ments that are considered to be universal, which reinforces Western aesthetic ideals of narration, of both third-person omniscience and realist representa-tion. As an oral historian, Marley uses speech in order to escape the subjectiv-ity of the written.[51] Homi Bhabha points to the two wrenchingly different registers at work in Jacques Lacan's theory—which has significance to the ma-terial history of Jamaican orality and of its specific practices, rhythms, tex-tures and the dialectical problematic between language/speech and the subject. Lacan argues that there is a temporal break in speech wherein "there exists a world of truth entirely deprived of subjectivity" that is "manifestly directed towards the rediscovery of truth which lies in the order of sym-bols."[52] Bhabha explains that Lacan's genealogy of historical discourse and narrative agency unearths the denied subjectivity that is intersubjective in relation to the sign: "It is in the 'contingent' tension that sign and symbol overlap and are indeterminately articulated through the 'temporal break.' Where the sign is deprived of the subject—intersubjectivity returns as sub-jectivity directed toward the rediscovery of truth, then a (re)ordering of sym-bols becomes possible in the sphere of the social."[53] Anthony Wilden explains that in Lacan's attempts to respond to the issue of *movement* in discourse,

Lacan challenges the commonly held linguistic notion that speech is static. For Lacan, as Wilden argues, "speech was a movement toward something, an attempt to fill gaps without which speech could not be articulated." Wilden notes that Lacan does not "distinguish thought from speech" and thus speech in the Lacanian sense suggests the articulation "in time and space something already 'given' in thought."[54] Speech, therefore, suggests a radical linguistic intersubjectivity as the dynamic aspect of both social code and individual message.

In the song "Concrete Jungle" from the Wailers' 1973 album *Catch A Fire*, the lead singer Marley depicts the importance of speech, aurality, and temporal breaks as a demonstration of Bhabha's notion of subaltern agency. By using practices of rhythm, sonic reverberations, and emotional textures that connect to the body, Marley challenges Western representations of the sublime and its supposed limitations within language by filling in the gaps between the sublime and its failure of representation to articulate the overwhelming magnitudes of pain or terror. "Concrete Jungle" speaks to the affect surrounding both the denigration of selfhood and exile in Jamaica that result from the colonial ideologies. In this song, Marley plays with the contrasting imagery of "light" and "dark," and he critiques the colonialist rhetoric about the mission of bringing light to African people. Europeans perceived Africa as the dark continent, a place of primitive jungles and the uncivilized human "Other."[55] In shifting the positivist discourse supporting slavery and colonialism, Marley shows that the New World where Africans were taken—in Jamaica, for instance—to be civilized and humanized is actually a "concrete jungle." Despite the end of slavery, as Marley suggests, postcolonial Jamaica is a place filled with darkness, as signified by his assertion that "No sun will shine today" and that "The high yellow moon won't come out to play." It is an experience in which he has "never known what happiness is" and "never known what sweet caress is."

This unrequited desire is conveyed as a void, a dark liminal space between slavery and freedom. Thus, through his extensive light and dark imagery, Marley employs paradox, a kind of discursive reversal. From a European worldview, light equates with the concept of enlightenment and its associated freedoms.[56] Instead of freedom and dignity, what Marley experiences "continually" is a subjugation to colonial systems that negate his humanity and selfhood: "Darkness has covered my light / And has changed my day into night." It is not until the last verse of the song that Marley reveals the catalyst for the overwhelming darkness that has taken over: it is the "illusion" and "confusion" that stem from the Enlightenment's colonial legacy in Jamaica's ideological systems, institutional practices, and social constructs—the dark forces of Western modernity —which he dubs "the concrete jungle."[57] The Western ideologies that abound in Jamaica have created a structure in which he feels as if he is "bound here in captivity," and even though there are no physical "chains around" his "feet," he's "not free." In "Concrete Jungle" Marley challenges the colonialist rhetoric of the Enlightenment by equating the plantation systems and social constructs about Black inferiority with the jungle Europeans created, which has brought darkness to his life.[58]

The guitar solo riff in the dub break in "Concrete Jungle" brings a melancholic sound that enacts a sonic representation of the ontological despair (of being) and material loss (of the before self) in the themes of alienation, exile, and loneliness in a manner that conveys deep realms of sublimity. In the sonic break from the album version, the imagination intercedes in this moment of sublimity, focusing on sentiment to destabilize a rationalistic mode of understanding by allowing the listener to fill in the imagery of the spaces left vacant by the suspension of vocals. Highlighting the phonocentric mode of communication that privileges sound, this instrumental break provides an emotional representation of the paradoxical experience of having no "chains around my feet" but nonetheless being "bound here in captivity" and surrounded pervasively by "darkness."[59] As Fred Moten posits in *In the Break*, such breaks are about when "the question of being and the question of blackness converge."[60] The sonic break in "Concrete Jungle" conveys the attempt to express the turmoil in postcolonial Jamaica by allowing the listener to experience through the imagination the magnitude of the mathematical elements of the slave sublime—that is, the immeasurable awe affiliated with the associative imagination's perception of the infinite plantations systems that occur as the changing same. To put it differently, unlike the Kantian premise, in the slave sublime the associative imagination provides conceptual unity and perception of the Real of unfreedom on a transhistorical level.[61] I am reminded of Njelle Hamilton's astute phrasing that "dub uses music-engineering technology to rearrange and shift suffering to new spatio-temporal dimensions" as a "quantum temporality."[62] The emotional textures of loneliness, despair, exile, alienation, and melancholy are what Kant attributes to the mental "terror" underlying the sublime in *Observations*.[63] As the slave sublime in Marley's representation, these emotions have a negative physiological impact with regard to his realization of his "bounded" subject position.

The instrumental break's focus on the guitar solo makes possible a shift from the pulsating drum and base reggae signature to capture the heightened sensation of despair through a modulating blur of sounds that almost drown out the underlying riddim. Chris Blackwell, who signed (Bob Marley and) the Wailers to Island Records, wanted to incorporate a rock sound so as to garner international appeal for the group's reggae music. Despite the impact that Blackwell's engineer had in creating this sound from the instrumental break, we must think about the underlying homegrown[64] Afro-Jamaican dub aesthetic that he draws upon.[65] To understand that the rock-inspired sonic break is actually an aesthetic trait of the slave sublime, we must consider the process of dubbing as initiating a challenge to order and boundaries in its embracement of chaos through dissonance and excess through modulation. Indeed, it is a slave sublime aesthetic that challenges boundaries: in some instances, Jamaican sound engineers damaged their equipment in the process of dubbing, thereby extending the machine "beyond its intended limits" in order to challenge "aesthetic norms" of "Westernized musical thinking," and, in this process, they produced a "new musical language" with a "constellation of meanings."[66] In addition to this understanding of dub's sonic power in its challenge to Western aesthetic modes, we must consider its opposition to perceptual models as well. Edwin C. Hill's argument about New World soundscapes that defy the European "writing subject" and their imperialistic and hegemonic gaze is noteworthy in relation to dub. As a sound text, dub "cystallize[s] fraught encounters between meanings and institutions of writing and sounding, resonating with the struggle over New World space."[67] Certainly, the effect of echo through reverb in "Concrete Jungle" is about giving a feel for the texture of New World space in which one is imprisoned ("bounded")—as in the simulation of echoing sounds that bounce off those socially constructed prison walls while wailing about the inconsolable and immeasurable levels of utter despair.

Nonetheless, there is beauty in the sonic reverberations, which amplify and distort spatial elements through echo to covey the emotional textures of the slave sublime. These contrasting elements of pain and pleasure speak to the paradox that functions as a defining element of sublimity. For the listener, there is the pleasure that comes from the aesthetic appreciation of the sonic elements, and, simultaneously, on a somatogenic level we are able to feel and explore through the senses the depth of these emotions that the echo chamber of the studio makes possible. Part of the beauty comes from each replay of the recorded sound that, to use Moten's phrasing, "reproduces agony as pleasure differently."[68] This pleasure/pain paradox in "Concrete Jungle" is achieved by the stretching or overdubbing of the guitar solo, as facilitated by the use of sustain pedals, which hold, prolong, and extend the guitar's wailing in successively higher octaves until it overflows into the returning vocals.

This manipulation of sound conveys how the transcendent moment in the beautiful is temporary as the listener is released back into the sublime iterations about the unrelenting desire for freedom: "I said that life (sweet life) / Must be somewhere (sweet life) to be found . . . / Instead of concrete jungle (jungle)," a place "where the living is hardest." By accessing the Real, the instrumental break provides a fleeting, transcendent moment in an alternate sonic space outside of Jamaica's social reality—outside Babylon, toward an ephemeral vision of freedom and, in that very instance, its negation. Because the magnitude of colonial violence has never been permanently resolved, the music provides only fleeting moments of catharsis. In moments such as this, we witness the function of dub's sonic distortion and mediation to achieve a quiet sublimation of violence through the evanescent bleeding of the sublime into the beautiful before returning to the realities of unfreedom. In "Concrete Jungle," this occurs when the shrillness of the guitar solo modulates to its highest octave and then eviscerates, as signaled by the morphing of the instrumental as it fades texturally and dimensionally into the vocals. Here we see a reversal of the trajectory from the Kantian sublime: in the slave sublime, there is a movement toward rather than away from beauty.

In many ways, the pleasure or the appreciation of beauty stems from the importance of the sonic rupture in the dub break, through which we are able to hear and, through the imagination, access the Real.[69] I return here to Moten's *In the Break* in which he offers the term "*second* iconicity" to denote the phenomenal moment during which there is a "fullness of the sign" that provides a "constellation of meaning, understanding, music, phrase, feeling, variation, and imagination." His use of the word "imagination" is pregnant with meaning in that it conveys a second-level iconicity that is not bound to logical structure but rather to an empirical knowledge that facilitates a "temporal" and "ontological sense" of a phenomenon.[70] In the context of "Concrete Jungle" this phenomenon is the representation of sublimity as the slave sublime that harnesses the powers of the imagination and the body for its empirical basis of knowledge. The dub break's suspension of vocals in this song transforms the song from a logocentrically driven representation of sound to one that communicates somatically—that is, directly to the body, highlighting the empirical characteristics of the slave sublime that are formed by the orientation of the body as an important faculty of cognition. This somatic aspect emphasizes the body's key role in the slave sublime moment and the ability to access the Real, wherein the associative imagination forms images and perceptions that are based on the intuition, senses, and feelings. It is an aesthetic transformation in which the sublime is momentarily perceived as positive without eliminating negativity—an effect of the slave sublime's vitalizing force to create spaces of resistance while realizing that the effects of slavery linger as repeating forces of historical materialism.

In my analysis of Marley's music, I have explored how the aesthetic judgment of the slave sublime—the reappearance of plantation structures and the related magnitudes of terror experienced—can be communicated effectively through a bodily representation, a key departure from the Kantian sublime. Whereas Kant situates the sublime within the rational faculties of the mind,[71] the slave sublime underscores the judging subject's embodiment. That is to say, the Kantian sublime is neither bound to content nor form, but only to the impression of reason's limitations. While this negativity in the Kantian sublime is contained by disciplining the imagination, the slave sublime gives autonomy to the associative imagination, which is able to make conceptual links across time and space.

While the slave sublime concerns how the after-effects are still with us and that there is an ongoing relation to the violence of slavery and coloniality, it indicates that there is something transformative in this aesthetic, especially in the way Marley intervenes into his subject matter, using the tools of voice, rhythm, dub, etc. This is a marked contrast with Kant, for whom aesthetic and form are tied solely to the experience of beauty since he regards them as sensual experiences and, therefore, not properly under our judgment. This separation of the beautiful from his notion of the sublime seems to be informed by a different logic, one that is founded upon the false claims of the Enlightenment, a marked contrast to the slave sublime's embracement of the imagination. There is a sense in which Kant wants the sublime to keep Imagination in its place, to discipline it with Reason, but there is an important way in which Marley liberates our imagination while remaining faithful to the trauma of how it is tied to a bodily experience. One can understand why he uses the imagination to evoke transhistorical memory and draws parallels between the political landscape during slavery and that of his lifetime. For Marley, the past and the present are interconnected in more tangible ways than they usually are perceived from a European worldview.

CHAPTER FOUR

The Real (and) Ghetto Life

Excess Violence and Manichean Delirium in Marlon James's A Brief History of Seven Killings

What is called real . . . is by definition dispersed and elliptical, fleeting and on the move and essentially ambiguous. The real is composed of several layers or sheets, several envelopes. It is an uncomfortable thing, one that can only be seized in bits, provisionally, through a multiplicity of approaches. And even if seized, it can never be reproduced or represented either fully or accurately. In the end there is always a *surplus* of the real that only those endowed with extra capacities can access.

—Achille Mbembe, *Critique of Black Reason*

There's a reason why the story of the ghetto should never come with a photo. The Third World slum is a nightmare that defies beliefs or facts, even the ones staring right at you. A vision of hell that twists and turns on itself and grooves to its own soundtrack. Normal rules do not apply here. Imagination then, dream, fantasy. You visit a ghetto, particularly in West Kingston, and it immediately leaves the real to become this sort of grotesque, something out of Dante or the infernal painting of Hieronymus Bosch. It's a rusty red chamber of hell that cannot be described so I will not try to describe it. It cannot be photographed because some parts of West Kingston, such as Rema, are in the grip of such bleak and unremitting repulsiveness that the inherent beauty of the photographic process will lie to you about just how ugly it really is. Beauty has infinite range but do does wretchedness and the only way to accurately grasp the full, unending vortex of ugly that is Trench Town is to imagine it.

—Marlon James, *A Brief History of Seven Killings*

Similar to Bob Marley's music, Marlon James's novel *A Brief History of Seven Killings* reveals the weddedness of the beautiful to the slave sublime and the significance of the imagination for accessing the Real that is associated with the continued unfreedom and violence in Jamaica during the 1970s and 1980s. Nonetheless, James concedes to the limitations of particular artistic mediums for representing the Real. The photographic image and written language, he suggests, cannot convey the complete scope of the awfulness that characterizes the Jamaican ghettos in West Kingston, such as Trench Town where

Marley once lived. These artistic forms reach a limit, signaled by their failure to represent the Real because of excessive and surplus violence.

The Real, within the context of the slave sublime, is linked to an infinite and overwhelming surplus of violence that emanates from plantation structures and the stark realization of unfreedom during the post-slavery eras, which challenge textual representation. Dennis A. Foster defines the Real in relation to the Lacanian notion of that which is prior to symbolic representation. Foster points out that the Real is "evoked by the implicit limits of symbolic representation" because "something is always excluded." Very significant in Foster's exposition of the Real is its connection to the "mad other" because of its "limits" and "silence," which ensue from the "failure" of finding a mode of representation that is "adequate to one's experience of it."[1] If, by a stretch of the imagination, madness in the symbolic sense relates to the failure of articulating an encounter with the Real, then we can venture to suggest that the Manichean delirium of ghetto life in Jamaica exhibits slave-sublime levels of psychic despair, poverty, and physical violence in its symmetry with plantation life. Pertinent questions to consider are: Can literature or other artistic forms convey the magnitudes of the slave sublime experience by accessing the Real that is connected to the West Kingston garrisons, which continue to have one of the highest per capita murder rates in the world? What happens to people who are trapped in this unrelenting despair, and how do they find a mode of expression to articulate their experiences of infinite violence?

While literature can represent elements of the slave sublime, it is not fully equipped as music is to convey the dimensions of social dissonance and excess violence that characterize the Real. The key to accessing the Real is through the sensuous realms of sound and performance, that which literature cannot convey in its devotion to textuality and its resulting inability to convey the excesses of violence that connect to the slave sublime. Unlike Dennis A. Foster's viewpoint that the Real is wholly inaccessible in its connection to the symbolic realm and the unrepresentable, Achille Mbembe suggests that the Real can be accessed by "those endowed with extra capacities." Because of its pervasive surplus or "excess," Mbembe argues, the Real can be "entered" through "orphic states reached through dance or music, possession or ecstasy." He goes on to suggest that an "encounter with the real can only be fragmentary and chopped up, ephemeral, made up of dissonance."[2] What Mbembe describes is an orphic musical context in which sound and the body are very important for accessing the Real. In psychoanalytic discourse, the mythical figure Orpheus functions as a leitmotif for creativity and madness because of unfathomable forces beyond his control. His psychic break was marked primarily by his journey to the underworld, where both his body and mind were affected by the liminality between life and death and unfulfilled desire— the unspeakable loss of almost rescuing and reuniting with his wife. Similar to Orpheus's mythic journey to and hapless return from Hades, Marley descends imaginatively into the underworld of the slave ship and plantation life only to return to a contemporary society that replicates the horrors of the past.[3] His music captures the full scope of the slave sublime condition by accessing the Real through performative bodily language, albeit in fleeting moments, which is usually absent from literature. In Marley's case, his creative abilities align with the imagination and the unfettered creative freedom it provides for accessing the Real, despite the Lacanian belief that it exists beyond representation. To convey this despair over the postcolonial situation in Jamaica, Marley engages in an embodied and sonic performance language that fuses beauty with the slave sublime in order for his listeners to access the Real, despite the overwhelming magnitudes of trauma and violence.

Given that the novel's origin was tied to the middling condition and the socialization of the emerging middle class in the nineteenth century, the novel as a form was not intended to convey the extant and the excess. Within this context, we may consider Joseph Roach's characterization of all violence as "excessive." Particularly excessive is the violence from the geo-economic terrain of the circum-Atlantic region, which occupies a space between life and death in its "economy of superabundance" because of its history of "slave-produced abundance."[4] There is certainly an economy of violence in this region, and especially in the case of Jamaica, which, as many scholars including Terry Lacey, Leonard E. Barrett, and Trevor Burnard have suggested, was perhaps the most violent slave society in the Americas. As early as 1740, Charles Leslie noted that "No Country exceeds them in a barbarous Treatment of Slaves, or in the cruel methods they put them to death."[5] Burnard notes in his discussion of Thomas Thistlewood's diary that "Jamaican society was especially brutal even by the elevated standards of New World brutality." Thistlewood's diaries reveal his slave-holding penchant for sadistic punishments, which included rubbing salt, lime juice, and pepper into the wounds of slaves after they had been flogged and then allowing another slave to defecate into the victim's mouth, which was then gagged with the fecal specimen for "4 or 5 hours."[6] Also particularly noteworthy was the theater of violence that Vincent Brown describes, which relied on "spectacular" displays of violence against both the physical body and spiritual imagination of slaves in order to maintain control over the slave population, even in death, as dismembered bodies were hung to decompose on poles without proper funereal rites.

Such violence in its excess and as performative practices against the imagination and bodies of slaves were tied to labor and production both during and after slavery, primarily because Jamaica—where Blacks outnumbered whites in a 9 to 1 ratio—was the centerpiece of Britain's slave economy. Also very significant to the production of violence, labor, and material surplus was the treadmill from the post-slavery apprenticeship period in which violence and performance were integrally linked, forcing the victims to "dance" while being tortured as they hovered within a liminal space between life and death and its related aesthetics of sublimity. Indeed, it was a condition in which performance was essential for survival. The paradox is that within this terrain of dancing, "violence occupies a portion of the cultural category that includes the aesthetic," which connects to a "symbolic economy of performance that mobilizes the beautiful."[7] These aspects of violence underlying the slave sublime align with performances that are crucially important for survival in its fusing together of the body and memory—as well as beauty and sublimity in its triumph of the imagination over reason, given that catharsis does not occur.

While Kant links reason to the sublime as the faculty by which one is able to transcend displeasure, Marlon James seems to suggest in *A Brief History of Seven Killings* that the magnitude of plantation-era violence remains for ghetto dwellers. The legacy of slavery and the continued practice of a master-slave power structure and attendant racial ideologies maintain the slave sublime presence of plantation systems that are patrolled and kept in check through structural neglect and violence. In Kant's definition of the sublime the philosopher points to the "feeling of displeasure" that arises from the "inadequacy of imagination in the aesthetic estimation of *magnitude* to attain to its estimation by reason" and the simultaneous awakening of "pleasure" (italics mine) that results from the judgment of the sublime object.[8] In this sense of the dynamic sublime, fear or terror is rendered pleasurable in the preeminence of Reason over sensuous Imagination. Interestingly, Aristotle characterizes tragedy in *Poetics* "as having *magnitude*, complete in itself" and as that which is represented in "language with pleasurable accessories" (italics mine). These pleasurable accessories arguably denote the elements of catharsis as resolution for the sublime contemplation of the "incidents arousing pity and fear."[9] However, these (neo)classical formulations from Aristotle and Kant do not hold true in a Jamaican setting. As represented in James's novel, a sublime judgment of the tragic circumstances surrounding (post)colonial terror suggests that catharsis is forestalled, not only because there is no rendering of "displeasure" as "pleasure" in the triumph of Reason over the sensuous Imagination, but also because the "magnitude" of plantation-derived violence has not been resolved. As such, the judgment of violence in the (post)colonial sphere cannot be regarded as sublime in a strict Kantian sense but rather as the slave sublime, which takes into account the lack of resolution or catharsis.[10]

James tackles the issue of madness in relation to the absence of catharsis and the Real of post-emancipation unfreedom in ghetto life in *A Brief History of Seven Killings*. It is a critical discourse that calls into question the faculty of reason and its negation vis-à-vis the abysmal impoverished conditions of slum life that produce madness as Manichean delirium in this encounter with the overwhelming awe underlying the slave sublime realization that plantation structures persist. In a sense, by addressing the concept of unreason, James switches from the racial imperative latent within Kantian philosophy to one about socioeconomic conditions, albeit that class and race are interconnected in Jamaica. Along the lines of what I discuss in chapter 1, James reminds us that Enlightenment thinking and its plantation rationale links whiteness to reason and Blackness to its negation. Consider, for example, the following quote in which Peter Nasser, a character of Middle Eastern descent who is considered white within Jamaican society, denigrates a Black character's intellect because of his racial identity: "Josey Wales, I me ever hire you to bombocloth think? Does it look like when I need thinking done, I call the naigger man to do it?"[11] In this quote, Peter Nasser subjects Josey Wales to what Frantz Fanon calls "sovereign discourse" based on a racialist notion of reason in order to place him in a subordinate position in the racialized social order and to provide justification for the status quo. Rather than the racialist discourse that links reason to race as an inherent biological factor, a belief that stems from Enlightenment ideology, James connects the issue to class within the Jamaican context: "And killing don't need no reason. This is ghetto. Reason is for rich people. We have madness."[12] The paradox is that the colonial delirium and Manichean divide that relate to poverty are the source of what James characterizes as madness, but to the casual reader it would seem as if it is linked simultaneously to color because of the racial dynamic of poverty and wealth in the Western hemisphere. As Fanon puts it in *The Wretched of the Earth*, the colony is a Manichean world, a place where race dictates one's position in the social order: "You are rich because you are white, you are white because you are rich."[13] Catharsis does not occur under Manichean socioeconomic conditions and hegemonic belief structures that replicate the experience of slavery.

The slave sublime's attraction to the beautiful is an attempt to challenge Manicheanism—that is, its false divisions and language of violence with a

purported connection to reason. Manicheanism includes the socially constructed divisions between light and dark, the beautiful and the sublime, civilized and primitive, etc.—divisions that are not arbitrary but rather driven by
underlying racist ideologies and social formations to dictate privileges and
exclusions. Such bifurcated divisions also connect to Kant's notion of *a priori*
categorizations that are essentially "deceptions of reason," "forms of ideology" seeking to "legitimate modes of oppression justified by the exclusion" of
many.[14] In *The Wretched of the Earth*, Fanon discusses the issue of the Manicheanism that exists in the colonized world and the physical divisions between the colonists and the dominated, who are kept apart by "rifle butts and
napalm." As Fanon puts it, the police and soldier as "the agents of government speak the language of pure force" and are "the bringer of violence into
the home and into the mind of the native."[15] In *On the Postcolony*, Mbembe
helps us understand that this divide is "sustained by an imaginary" through
"an interrelated set of signs that present themselves, in every instance, as an
indisputable and undisputed meaning. The violence insinuates itself into the
economy, domestic life, language, consciousness."[16] To maintain the divisions
and fear through his agents, the colonial master constantly announces his
power in a symbolic language involving what emphasizes not only his presence but also his tremendous propensity for violence in order to maintain the
physical and economic divide. That is because the language of violence is de-
ceptively steeped within reason and Enlightenment discourse. Reason provides the "logic of exclusion" and is the discursive "mechanism through which
that oppression is made a reality."[17] As Fanon explains, "colonialism is not
a machine capable of thinking, a body endowed with reason. It is naked
violence."[18] The Manichean containment in the ghetto allows for the control and surveillance through violence, which James rightly characterizes as a
"chamber of hell."

The current confinement of the lower stratum of the Kingston population
into ghettos that are "chamber[s] of hell" speaks to the enduring plantation
rationale of denying basic necessities because of a belief in their animality,
idleness, and immorality, not to mention a corresponding belief in the insanity of their unreasonableness. In *Madness and Civilization*, Michel Foucault
provides a historical genealogy of madness (from the classical period to the
eighteenth century) and its characterization as unreason, as animality, and as
enslavement to passions, particularly in the absence of labor. Foucault focuses on the issue of "confinement," noting that there is a long history in
which the insane were locked up "in the cells of prisons" along with the poor,
unemployed, and convicted.[19] As it was thought during the Enlightenment

period, these particular groups of people were ruled by "sensibility" in their unreason. The "locus of confinement," therefore, was linked to the "power of segregation" from society for those who supposedly could not fulfill their moral obligation against idleness and other forms of behavior lacking "constraint."[20] Arguably, there is also a historical genealogy in Jamaica that can be traced back to the slavery and post-slavery periods: a prevailing plantation logic was applied to the newly emancipated in Jamaica who refused to work— which compounded an already existing belief that Africans/Blacks, as the subhuman "Other," occupied the sensible realm and were not ruled by reason, and were, therefore, more properly designed by nature for hard labor.

In order to maintain a civilized society, the assumption was that containment and labor were necessary disciplinary measures for those who lacked reason. The belief was that their unchecked freedom would lead to the dissolution of civilized society. The language that Foucault invokes is very similar to the concerns raised in Great Britain during the nineteenth century surrounding debates on the abolition of slavery in the West Indies because of an apprehension about labor shortages since many ex-slaves were refusing to work on their former masters' sugar plantations. As a result, they were characterized as lazy and idle. One only needs to think of the image that Thomas Carlyle raises in his essay published in 1849, "Occasional Discourse on the Negro Question," in which he presents an impression of the West Indian ex-slave in "his ugliness, idleness, rebellion" and freedom as unrestrained liberty: "Sitting yonder, with their beautiful muzzles up to the ears in pumpkins, imbibing sweet pulps and juices."[21] As far back as two centuries before Carlyle's indignant branding of the West Indian ex-slaves as having wanton submission to passion and corporeal desires in the absence of work, "mendicancy and idleness" were considered "as the source" of all mental disorders.[22] Even more striking, "madness was perceived on the social horizon of poverty, of incapacity for work" and as immorality having the potential for social danger. It was a clear case of what Foucault calls "classical rationalism," which had to "watch out for and guard against the subterranean danger of unreason, that threatening space of absolute freedom" in the unrestraint or wanton "surrender" to desire or passion.[23] By using the word "muzzle," Carlyle painted a mental picture that relegated West Indian Blacks to the domain of animals lacking the ethical principles on which freedom is premised because they supposedly also lacked restraint and were thus ruled by bodily desires.

A crucial issue here that I am attempting to unravel is that these ideas about madness reside within the philosophical formulations about the sublime and Cartesian dualism, not only with regard to the respective role of reason and the imagination but also in relation to the human, freedom, and morality.[24] In the philosophical ideas of the eighteenth and nineteenth centuries, passion and desire were linked to corporeality, to the body and its vices. Therefore, the issue of madness as existing within the domain of unreason was also a suggestion that madness was connected to the imagination within a larger understanding of Cartesian dualism. As Foucault explains, madness was thought to be "'the derangement of the imagination' . . . at the level of *unreason*" that "quickly escapes reason of the mechanism and becomes, in its violences, its stupors, its senseless propagations, an irrational movement."[25] It was believed, as Foucault suggests, that this "irrational movement," as a departure from reason, was one toward nonbeing, away from the human and toward animality.[26]

It is under these Foucauldian lenses that I argue that the planned failure of emancipation in Jamaica through structural neglect (in the lack of proper housing, sufficient food, adequate education, etc.) and the current containment in ghettos are premised on the assumption of a correlating set of variables, namely Blackness, idleness, madness, and animality. For centuries, a belief was held that madness corresponded to animality, which supposedly "inured the madman to hunger, heat, cold, pain . . . indefinitely," meaning that there "was no need to protect them; they had no need to be covered or warmed."[27] Instead, the concern was about reducing the traces of the human to a pure animal condition as they were held in pigsty and rat-infested conditions. Foucault describes a process of nonbeing in which humans classified as insane were reduced to an animal-like existence through the disciplinary mechanism of state-sanctioned violence and work as beasts of burden. In dealing with the so-called human animal, the process of "confinement," Foucault tells us, was a "police matter" that could be "mastered only by discipline and brutalizing."[28] Discipline was not about restoring humanity, "not to raise the bestial to the human, but to restore man to what was purely animal in him."[29] What Foucault describes is no less than what Orlando Patterson talks about in *Slavery and Social Death* as the transformation of humans through violence and dishonor as well as legal and social alienation to a liminal state of nonbeing, their social death.

James's characterization of the ghetto as a "chamber of hell" also calls to mind the notion of a "torture chamber" that Elaine Scarry describes in *The Body in Pain*. Through torture, victims from the ghetto are trapped and disciplined both physically and psychologically to remain within the bounds as the socially dead that are ebbed in and confined. This is especially the case when the society provides neither social mobility nor avenues of escape for those who have to "see and wait" indefinitely for change that is hopeless: "every time you reach the edge, the edge move ahead of you like a shadow until the whole world is a ghetto and you wait."[30] Suggesting a slave sublime dimension, "wait" is characterized as a hopeless "void" that is infinite, and, as James puts it, "the only thing that ghetto people can fill a void with is void."[31] It is also an infinite psychic violence that provides no end nor outlet for the pent-up Manichean delirium. It is a kind of unrelenting torture, especially when there is no escape from the stygian conditions, a product of structural neglect; this is what manifests superficially as madness, but in reality as deep socioeconomic despair about entrapment:

> Under the gully you just never know how the stink can drive a man mad. How he can think crazy shit and wicked shit and nasty shit, kill a baby shit or fuck a little girl shit or shit in church shit because the stink so stink all you can think is that the stink must be easing into you like water through a strainer and now you must be stink too. And I just want to wash it off, I just want to wash the whole thing off but the water running through the gully stink too.[32]

James invokes grotesque imagery in the passage above to elicit the readers' empathy, disgust, and horror about the social conditions of the ghetto, the gully life of excess in its complete awfulness.

Offering an ambivalent stance that acknowledges the "idiosyncratic" nature of James's novel, noting that it "is a work that wears its ambition extravagantly," Nadia Ellis also critiques it as having "flights into rhetorical excess"—what she characterizes as a "poetics of excess" that "sacrifices the potential for *empathy*."[33] While conceding that James's strategy is purposeful, the complaint about the novel's "excess" overlooks the sublime levels of violence and social despair that necessarily call for such authorial maneuvers in which even the supposed lack of "readability" is an announcement about the crisis of textual representation to convey the ghetto as a "chamber of hell." Because of what appear to be abnormal living conditions, the reader is not only horrified but repulsed that human beings can exist is such conditions. We may take into account Terry Eagleton's idea that tragedy should have "some horrific quality that shocks and stuns."[34] The grotesque imagery conveying this tragic scenario, thus, relies on the readers' lack of familiarity with such abysmal existence. As a concept, the grotesque gained popularity during the Enlightenment to "denote" what was perceived to be "aberrations from the desirable norms of harmony, balance, and proportion."[35] It is in this vein that Sheri-Marie Harrison counters Ellis's stance by arguing that "*A Brief*

History is thrilling in its excess, because its referential, seemingly haphazard and overwhelming narrative framework . . . participates in broad critique of (late) global multicultural capitalism."[36] As one element of excess, James evokes the grotesque in the context of the slave sublime to convey notions of social dissonance—that is, as a contrast to the normative notions of concord and harmony. Moreover, as a contrast to what is common in literary depictions of the grotesque as comical, James departs from such satirical renderings in order to call attention to the realistic depiction of what would otherwise appear as distorted and marvelous. The character Papa-Lo, a ruling don from one of the garrisons, helps us to understand the grotesque imagery of "shit" as normative, as what results constantly from Babylon's execution of power: "Babylon is a country. Babylon is a shitstem, Babylon is oppressor and Babylon infiltrate with police."[37] In essence, what James represents is not the Rablesian vein of grotesque realism for comic relief but rather tragedy in its raw sense, stemming from excess structural neglect as the systemic and physical violence associated with the Manichean divide, the "shitstem," in other words.

In his novel, James offers a counter-Aristotelian writing of history in which he appeals to tragedy and elements of pathos while foreclosing the possibility of catharsis, a concerted strategy of writing a tragic history of the ghetto. In *Poetics*, Aristotle provides a distinction between tragedy and history based on the notion that tragedy evokes catharsis through pity and fear, while suggesting that history in its fidelity to the particularities of truth and facts should not attract the readers' attention through the marvelous or sensational. Aristotle's demarcation between tragedy and history correlates to what he envisions, respectively, as a difference between fiction and fact[38]—and by extension the imagination and reason. However, in his representation of the marvelous real, James violates the Aristotelian distinctions, which he announces in the very title of his book, *A Brief History of Seven Killings: A Novel.* Traditionally, history as a narrative form existed in a decontested terrain as a hegemonic, master-narrative system because of its supposed basis of conveying truth and reality, especially in colonialized settings. Along with NourbeSe Philip's critique of history in *Looking for Livingstone*, as I've discussed in chapter 2, James enacts boundary crossing, blurring the lines between truth and fiction to call attention to the marvelous real in his rendering of the (un)believable tragedy surrounding gully life in the Jamaican ghettos of West Kingston. James even intimates toward this idea in his epigraph, echoing a well-known proverb in Jamaican culture, "If it no go so, it go near so." In his literary representation, violence supersedes verisimilitude, which was the early desire of realism. Verisimilitude is rooted in structure and the internal logic of a text; for instance, a plot focusing on the creation of a logical and internally embedded web that then reinforces its own overarching structural logic. However, postmodern critics have argued that truth or significance lies beyond verisimilitude and that the truth and meaning could be ascertained only by nondiscursive means.[39] James places the marvelous and incredible alongside the realistic as a revision to historical writing involving the slave sublime. James's suggestion is that history is not simply a conveyor of scientific-leaning truth as Aristotle believed but rather an art form laden by the tools of rhetoric for appeal and persuasion. Thus, James renders the tragedy of a psychological drama in novel form and as historical writing.

While the Aristotelian precept for tragedy also calls for key elements such as characters of noble birth, James's novel, on the other hand, depicts characters who lack nobility and engage in the prosaic aspects of ghetto life, which is "shitty." Despite a lack of nobility, the central character in a novel is usually representative, being able to appeal to the middle class, thus functioning "as an exemplary of the achievements . . . beyond political, class and sectarian divisions."[40] However, there is no central character in *A Brief History of Seven Killings* and all of them are unrepresentable because of their debased socioeconomic condition—therefore, they do not provide a socialization model or script for the exemplary individual. The novel is long known for its rule-breaking tradition, but James is not simply breaking the rules of a generic tradition; instead, he is demonstrating the ineffectiveness of that particular genre within the peripheral (neo)colonial space of the Caribbean. That is to say, James represents the extant aspects of (neo)colonial violence that lie outside the capabilities of either the novel or classical notion of tragic drama. Nonetheless, James fuses together the novel with the dramatic tradition of tragedy to introduce the potential nobility of his characters, yet he demonstrates their failure to achieve nobility, precisely because of the challenges they face as neocolonial subjects. His characters have no claim to nobility because they lack the political or social power to change their circumstances (their tragic fate), especially because of the cycles of maddening violence that they endure as a collective—not as individuals.[41] Despite the tragic circumstances, James's prose conveys elements of slave sublime conditions including its movement toward the beautiful in an attempt to convey the Real.

Nonetheless, *A Brief History of Seven Killings* reveals that the photographic image and literary text, while being able to convey the slave sublime levels of ghetto life, reach a limit. The impoverished slum conditions of the ghetto convey such sublime magnitudes that they supersede the possibility of conveying the Real. As Alex Pierce puts it, "*it cannot be described*" or "*photographed*" because it is a *"rusty red chamber of hell."* Later in the novel, Alex Pierce returns to this encounter with the slave sublime conditions of the ghetto that seem to escape its representation of the Real, no matter how familiar you are with this experience: "And it's the kind you've never seen before despite the hundred times you've seen it. I tried drawing parallels before but you just can't when you're there."[42] Through his character, James attempts to describe the Real and what happens to (written) language in the contemplation of the slave sublime conditions of West Kingston ghettos in Jamaica.

A perceived madness prevails in this ghetto context, as the novel suggests, because of the challenges to conveying the experience through language and because of the slave sublime's attraction to the beautiful, which it transforms into the grotesque. In the Jamaican ghetto, madness seems to erupt as the paradoxical attraction to and repulsion of the beautiful, particularly when it stands on its own, when it does not accompany the harsh realities associated with the slave sublime: "Madness is walking up a good street downtown and seeing a woman dress up in the latest fashion and wanting to go straight up to her and grab her bag, knowing that it's not the bag or the money that we want so much, but the scream, when she see that you jump right into her pretty-up face and you could slap the happy right out of her mouth and punch the joy right out of her eye and kill her right there and rape her before or after you kill her."[43] Here James commingles the beautiful with the sublime in relation to the awful conditions of ghetto life, a situation in which the beautiful cannot exist by itself. The narrator in this passage wants to produce a "scream" that is primal in order to bring the scenario back to reflecting or reenacting the spectacular violence that is associated with the true nature of ghetto angst, given the social conditions in which the "scream" is a lived, horrific reality. The "scream" is part of the grotesque soundscape that has a historical genealogy from slavery to contemporary times, namely the sound of the whip, the sound of rape and torture, the sound of the dying within the scenic and beautiful tropical backdrop. But it is the sound that takes centerstage with the outcries of gut-wrenching loss in all its "unending vortex." The previously quoted passage begs the question as to why there is a repulsion of beauty in the absence of the "scream" of the slave sublime when contemplated by those who live in the squalor of the ghetto. The answer to this question is revealed when the character Bam-Bam speaks of "the Singer" (Bob Marley) in 1976 before he was famous, when he lived in Trench Town and tried to land a record contract in a manner that calls forth the importance of tethering the beautiful to the slave sublime: "You cut a tune, but not a hit song, too pretty for the ghetto even then, for we past the time when prettiness make anybody's life easy."[44]

A repulsion of beauty ensues because it has to be commingled with the harsh realities of the slave sublime in the West Kingston garrisons to provide a realistic texture of the environment. With time, however, Marley was able to fuse the beautiful with the slave sublime in his later works that reflect his mature critical and imaginative abilities to convey the Real.

These representations of the ghetto in its intermingling of the beautiful and the slave sublime call to mind a significant passage from Jamaica Kincaid's *A Small Place*, which similarly describes an encounter with sublimity and its transfiguration, as the beautiful, in the distressed physical environment of the Caribbean. In Kincaid's description, the slave sublime manifests as a paradox involving a merging of the extremes of beauty and "pauperedness" that is the island of Antigua, another former British slave colony:

> [N]o real lily would bloom only at night and perfume the air with a sweetness so thick it makes you slightly sick; no real earth is that colour brown; no real grass is that particular shade of dilapidated, rundown green (not enough rain); no real cows look that poorly as they feed on the unreal-looking grass in the unreal-looking pasture, and no real cows look quite that miserable as some unreal-looking white egrets sit on their backs eating insects . . . No real village in any real countryside would be named Table Hill Gordon, and no real village with such a name would be so beautiful in its pauperedness, its simpleness, its one-room houses painted in unreal shades of pink and yellow and green . . . It is as if, then, the beauty—the beauty of the sea, the land, the air, the trees, the market, the people, the sounds they make—were a prison, and as if everything and everybody that is not inside it were locked out.[45]

Kincaid also highlights a bounded subjectivity similar to Marley's and James's representations due to the legacies of slavery and (neo)colonialism that maintain a prison-like structure in the postcolonial era. What Kincaid describes is the slave sublime condition in which "ordinary people" are trapped without resolution to the magnitudes or overwhelming extremes of "pauperedness" that move toward the beautiful. As she puts it, "no real village with such a name would be so beautiful in its pauperedness." Because the people are imprisoned within such bleak social conditions, Kincaid asks, "And what might it do to ordinary people to live in this way every day? What might it do to them to live in such heightened, intense surroundings day after day?"[46] We may consider the ghetto as a bounded space, similar to a torture chamber, slave ship, plantation, or prison in which the social death and the devaluation of the human dignity of its inmates or inhabitants are emphasized in the denial of their pain and structural neglect. The "scream" under this light, as one can imagine, is also what happens in the slave sublime moment of contemplating freedom and its unfulfillment. The "scream" is also a symbol of great orphic loss, loss of epic proportions that can produce madness or actions that can be characterized as such.

In the case of *sufferahs*, the impoverished people in West Kingston ghettos who lack social and political power, James uses madness as a concept to symbolize their liminality—their occupying of an in-between space between emancipation and freedom, their social death and despair over the desire for freedom, and their waiting in vain to recapture the hope that almost was and for change. Throughout the novel, James evokes the concept of the changing same. For instance, in the opening episode of "December 2, 1976" the ghost Sir Arthur George Jennings, a dead narrator, comments on the sociopolitical climate and conditions of Jamaican society in its sameness over time: "Look hard enough or maybe just to the left and you see a country that was the same as I left it."[47] Later in the novel, another character Kim Clarke offers a similar commentary: "Two years since the election. Jamaica never gets worse or better, it just finds new ways to stay the same."[48] It is a liminal context in which people "wait and see" for change that does not happen, as Bam-Bam tells us:

> Sweet-talking voice on the radio say that crime and violence are taking over the country and if change ever going to come then we will have to wait and see, but all we can do down here in the Eight Lanes is see and wait. And I see shit water run free down the street and I wait. And I see my mother take two men for twenty dollars each and one more who pay twenty-five to stay in instead of pull out and I wait. And I watch my father get so sick and tired of her that he beat her like a dog. And I see the zinc roof and rust itself brown, and then the rain batter hole into it like foreign cheese, and I see seven people in one room and one pregnant and people fucking anyway because people so poor that they can't even afford shame and I wait.[49]

Within this liminal space, the *sufferahs* occupy a threshold in which there is also a lack of division between public and private that draws upon a grotesque, bodily aesthetic, similar to the previous imagery of seeing "shit water run free down the street." Corresponding to James's representation, Fanon notes that the world of the dominated in which the poor are relegated, abandoned, and confined in a state of hunger for food and material necessities is a place that lacks "spaciousness; men live there on top of each other."[50] Under these conditions of structural neglect, there are different ways in which private matters (in all aspects of the word) are rendered public for all to "see." "Wait and see" also involves the suspension of action, of passively waiting to see what will happen. We must consider Sir Arthur Jennings's revelation that "Living people wait and see" and that "Dead people see and wait."[51]

"Wait and see" for the living, in its transposed mirror image of "see and wait" for the dead, articulates a position of social death, a term Orlando Patterson coins in *Slavery and Social Death* to denote the lack of agency under the material conditions of slavery. In the West Kingston ghettos, the infrastructural violence and dehumanizing conditions—the absence of a sewage system, the inadequate housing, the continued selling of bodies as commodity, and the lack of socioeconomic power or political and legal recourse—maintain the base conditions of poverty and dishonor as social death as it was under slavery. As Papa-Lo tells us, slavery continues on in Jamaica: "me drive past plantation still standing."[52] The quote below also suggests the enduring presence of the slave plantation system through Babylon's paradigmatic substitution of the ghetto as the changing same to indicate a liminal status between emancipation and freedom. In this perseverance of paradigmatic plantation structures, there is no long-term cathartic resolution to the social injustice, as the situation just gets infinitely worse in magnitude as the ghetto moves ahead of its inhabitants and provides little to no means of escape. Oftentimes education fails to provide social mobility because of the master-slave power structure that remains in Jamaican society. As James suggests, Babylon holds a "leash" that keeps everyone in place: "But a man can only move so far before the leash pull him back. Before master say, Enough of that shit, that's not where we going. The leash of Babylon, the leash of the police code, the leash of the Gun Court, the leash of the twenty-three families that run Jamaica. That leash get pull two weeks ago, when the Syrian pussyhole Peter Nasser try to talk to me in code. That leash get pull one week ago, when the American and the Cuban come with a colouring book to teach me about anarchy."[53] The ruling elite's production of scarcity to create competition over scant resources onward from the post-emancipation era has been a tactic of sociopolitical control over the masses. The contemporary creation of garrison communities that are confined through poverty and policing and which bend to the dictates and whims of political leaders is just one point in case.

Marley's song "Ambush in the Night," which James uses as the title of his novel's second section, articulates what happens in the process of politicians "fighting for power": they "bribe" with "guns, spare parts, and money." Marley sings about the actual situation of his failed assassination in which he was "ambush[ed] in the night" with "guns aiming at" him. What he describes is a "political strategy" that replicates (post-)slavery maneuvers of structural abuse and insufficient resources through which the poor are "kept hungry": "when you gonna get some food / Your brother got to be your enemy."[54] Fanon explains that in the colonial context the lack of material necessities—adequate food, consistent work, and proper shelter for children, who look "like skeletons"—forces the natives to "fight" each other and "to commit murder every day." As a result, "the native comes to see his neighbor as a relentless enemy."[55] Within the context of slavery, as Mbembe argues, the shifting aspect of slaves' subjectification also made it difficult for them to form alliances with other slaves because they "were socialized into the hatred of others, particularly other Blacks" and the "plantation was characterized by its segmented forms of subjugation, distrust, intrigue, rivalry, and jealousy, ambivalent tactics born out of complicity."[56] It was an instrumental way in which some slaves would be rewarded for carrying out the master's brutality toward other slaves in the name of self-preservation.[57] This socialization was important for maintaining the plantation structure.

When we take into account the ideas from Fanon and Mbembe, we can understand why Marley's decolonial strategies of fostering ancestral and communal bonds toward achieving peace and to challenge Babylon's divide and rule tactic were regarded as threatening. As James suggests in his novel, Marley was considered as a political threat as "neither the JLP nor the PNP fucking with the peace treaty. Peace can't happen when too much to gain in war."[58] According to Marley, the assassins were "Protected by his majesty."[59] Given the political climate in Jamaica at the time and James's suggestions in his novel, we can surmise that "his majesty" refers broadly to political leaders in Jamaica and the CIA from the United States:

> The two men who bring guns to the ghetto watch you sing yourself out of their hands and they not happy at all. Nobody uptown singing thanks and praises for you. Not the man who brings guns to the Eight Lanes, still run by Shotta Sheriff. That man know him party going up for re-election and they need to win, to stay in power, to bring power to the people, all comrades and socialists. Not the Syrian who brings guns to Copenhagen City and who want to win the elections so bad that he will move God himself if God in the seat. The American who come with guns know that whoever win Kingston win Jamaica and whoever win West Kingston win Kingston, before any man in the ghetto tell him.[60]

The state of rivalry is needed to maintain the plantation structure that, on another level, reenacts the divide and rule strategy from the old playbook on the best tactics for sustaining colonial conquest.

James compares the creation and maintenance of garrison districts by Jamaican politicians to the "Scramble for Africa" in the nineteenth century when Europeans carved up the continent, creating artificial divisions and rivalries among existing tribes and linguistic groups: "In 1966 they carve up Kingston and never ask we what slice we want. So every land that hit midway on the boundary, Rema, Jungle, Rose Town, Lizard Town, they leave it to we to fight over. Me fight hard until me get tired. I raise the men who now run with Josey Wales and nobody ever badder than me. I swell Copenhagen City two times in size and eradicate robbery and rape from the community. This is election year and nothing left now but war and rumour of war."[61] Through the creation of garrison districts, the political leaders employ a divide and rule strategy, as slave and colonial masters did previously. As a result, the ghetto is always in a state of war—a place where a good night's sleep doesn't normally happen because of gang rivalry and raids by the police and soldiers, who "act like we is enemy and this is war."[62] Moreover, when we think about garrison structures in West Kingston, we can think of political stratagems to maintain a slavery-like structure of competition in the midst of scarcity. Along with what is considered political tribalism in the violence perpetrated by gangs, politicians are able to secure votes by promising food and school supplies,[63] but they only provide these resources and jobs for those in their loyal garrison communities.[64] However, not much is done for loyal voters and gang members who carry out voter intimidation schemes through violence and bribery between elections, as Demus suggests: "white man who live uptown and don't care about we until election time."[65]

Jamaica is a place where wealth remains in the hands of a small non-Black population who "live uptown," among them "the twenty-three families who run Jamaica," mainly because of their color and connections to the *ancien régime* from slavery, who continue to use the "leash of Babylon"—the police, namely the Jamaican Constabulary Force—for disciplining and confining the poor. The constabulary is a name that echoes the police's historical genealogy in their paradigmatic relationship to slave drivers and constables during the periods of slavery and apprenticeship as evidence of Babylon's transhistorical, metamorphic power and *ipse* identity to change while remaining the same throughout time.[66] As historian Terry Lacey notes, during slavery, the Jamaican planters (slave masters) used the local British army "and a system of parish constables" along with their "own army of professional terrorists—the overseers and slave drivers." It was a situation in which "Brutality against the slaves reflected a general style of social control."[67] James Williams reports in his 1834 *Narrative* that under the apprenticeship system the former slave drivers became known as constables and were granted the power to control their fellow apprentices through the use of violence. Because there were no checks and balances, there was systemic abuse of power. In the workhouses (prisons) the constables' lack of regard stemmed from the fact that they had all received life sentences.[68] In the ghetto, the constant presence of the police and soldiers is a reminder, not only of their power to confine and discipline, but also the notion that "power dance[s] with the shadows"[69] because of its metamorphic ability to change its name over time while remaining the same in its practices. In *Exceptional Violence*, Deborah A. Thomas characterizes such instances of the changing same as "repertoires and cyclical histories that expand to incorporate and accommodate the new while always giving us the sense that we have somehow seen this before."[70] From an anthropological stance, Thomas articulates how Jamaica's contemporary violence can be understood as transhistorical reiterations and reenactments from the colonial past but cautions that this violence should not be read as culturally embedded. James, however, in his chapter "Shadow Dancin'" conveys the idea of performative violence and the historical connection between performance and the sublime elements of violence that transcend the plantation space. The systemic use of the police to inflict physical violence in the interest of the wealthy in the contemporary era is also connected to the continuation of structural violence that stems from the planned failure of emancipation in order to prolong the abuses from slavery under a capitalist system.

The current conditions in West Kingston are not simply a product of criminality (in its fallaciously assumed link to Black pathology): these conditions emerge from the very actions of social elites and politicians who protect their interests in order to preserve the status quo and bounties gained from slavery and colonialism. In essence, the poverty and abysmal social conditions of gully life in the ghetto stem from Babylon's fervid attempt to maintain the status quo, to preserve the Manichean legacies of slavery and colonialism. Within this socioeconomic and psychological turmoil for the dispossessed, there is a perceived elision between criminality and madness. Madness is characterized not only as a killing for money, but also as the fratricidal violence of purging pent-up frustrations. Fanon tells us that "criminality" is "the direct product of the colonial situation."[71] In the "Preface" of *The Wretched of the Earth*, Jean-Paul Sartre explains that auto-destruction occurs because when the "suppressed fury" of the colonial experience "fails to find an outlet, it turns in a vacuum and devastates the oppressed creatures themselves" and that in "order to free themselves they even massacre each other."[72] As one character from James's novel tell us, "Sometimes a man get killed because he look at another man in a way he didn't like."[73] Needless to say, the Jamaican state fails to take responsibility, especially because many politicians protect their personal interests and are also in collusion with neocolonial forces.

The "colouring book" mentioned in a previous block quote functions as an ideological tool for instilling the values of American capitalism and for preserving their hegemonic power, as part of the imperialist Babylon system. Through the distribution of coloring books, we can see a (neo)colonialist strategy being implemented in targeting children who can be indoctrinated from an early age in capitalist values. This colonialist strategy mirrors what Chinua Achebe describes in *Things Fall Apart*. In Achebe's novel, Mr. Brown, when realizing that evangelizing and colonial brainwashing would not work as surface-level coercion through conscious means, decides to build a school. Similar to the colonial school system, the coloring book displaying images of America and its standards of living as a capitalist utopia functions as an ideological apparatus that works toward transforming the collective unconscious through discursive means and semiotic systems as part of a wider naturalizing process. We must also consider the impact of North American neoliberal ideology about the relationship between democracy, "progress, markets, [and] freedom," as revealed in the CIA agent Mr. Clarke's statement in James's novel. An important issue raised in the novel is the concern that the CIA strategies were not about bringing "democracy" to Jamaica, but more about preserving the American way of life under a capitalist system, which, as is characteristic of its vampiric nature, drains the lifeforce out of other countries to secure its own notion of freedom. Thus, the West Kingston ghettos are a material manifestation of Babylon's power, both domestically and internationally, in its furtherance of plantation structures that maintain an economic and color caste hierarchy in which "nasty naigger must always know them place."[74] The goal is to extend the slave sublime conditions with the continuance of plantation structures that leave the poor in a liminal status characterized by social death.

Eventually, James reverses the social death underlying "wait and see" and "see and wait" to suggest a position of power or agency for the dons, gang leaders who have come to function as surrogate heads of state in the West Kingston ghettos. As one don explains, "People with no plan wait and see. People with a plan see and wait for the right time."[75] In James's novel we see the evolution of dons as symbols of power that can even supersede the state in its violence. Dons have acquired a problematic agency as they harness violence linked to the repression of drives and desires. On another level, their mimetic embracement of violence is also a learned behavioral language that utilizes the body in its reenactment of plantation-derived violence. The dons are known for their swift measures of extralegal justice through brutal death campaigns. Thus, the dons are, without a doubt, paradoxical figures: they are the perpetrators of violence and the peace-keepers in the ghetto; as the law-breakers and law-enforcers, they function as moral compasses and socio-economic benefactors to their respective garrison communities. The reason for this is that the West Kingston garrisons operate almost autonomously outside the Jamaican state, which, through planned structural neglect, provides little to no resources or infrastructure for people that live there. As James's novel suggests, it is a place of joblessness, where shit runs down the street as a normal occurrence. The minions under the dons have also evolved from *rudies* to *shottas*, as not just a change in name only but an announcement of their enlarged power as they lose the gang affiliation to become members of a posse who "answer phone call from America," who have escaped their ghetto confinement to become part of a transnational network of under-ground economies that include the drug trade.[76] It is almost as if, as Laurie Gunst intimates, the posses headed by dons have become corporations—as if wealth and death are included in their business plans and mission statements. Their relationship to the United States is crucial in thinking about their evolution and mimesis of American violence, precisely because of the United States' ascension as neocolonial master in Jamaica.

As the neocolonial master, the United States has extended the Babylon system from slavery as a new capitalist frontier in Jamaica—the "Wild, Wild West Kingston"—marked by lawlessness, gun violence, and an escalated dissolution of order and wellbeing. My argument here intersects with Michael K. Walonen's discussion of *A Brief History of Seven Killings* and his point that "'frontier' spaces" are not only marked by violence, but that such "spaces subject to imperialism equally serve as arenas in which masculine identities can be formed and asserted through particularly egregious acts of violence," which "manifests itself in local acts of killing and assault that perform masculinist identities."[77] Part of the violence stems from the fact that guns were made available to gang members through CIA clandestine endeavors to destabilize the social democracy that was brewing under Michael Manley's government during the 1970s. Because of these guns, there was no longer a need to dabble in knife fights as Jamaica devolved into a frontier zone. In its efforts to undermine the Manley government, the CIA intervention and instigation of political conflict or tribalism during the 1980 election led to the death of close to 800 people. Below, James demonstrates in italics how the Wild West became a motif and narrative tool to articulate the Real of violence and lawlessness for those living in West Kingston ghettos:

> This is the story of the gunmen of Wild, Wild West Kingston . . . Every sufferah is a cowboy with a house and every street has gun battle written in blood in a song somewhere. Spend one day in West Kingston and it makes perfect sense that a Top Ranking calls himself Josey Wales. It's not just the lawlessness. It's the grabbing of a myth and making it theirs, like reggae singer dropping new lyrics 'pon di old version. And if a western needs an O.K. Corral, an O.K. Corral needs a Dodge City. Kingston, where bodies sometimes drop like flies, fits the description a little too well.[78]

Through mimesis, the posses imitate the neocolonial master's violence, particularly the symbolic representation in cinematic and musical depictions of the American Western frontier. Moreover, the adoption of an American mythos, conveyed as cinematic beauty in shootouts in the OK Corral, becomes a representative medium through which they make sense of the lawlessness and wanton gun violence confining them to their real-life situations in West Kingston ghettos.

Writing an entire opening passage in italics from his character Alex Pierce's perspective, James calls attention to the Real and the failure of textuality for representing this drastic state of ghetto life in the frontier zones of garrison communities. The West Kingston ghetto is place of paradox and it conveys the ambiguous and extreme in all forms. There is even an intermingling of beauty and slave sublime levels of poverty, which Alex Pierce consigns to a grotesque imagery: "There's a reason why the story of the ghetto should never come with a photo. The Third World slum is a nightmare that defies beliefs or facts, even the ones staring right at you. A vision of hell that twists and turns on itself and grooves to its own soundtrack. Normal rules do not apply here. Imagination then, dream, fantasy. You visit a ghetto, particularly in West Kingston, and it immediately leaves the real to become this sort of grotesque."[79] It is a context in which the imagination is imperative to facilitate the reader's ability to fully grasp the conditions of the ghetto in its extreme magnitudes of violence—the structural neglect and psychic despair—which seem to overwhelm and transcend representation both in the photographic image and written text. Under normal circumstances, the photographic image is intended to enhance our understanding of a story, but it fails to accomplish that goal in the context of the Jamaican ghetto. Indeed, as Walonen argues, "Any text that attempts to approach violence in any sociohistorical context through any discourse will inevitably run into the fact that in its raw intensity, sheer emotionality, and essential Dionysianness violence will out-strip any attempt of language to capture it or do more than obliquely evoke it."[80] Part of the difficulty of conveying the Real of West Kingston ghettos through textual or photographic representation stems from the fact that spaces of domination are marked by violence, which is "linked to the exercise of language, to a series of acts, gestures, noises, and sounds,"[81] best captured through a performative medium. Alex Pierce tell us that the slum conditions of ghettos such as Rema and Trench Town in the West Kingston garrisons are in a state of "bleak and unremitting repulsiveness that the inherent beauty of the photographic process will lie to you about just how ugly it is." "Beauty," he suggests, "has infinite range but so does wretchedness and the only way to actually grasp the full, unending vortex of ugly that is Trench Town is to imagine it."[82] The slave sublime elements and its transfiguration are clear in James's coalescing of beauty and sublimity and his suggestion about the importance of the imagination for understanding such enormities of violence. In James's representation, beauty is not bound to form as it is in Kantian philosophy because it transcends limitations to become "infinite" when linked to the slave sublime. In contrast to a Western framework in which beauty would have no place, in the Jamaican social reality that is tethered to sublimity, James's novel suggests that the imagination is crucial to understanding this apperception in which the beautiful is intermingled with the slave sublime elements of excess violence.

The neocolonial role of the United States during the Cold War era and the overt manifestation of excess violence in the new Jamaican frontier led to an abrupt ideological change in the society, marking a major social, economic, political, and artistic upheaval. What James characterizes as "Wild, Wild West Kingston" is as an even more harrowing situation than the "concrete jungle" that Marley describes because the West Kingston ghettos faced increasing magnitudes of poverty and violence. By the mid-1980s, the American installation of the Edward Seaga government, global markets, and economic restructuring through the IMF made matters even worse. James describes a situation in which Marley's reggae music no longer held sway, not only because of his untimely demise in 1981. Unlike the overt elements of violence rendered in Marty Robbins's *Gun Fighter Ballads*, which captured the imagination of *rudies* during the 1970s and the carnivalesque aesthetic in Jamaican dancehall music that emerged in the 1980s, Marley describes the feelings associated with the slave sublime aspects of life, relying instead on the use of metaphor and indirect representation. It is a tactical way in which Marley appeals to a wide audience, maintaining double voice yet still able to convey the harshness surrounding the slave sublime while providing moments of sonic beauty to convey the Real of unfreedom in Jamaica. Nonetheless, because of the even more overwhelming, gritty social environments of West Kingston in the 1980s, the Jamaican underclass of Black *sufferahs* were looking for a new artistic medium to represent their slave sublime conditions under globalization, as Jamaica became a new frontier zone for North American capitalism that replicated the Dionysian elements of colonization.

CHAPTER FIVE

The Ogun Archetype in Jamaican Dancehall Music

Harnessing Ogun's Combative Will to Challenge Globalization's Dionysiac Nature

There is thus something Dionysian about the act of colonization. It is a grand, narcissistic outpouring. The mix of voluptuousness, frenzy, cruelty, drunkenness, and dreaming that is one of the structural dimensions of the colonial enterprise can be understood only in relation to that form of enchantment that is both unrest and turmoil. The colonial world, after all, includes many of the characteristics that Friedrich Nietzsche recognized in Greek tragedy.

—Achille Mbembe, *Critique of Black Reason*

Music is the intensive language of transition and its communicant means, the catalyst and solvent of its regenerative hoard. The actor dares not venture into this world unprepared, without symbolic sacrifices and the invocation of eudaemonic guardians of the abyss. In the symbolic disintegration and retrieval of the protagonist ego is reflected the destiny of being. This is ritual's legacy to later tragic art, that the tragic hero stands to his contemporary reality as the ritual protagonist on the edge of transitional gulf.

The source of the possessed lyricist, chanting hitherto unknown mythopoeic strains whose antiphonal refrain is, however, instantly caught and thrust with all its terror and awesomeness into the night by swaying votaries, this source is residual in the numinous area of transition.

—Wole Soyinka, *Myth, Literature and the African World*

Louis Chude-Sokei has asked the question, "how can nationalism—race-based or otherwise—exist in a context of multinational corporations where Babylon itself—late capitalism—is increasingly mobile and decentered? Where now is the site of struggle, and how is resistance to be formulated?"[1] While the site of struggle still needs to be fully carved out, the subversive power of Jamaican dancehall deejays who enact their form of ideological violence through sound and performance that draw upon the Yoruba god Ogun as an archetype of tragedy and combative Will suggests a movement toward that goal. As Julian Henriques proposes, it is important for us to shift from an understanding of *logos* solely as word to include the significance of sound and visual semiotics encoded through the body.[2] Using sonic and somatic discourse as logos, dancehall music functions as a subaltern weapon, albeit a limited one, as it challenges the economic and political hegemony of the ruling classes who have maintained structural violence. Jamaica's structural violence results from the historical legacies of slavery and colonialism, in particular the disproportionate distribution of wealth and the perseverance of the *ancien régime*, a group of twenty-three families (consisting of Syrian, Lebanese, Jewish, and Chinese people, as well as Jamaican browns and whites) who comprise the racial oligopoly, who dominate the capitalist superstructure, and who have little interest in developing the lower sectors of society. The perpetuation of the *ancien régime* in Jamaica allows for social, economic, and political abuses, and, in the transference of power after slavery and independence, they have assumed the residual, hegemonic position as the new plantocracy. The emerging middle class of Afro-Jamaicans has adopted the values of the ruling class. In giving a general description of power relations in the West Indies, Gordon K. Lewis characterizes the class oppression as one based on "social bullying and economic intimidation": "The truth is, frankly, that West Indian society is based, primarily, on class oppression and paternalism (whether within or outside the graded culture-class hierarchies) in all of its strategic areas: government, education, the police system. Social bullying and economic intimidation are pretty much the order of the day in the life of the masses."[3] The lower class endures oppression not only from within but also from the external forces of globalization. For the lower sectors of Jamaican society, the 1980s economic and social frustration functioned as an implosion that had virtually no outlet except for the symbolic utterances of dancehall music, which conveys both the psychic and the physical violence that punctuates their daily existence. In so doing, dancehall practitioners translate the physical resistance that marked the slave era and the post-emancipation periods in Jamaica to the level of sound in the decades after the 1980s.

While 1980s dancehall music typifies the carnivalesque aesthetic, the newer mode of music that followed during the 1990s and 2000s points to a shift in radical democracy with an overt political voice that reflects upon the causes and nature of violence in Jamaican society. As organic intellectuals, prominent dancehall deejays such as Mavado, Bounty Killer, Damian Marley, Popcaan, and Busy Signal bring about a shift in public discourse.[4] A struggle is played out through the state apparatus of policing and legislating, both of which function as oppositional forces against dancehall culture. In turn, dancehall aesthetes' public displays of symbols (attire, speech, and bodily language as logos) encode their resistance and affirm their agency as "pedagogical actors who reshape the world through their everyday practices," to use Nadine Dolby's term.[5] Dolby notes that "liberal democracy embraces the division between the public and private spheres" while "radical democracy presumes that private acts (of consumption, of cultural production, of identity) are inherently a part of the public domain—which reaches far beyond the strictures of state politics."[6] Here, Dolby also makes reference to the intertwining relationship between the values and practices of democracy and consumption.

In a similar manner, the agency derived through dancehall culture lies in its function as an expression of radical democracy, that is, the ability to negotiate and transform everyday practices—i.e., the social, economic, political, and cultural—and to erase the demarcation between the private and public domains.[7] This elision between the public and private signals the slave sublime aesthetic and an attempt to challenge the ruling classes' hegemonic ideologies. The class-based ideological struggles are discernible through police surveillance and the enactment of legal statutes such as the 1997 Night Noise Abatement Act (known also as the Night Noise Law) in order to contain and censor music in dance halls. As I discussed in chapter 1, a similar tactic of censorship was used during slavery and the early decades following emancipation to censor Pocomania, Obeah, and other African-derived religious practices.

This recourse to censorship during the 1990s may indeed suggest not only the paradigmatic relation between slavery and globalization, but also an equivalence between African-derived spiritual forms of worship and dancehall music. Arguably, dancehall music can be characterized as a secular religion having a comparable potential for revolt. In Jamaica, the Night Noise Law unwittingly acknowledges the subversive potential of dancehall music as a weapon, having the power to provoke and to disturb. In her discussion of rap music in the United States, Tricia Rose notes that in ideological struggles, dominant groups use censorship as a tactical maneuver and as a form of social containment.[8] She points out that "During the centuries-long period of Western slavery, there were elaborate rules designed to control the slave population. Constraining the mobility of slaves, especially at night and in groups, was of special concern; slave masters reasoned that revolts could be organized by blacks who moved too freely and without surveillance."[9] For the Jamaican middle and upper classes, the Night Noise Law functions as a form of "social bullying," to use Gordon K. Lewis's term, and as a means of protecting the society from what they as the status quo regard as Black lower-class immorality and the music and its cultural icons as symbols of that moral depravity. Moreover, they use censorship as a hegemonic tool to stifle the lower-class demand for political and economic redress and as a means of transitioning from the margins to the center, from cultural marginality to empowerment.

In Jamaica, noise functions as a highly contested aesthetic boundary between so-called legitimate culture and dancehall practices, as it incites a challenge to the established power relations by transcending the containment of the dance hall (club) as it spreads to everyday culture and its *loudness/lewdness* encroaches upon upper-class sensibilities. What results in Jamaica is a clash that has synchrony along racial and social lines. Dancehall culture in Jamaica is a mass activity that is considered threatening to the legitimate, normalized, or accepted code of conduct and behavior, but the deregulation of the media has made the job of containing dancehall music difficult for censors. Donna P. Hope offers a vivid and lively description of dancehall, which takes into account the music and its attendant aesthetics: "It is loud and colorful. Its heavy bass, catchy slang, flashy regalia, colorful and daring costumes, vibrant dances, and defiantly arrogant attitudes are hard to miss."[10] Hope reports also that the loudness, the oral and visual abundance of dancehall culture, "guarantees that many individuals from different socioeconomic backgrounds consume dancehall culture both consciously and unconsciously," and the unconscious consumption of dancehall culture is fostered by posters that "blaze colour and hype across visual spaces . . . [I]ts overall noise and publicity is a riot that continuously disturbs the peace."[11] Norman C. Stolzoff adds that during the day "one confronts dancehall music while crammed into public buses; while walking down the street coming from record shops and small sound systems used by music vendors; while socializing at bars" and so on.[12] In its proliferation, dancehall culture transcends the dance hall, no longer existing on the fringes as a rite to be observed by the disenfranchised. As such, the "code-structuring messages"[13] of this musical genre can be understood as analogous to the ideological messages of the lower class allowing them a sphere of influence that extends to the political and socioeconomic sector.[14]

The lower class has harnessed the power of noise by offering dancehall music as a symbolic weapon to cast out and to overturn existing spheres of influence. Noise in the typical sense denotes the amorphous and the unformed; however, in regard to dancehall, it can be read as a highly structured metalanguage, yielding thoroughly organized information and connotations. Thus, the aesthetic practices and radical democracy of dancehall music suggest that its noise is itself a conveyor of systematically organized messages. Music is thus capable of channeling the power of noise and can function as a weapon, thereby making it possible to disturb the hierarchy of social relations and to sublimate symbolically the violence through the imaginary.

Given the interrelation between music/noise and politics, I argue that dancehall music confers to its participants the agency that is limited for them in the legitimate socioeconomic and political structures of Jamaican society. Functioning also as a secular rite, the music allows dancehall adherents to channel the "imaginary and violence" that disturbs "the social hierarchy." The music therefore functions as "a strategic consumption, an essential mode of sociality for all those who feel themselves powerless."[15] In other words, there is a link between dancehall music's function as both secular religion and popular culture and the possibilities it holds for liberation: it allows followers to engage in it not only as a secular religious ritual but also as an expression of public cultural citizenship, allowing them to move from the private domain of the dance hall to the public sphere. In a sense, this movement from the private to public is a way to reclaim the commons from privatization—a symbolic gesture that articulates their dissension toward the privatization of public resources through the mandates of neoliberal structural adjustments.

However, there is a two-fold challenge to viewing dancehall music as a vehicle of liberation because of the paradoxes underlying its counter-hegemonic strategies. First, the artistic quality of the music has been dismissed as mere "excesses" of noise and as an art-form that promotes violence. Second, it embodies a lower-class aesthetic that reaffirms the middle and upper classes' judgment of it as loud/lewd (as evidence of cultural decadence because of sexually explicit lyrics and the adherents' slack deportment, not to mention the recurring expressions of overt violence) and that, in their view, impedes agency and socioeconomic mobility because of the inherent paradoxes and contradictions. Natasha Barnes explains that for social elites and even some leftist academics "dancehall is at best a conundrum, at worst a refractory lens of all that has gone wrong" as suggested by their "disappointment and confusion over the form's political imaginary."[16] Put simply, the "conundrum" involves, for instance, the connection between a representation that protests violence and its consequences and causes, yet also seems to emulate it. This paradox, I argue, is at the heart of dancehall practitioners' counter-hegemonic stance. A key issue that I explore in this chapter is how we can account for the movement from miming the slave master's violence to channeling the Ogun archetype—the divine figure of paradox itself—in secular religious ritual and as a symbol of sociopolitical contestation, for which noise as sonic disturbance and as somatic discourse are important. I also interrogate why the challenge to neocolonialism is done through performative means, and I address the question as to what this says about the nature of dispossession and the lack of political power.

Ogun is significant in Jamaican dancehall musical narratives as a fitting archetype to combat and challenge what Achille Mbembe dubs the Dionysiac character of colonization. In *The Birth of Tragedy*, Friedrich Nietzsche defines the Dionysiac in a manner that captures the quintessential traits of slave masters in the Caribbean. The Dionysiac, according to Nietzsche, entails "an extravagant lack of sexual discipline, whose waves engulfed all the venerable rules of family life." Nietzsche also characterizes the Dionysiac as a "grotesque," "barbaric," and "most dangerous force" that has a "repellent mixture of lust and cruelty."[17] In a Caribbean context that stems from the transatlantic crossing, Ogun practices transform in order to mitigate and mediate the slave sublime condition, an overwhelming experience that is marked by the terror of the Dionysiac. The tragic social circumstances and historical aftermath that prolong and replicate slavery in the Caribbean call forth the Ogun spirit and the tragic Will, expressed as both creative and destructive forces, to combat the Dionysiac terror and oppression. It is important to note that "Ogun represents empowerment to conquer seemingly insurmountable transitions or challenges through the power of one's will."[18] In Haiti, for instance, Petro spirits represent Ogun and "an effort to expropriate the power of slaveholding" through mimesis and "to use that power against itself."[19] This repetition of the master's violence is not simply mimetic as it also involves a change in sociopolitical dynamics, for Ogun is the god of retribution and protector of the dispossessed.

The mimesis of the slave master's Dionysiac power puts forth the sonic and somatic as logos—as reenactments of the trauma in the transference of language to the body, which provides insight about the performance aspect of violence that is central to the slave sublime aesthetic, which subordinates textuality. I draw upon Sandra T. Barnes's notion that Ogun is a "root metaphor" or "conceptual archetype" with "recurring patterns" and "structures of mind"[20] by suggesting that within dancehall culture Ogun functions as an emblematic figure with a translation from West African identity to fit the social context in the Caribbean, to make sense of and to deal with old and new forms of plantation structures, such as slavery and globalization. Barnes argues that Ogun in Africa was not originally part of a written tradition, that he was specifically found in performances and rituals in which he symbolized the forces of creativity and destruction.[21] In the Yoruba ìjálá chants, for instance, as Babalola writes, Ogun is represented "as a crusader against injustice."[22] Additionally, he "is looked to as a protector who will promptly respond to the appeals of the oppressed in their encounter with an unjust fate. In this respect, Ògún is a warrior against injustice within his own society, just as he is a warrior in battles against outside enemies."[23] Through performance, Ogun embodies combative Will in action. Despite his combative nature, in Africa he is not regarded just "as a ruthless figure, but as a social role model," "heroic leader," "provider," "protector," and "breadwinner."[24] Ogun's significance to "political resistance" is still meaningful today in spite of his origins during the Iron Age in West Africa.[25] Diasporic manifestations of Ogun have a political function as well, the reason he is linked to revolution, in Haiti, for example. These very virtues separate Ogun from his Hellenic parallels. Unlike Greek mythology, the landscape of Yoruba myth is conceptualized by the paradoxical tension that exists between the spirit of destruction, creative fulfillment, and the morality of reparation.

Dancehall music representations occur as a blurring between actual and performative elements of violence as the murderous, Dionysiac frenzy that artists bring to life for us by changing the slave master's violence into an act of repetition and distortion through Ogun rituals that serve as symbols of combative Will. As the god of iron, Ogun can be considered as part of the mechanized dub aesthetic in dancehall music's deejay artform as well as the figurative and literal gun that functions as a symbol of masculinity. Ogun functions as an iconic or archetypal figure in dancehall spaces and culture with an association with fire, metal, dance, and the color red and as a heroic figure of the abyss and transition. In Nigeria, "it is generally believed that fire is a spirit under the custody of 'Ogun'" and when he "is angry or [his] support is solicited by other gods to help avenge an offense against them, Ogun would send fire to the house of such persons."[26] In Haiti, Ogun is synonymous with Ogou who functions as a Petro spirit with "a fiery nature"[27] in the possession rituals of Vodou. Ogou is significant because of "several centuries of political and military upheaval, a historical legacy which transformed the African religious cosmos" to fit the sociopolitical reality.[28] As with Haiti, fire has played an important role in Jamaican history and cultural forms as it conveys resistance to the slave plantation power structure. Ogun was there all along throughout Jamaica's musical history as well, even in Bob Marley's music. In "Slave Driver," for instance, from the *Catch a Fire* album, Marley sings, "Slave driver, the table is turn / Catch a fire, you gonna get burn." Certainly, we cannot overlook the *Burnin'* album. Overall, the symbolism of fire and burning has been very pronounced in reggae music and in the dancehall music genre that would follow.

The Ogun ethos in the contemporary Jamaican dancehall musical genre, one could argue, is a counter-myth that is layered with the psychological issues that Fanon links to the experiences of coloniality. The Ogun practices suggest one way in which this divine figure functions as a revolutionary force and another way in which particular segments of the Jamaican population have articulated the fratricidal violence and dance of possession through this deific archetype by miming old rituals from the slave plantation and by excavating old memories about coping strategies from the reservoirs of historical memory and ancestral culture. In Jamaica, the Ogun archetype attached to the warrior figure is exhumed as noise and as visible practice, no longer on the margins of society, because of the historical moment of globalization—with its Dionysiac power of dispossession that has a far-reaching social, psychic, and political impact beyond the economic crisis.

Ogun as Don-Like Protector

Channeling Ogun in his 2009 album *Mr. Brooks . . . A Better Tomorrow,* Mavado points to the paradoxes and contradictions both in his personal life and in Jamaican society. The song "Don't Worry" is the exemplar of paradox, voicing both the wanton violence and yet the political agency of directly critiquing the Jamaican establishment, which preserves and condones old and new forms of domination. Mavado's deejay persona also embodies the contradictory characteristics of Ogun, as he identifies himself as protector of those in the ghetto. Setting up himself as a "gully gaad" (gully god), a kind of warlord protector, Mavado states that "every knee shall bow and every tongue confess to me." He tells those living in the ghettos, "don't worry," and his use of this refrain throughout the song takes on a double meaning, both as a means of consoling those dealing with the brutalities of slum life and as a way of warning those who would harm the people living in his protectorate. The overt expressions of violence are, however, tempered by the melodic sound of his voice, which varies from tenor to baritone as he wails "don't worry" and croons "Na na na noooo no" and "whoaii." The calm, wailing voice is counterposed with the rhyming and chilling echo of "retaliation in a hurry," an Ogunic reverberation that occurs throughout the song, which, furthermore, is intensified by the haunting and monotone drum and bass that accompanies the eerie sound made by a keyboard synthesizer. Mavado delivers his lyrics in a confident tone and takes comfort in his job as protector and revealer of what is happening in the gully: "But ah [I] sing some songs about

the gangs / Cause someone need to talk it." He talks about the police harassment and brutality, contemporary forms of oppression that typify the tragic
life in the gully—the West Kingston slums, in other words.

As Mavado states in "On the Rock," the simple fact of being born in the
"slum" is the primary reason for the high death rate among the youths who
live there: "Di yutes dem blood a run / Dung deh inna di slum." Here, Mavado
points to the problems that stem from structural violence (poverty, poor education, inadequate housing), and, as he sees it, the youths cannot escape their
fate because politicians have made campaign promises without delivering on
them. He attributes the politicians' and the upper classes' lack of concern
to their wealth, claiming that if a revolution should start they have enough
money to allow them to "fly out": "If revolution shoulda start dem rich
enough can fly out." This deejay warns that if the authorities censor his music,
which he believes has been a source of distraction for the *sufferahs* in the
ghetto, they must be prepared for the bloody uprising that will ensue: "Music
a gal over gun / Tell dem nuh stop the fun / Cause if dem stop the fun /
Dem mus prepare fi stop the gun."[29] Mavado uses an echo effect in various
parts of the second verse as a means of emphasis, in particular the line that
states his frustration with the poverty ("Mi tired ah di ... poverty"). The
word poverty itself is echoed after pauses or gasps in this verse as a means of
representing his frustrated and heightened emotional state.

Echoing the word poverty at the end of another song, "Overcome," is clev-
erly done, as it functions as one of the major factors that the novelist Roger
Mais and other dancehall deejays, such as Bounty Killer, have attributed to
the rising violence in Kingston ghettos. In Mais's 1953 novel *The Hills Were
Joyful*, one character, an English chaplain residing in Jamaica, provides credence to the significance of poverty as the major impetus for committing
crimes: "The population of our prison is made up almost wholly of people
who had no other alternative but to commit these crimes for which they are
being punished, and what is more shocking still, they will be forced to commit them again and again, each time they are outside. For they have no other
means of putting food into their hungry bellies."[30] Although a fictional character, the chaplain's observations linking crime to poverty are significant: his
identity as part of Jamaica's colonial superstructure functions as an authenti-
cating machinery. In this sense, the novel suggests a continued representation
of violence as being integrally related to the economic situation. Even as late
as the mid-1980s, poverty was still regarded as a motivating factor for committing crimes. After interviewing a representative sample of 3,000 prison
inmates, criminologist Bernard Headley provides empirical evidence in *The*

Jamaican Crime Scene that those who have been imprisoned "had little access, if any, to the basic necessities of life—things such as a regular meal and a sure place to sleep."[31] These perspectives from Mavado and Mais demonstrate that, whatever the immediate causes of violence, it is structured, both in the grammar of its practice and in the systems of representation that account for it, by a longer historical continuum that cannot be accounted for by any present sociology or criminology.

Similarly, in current popular musical representation, dancehall deejay Bounty Killer's song "Look" points also to poverty as a major cause for violent crimes:

> Look into my life, can you see my kids?
> Let me ask you this, do you know what hungry is?
> Well in this part of town, survival is my will
> For you to stay alive you've got to rob and kill.
> Look into my house, would you live in there?
> Look me in the eyes and tell me that you care,
> Well I've made up my mind to end up in the morgue
> Right now I'd rather die, cause man a live like dog
> Look into my eyes, tell me what you see?
> Can you feel my pain, am I your enemy?
> Give us a better way, things are really bad,
> The only friend I know is this gun I have.
> [...]
> You've been talking 'bout you want the war to cease
> But when you show us hope, we will show you peace

By characterizing the crimes as "war," Bounty Killer represents Ogun-inspired violence as a strategic and realistic response to genuine economic and social exigencies. Leonard E. Barrett Sr. argues that in 1981 the Seaga administration's adherence to a capitalist agenda had "had a detrimental effect on Jamaica's poor" and that the poor were "effectively kept at a distance by the arm of the law, whose duty it [was] to protect capital."[32] According to Barrett, the "criminal element emerged from the people who have been consistently denied a share in the wealth of their homeland, [who are] now determined to get a piece of the pie by any possible means. The means now utilized is violence . . . No one is excluded from this 'war.'"[33] Likewise, Terry Lacey attributes the violence in Jamaica to the social and economic conditions. He argues, "There are plain economic and social reasons . . . why Jamaican society in general was a violent and sometimes brutal society."[34] He is not alone in holding this viewpoint, as Claremont Kirton offers a similar explanation: "Whether in the squalid 'ghettoes' of Western Kingston or the impoverished rural communities of St. Catherine, the toll exacted by the economic crisis has many dimensions and takes different forms. In desperation, some people turn to crime. Burglaries, robberies, larceny, drug dealing are all on the increase. In response, the police resort to brutality and frequent killings; in 1989, 180 Jamaicans were killed by the police. The fastest growing economic sectors in Jamaica are now drugs—and the security industry."[35] Here, Barrett, Lacey, and Kirton echo Fanon's point that the "starving peasant outside the closed system, is the first among the exploited to discover that only violence pays."[36] While revealing poverty as the motivating factor for violence in the ghettos, many of Bounty Killer's songs have actually encouraged the youths not to resort to such bloody means. Nonetheless, given this deejay's overt revelation of the social conditions and fearing the revolutionary potential behind the lyrics, the reactionary government of Jamaica banned "Look" and other songs offering a social critique, such as "Fed Up" and "Anytime." In her discussion of "Anytime," Patricia J. Saunders points out that "the song provides an alternative historical background to the nature of violence in Jamaica" and that it "works effectively to institute another order of power, one that is exercised through the same modality" of the Jamaican nation state's own "violence." Such measures taken by Jamaica's poor are a means of survival, Saunders explains, especially given the government's structural neglect and brutal policing tactics. The "irony" of this "war" that reveals the sufferahs exacerbated victimization is the "fact [that] crimes are being committed against poor people by the government and its policies."[37] Like Bounty Killer, Mavado's songs draw attention to and lament over the social and economic conditions of those residing in the gully. The widespread structural neglect and incessant violence in the Kingston ghettos suggest why Mavado, typifying the Yoruba god Ogun, takes on the symbolic role of protector because the government has abdicated its responsibility. Mavado realizes that structural forms of violence are sanctioned by the government and, more importantly, he realizes that these forms of violence are not only contemporary but also transhistorical.

Given Jamaica's history of slavery, apprenticeship, and colonialism, Mavado characterizes contemporary violence as cyclical, as part of an unbroken historical chain—as something that was *already there*.[38] In the same manner that slave drivers and constables were employed, during slavery and apprenticeship respectively, to protect the planters' interests, Mavado attributes much of contemporary violence to the police who maintain the status quo as they enforce "top society['s]" policies. Because of this paradigmatic quality of violence in Jamaica and the manifestation of the slave sublime (the overwhelming magnitude of contemporary violence and the realization that slavery is ever-present through modes of substitution), Mavado expresses a great degree of futility and pessimism in "Chiney K." He points to many contradictions in Jamaican society and, as he sees it, "top society" and the police are to be blamed because the incessant violence has been in play even before he was born. In the chorus, he describes a scene of gunplay that starts during the middle of day and carries on throughout the night, as "Badman" (gangsters) and police shoot the "Chiney K." With very slight variation this incessant gunplay is portrayed by the repetition of key lines throughout the two-verse chorus. The line "all mama pray" is omitted in the second verse to show the futility of praying, while the line "life fade away" is substituted so as to explain again the futility of praying because the gunmen continue to "beat" the "Chiney K." As Mavado makes it known, it was "di law" (the law) that he saw first with a "big gun" when he was four years old and witnessed an incident involving their use of excessive force. Pointing to the garrison communities that the two leading political parties have created and maintained, he alleges that it is the politicians that are actually responsible for bringing the guns to the island in the first place, thus setting the stage for the surging levels of gun violence. Given the underlying political basis for the high crime and death rate, Mavado suggests that music is a weapon, a source of power that allows him to turn the tables—to voice and to draw attention to the structural causes of violence in Jamaican society: poverty, the formation of garrison communities, and police brutality.

In contemporary Jamaica, the excessive use of state-sanctioned police violence points to the historical legacies of slavery and colonialism, regimes during which the overseer, police, and army have carried out terror as means of maintaining power for the ruling classes. In *The Wretched of the Earth*, Fanon argues that the "colonial regime owes its legitimacy to force and at no time tries to hide this aspect of things."[39] Given Fanon's argument, it becomes evident that the colonizer uses violence as a primary means of communicating his paternalistic role as both master and teacher of violence.[40] Providing credence to the extensive use of violence both as a means of communication and maintenance of subjection, Winston Arthur Lawson notes that the Jamaican plantation system "was born and bred on violence," which it "maintained by the exercise or threat of unleashing merciless and overwhelming force," and that it was a system that "would always retaliate vigorously and swiftly against any challenge to its authority."[41] Genealogically speaking, and as historical testimonials suggest, the Jamaican police force known formally as the Jamaican Constabulary Force can be traced back to the institutions of slavery and apprenticeship when Black slave drivers and constables were trained to protect the planters' interests by inflicting wanton violence against fellow slaves. Henry Whiteley's first-hand testimonial, *Excessive Cruelty to Slaves: Three Months in Jamaica in 1832*, reports the degree to which Black slave drivers participated in the systemic violence on Jamaican plantations. Whiteley states, "I observed the drivers took great pride in being able to crack their whips loud and well."[42] Suggesting the substitutive, paradigmatic aspects of violence, the practices of violence under apprenticeship were no different from those under slavery, as James Williams reports in *A Narrative of Events*—the only difference was that the proper nomenclature had changed: slaves were called apprentices and slave drivers were called constables.

In present-day Jamaica, the Jamaican Constabulary Force as the police continues its abuse of power in order to protect the interests of the ruling classes. It was reported in the study "Human Rights in Jamaica," conducted by Americas Watch in both 1986 and 1992, that "the level of police violence is extremely high; killings by police during these four years constituted 22 percent of all homicides in Jamaica."[43] The report attributes the high level of homicide by the Jamaican police to the fact that the "police are trained and organized along paramilitary lines, to respond to violence." Additionally, this report points out that for the police there "is a persistent failure to protect life which demonstrates that deadly force actually is the instrument of first resort."[44] Another primary reason that Americas Watch cites for police violence is the "politicization" of the force.[45] It is also noted in these reports that "Jamaica has one of the worst records of police violence in the world, with official statistics listing an average of 140 people shot and killed annually." These figures are alarming, especially "[g]iven the country's small population."[46] As a percentage, the number of police homicide translates to "one-third of the total murders in the country, whereas the rate in the United States has been estimated at less than 4 percent."[47] A good percentage of the total homicides occur in the garrison districts.

The Jamaican government frames violent conflicts occurring in West Kingston garrisons as the result of political tribalism. This notion of "tribalism" is a loaded term that allows for the characterization of the violence as atavistic and as that which precedes the emergence of a civil society. It is considered, thus, that membership in a civil society is predicated upon the acceptance of the social contract and the ideals of civilization. In this regard, the Jamaican government represents dissenters in garrison communities as primitive tribes. The government can then justify the violent means of coercion they see necessary to implement as forms of control and discipline so that the dissenters will accept the so-called higher principles of the state over the tribe. What seems evident is that this colonialist logic allows state security forces to commit violence on their own people under the euphemism of a "state of emergency," calling to mind the atrocities of the 1865 Morant Bay Rebellion as the changing same.

The concept of a "state of emergency" in contemporary Jamaican jurisprudence is basically the implementation of martial law, though often through extrajudicial means. Martial law actually originated within the metropolitan sphere but was utilized during the colonial era as a means of protecting the crown's interests through the use of state-sanctioned violence under the logic of "necessity" during periods of turbulent social unrest. In his book *The Jurisprudence of Emergency*, Nasser Hussain argues that "the logic of necessity is deeply embedded in the rhetorical structure of a liberal-constitutional system's response to emergency" and that there are "changing rules for defining 'necessity.'"[48] As a rhetorical strategy for ensuring the implementation of state-sanctioned violence, the concept of "necessity" under martial law is vague. The current juridical system in Jamaica has adopted a similar semantic evasion in its definition of what constitutes a "state of emergency" for the implementation of martial law. In a 2003 article titled "A State of Historical Emergency" appearing in the Jamaican newspaper *The Daily Gleaner*, Melville Cooke, commenting on police officers' excessive use of violence, states that "imposing a state of emergency with them [the police] on the front-line is tantamount to getting a child molester to take a group of Girl Scouts on a long camp." Suggesting the ways in which there is a continued interplay between politics and violence, Cooke argues further that violence as practiced by the state has "blossomed [into] the culture of murder in which we have today." Cooke's point is evident in the more recent events of May 2010.

On June 4, 2010 the Human Rights Watch called again upon Jamaican authorities to conduct an impartial query into alleged extrajudicial killings during the previous month by state security forces in a joint military and police effort to apprehend drug warlord and trafficker Christopher "Dudus" Coke, a don who ran an international drug ring from his stronghold in Tivoli Gardens. Despite the United States' persistence, Dudus's extradition orders were not signed by Jamaican Prime Minister Bruce Golding because Dudus, as the area don of the JLP-controlled Tivoli Gardens garrison community, was instrumental in his election as member of Parliament. It was only when voters and Parliament threatened to remove Golding from office that he signed the orders. The *Daily Gleaner* reported that once Golding signed the order for Dudus's arrest, after dawdling for several months and seeking the aid of a U.S. lobbying group to fight the extradition request, there was a standoff between Jamaican security forces and this don's Shower Posse gang, who wanted to protect him from extradition to the United States for trial for his alleged association in the death of over 1400 people in the states, casualties of his Jamaica-based international drug trade. The violence spanned four days, starting on Sunday, May 23, 2010 and ending on Wednesday, May 26, 2010. Witnesses reported that the police was responsible for vigilante violence, the extrajudicial homicides of more than seventy people. The police killed indiscriminately at point-blank range a number of unarmed men who had no connections to Coke's Shower Posse gang. In general, the police's reign of terror against West Kingston posses and innocent people as a carte blanche had started decades before when the successes of the 1980s drug trade made the gangs financially independent and thus ended their dependency on politicians. Laurie Gunst argues that the "party leaders, menaced by an outlaw underworld they could no longer control, turned the Jamaican police in the ghettos to execute their former paladins."[49] Indeed, the problem of violence in Jamaica stems primarily from a legacy built upon the government's perpetuation of violence.

During the various stages of Jamaica's history, there have been cycles of violence and criminality that have become normalized in the social, economic, and political practices of the island. By design, the formal system of governance that was inherited from the British instituted both the structural violence of withholding basic necessities (education, adequate housing, healthcare, etc.) and the physical violence of maintaining law and order in a paramilitary fashion in which the police and army are used as state-sanctioned terrorists who inflict violence upon the poor, as they stand in paradigmatically as iconic remnants of the overseer and slave driver from the days of slavery. Because of the collusion between the government and drug warlords, dons such as Dudus have been able to control garrison communities that exist as independent states within the Jamaican state, where their constituents recognize them as the legitimate rulers. In a reciprocal fashion, these constituents are shared with the don's political backers, who are either seeking or hoping to maintain offices in government. The constituents who reside in garrison communities regard the dons as godfather figures with a mixture of trepidation and veneration, but their sense of dependency motivates their fierce loyalty, as seen in video footage from *Al Jazeera* of the May 2010 incident in which a placard sign taped to a dog reads, "Jesus die for us. We will die

for Dudus!!!"[50] An insidious sign such as what was taped to the dog is motivated by basic human needs: because the government tolerates such high levels of poverty through structural neglect, basic human needs drive individuals
to view criminals who provide resources to their respective garrisons as surrogate heads of state rather than the government. Contrary to what the placard suggests, Dudus, although perceived as a savior, is paradoxically no saint
at all, as the name of his gang, the Shower Posse, implies. He deals in swift
and deadly violence by showering bullets, similar to Lawson's description of
the way in which Jamaican planters (slave masters) displayed their power.
The paradox is that it is the dons who, through their underground economies
and legitimate business practices, provide the basic resources—welfare, employment, goods, and protection—that the government fails to grant, despite
their election or campaign promises. Even a businessman whose identity remains anonymous, according to a *New York Times* article, considers Dudus's
presence as "a stabilizing force" that benefits business: "Because of his
[Dudus's] ongoing and long-term presence he has been a stabilizing force
to allow business people and civil society in the area to exist in a way that suc-
cessive elected governments have been unable to guarantee . . . A lot of this
has to do with the failure of the government. He [Coke] shouldn't exist, but
until the government can take up the responsibility for proper governance of
Jamaica then we are better served with him existing, simply."[51] Can Ogun be
linked to the ruthless figure of the don who is both destroyer and provider?
What connections can be made given the economic, political, and social conditions in Jamaica that arise out of the context of myth, the neoliberal agenda
behind globalization that can be characterized as Dionysiac?

Describing Ogun's dynamics in dance and oral performance from Yorubaland and Brazil that captures the Shower Posse's brutal and swift violence,
Margaret Thompson Drewal explains that it is "Ogun's nature to be quick,
direct, and strong. Whether creative or destructive, his dynamic can be characterized as explosive."[52] Moreover, a possible link between the don/*shotta*
and Ogun points to the god's idiosyncratic nature when transferred to and
transformed within the slave societies of the Caribbean and Latin America.
Donald J. Cosentino argues that "under the social, cultural, economic, and
political circumstance of the Atlantic slave trade, his already complex persona
was twisted and turned into fantastic new shapes."[53] Despite the change, as
Cosentino argues further, Ogun's meaning within the New World context derives "from a remembered theme." To this theme he accords constancy in spite
of the proliferation of "modes of expression." Ogun is thus altered to fit the
new sociopolitical context and may lurk on the "margins of official culture"

where he is "being generated anew."[54] Cosentino urges us to consider that "If we want to trace the development of West African religions into world religions," it is imperative to "readjust our sights from the old votive sanctuaries to the wilds of a cosmopolitan and heterogeneous world culture," and that we ought to investigate and examine closely "those neglected margins of official culture reserved for scholars of folklore and popular culture."[55] We cannot overlook Ogun's creative/destructive side enacted symbolically through dancehall performance that draws from West Kingston gang culture.

In a state of normalized violence, the cultural production will bear its marks—the scars of intergang rivalry, police intimation and use of deadly force, state-sanctioned violence (including structural neglect), and collusion with gang leaders of garrison communities. Mavado's music involves a complex system of coded language and signification, as many of his songs about violence draw upon the don as an iconic Ogun figure and his lyrics demonstrate a semantic indeterminacy or shift between symbolic and actual violence. In its indeterminacy, the manifestations of Ogun can be read as a merging with Eshu (Anancy, the trickster figure), who was so important for techniques of survival during plantation slavery, particularly as subterfuge to the slave master's power. Mavado starts the song "So Special" with playful gun lyrics, referring to himself paradoxically as being "so special" because of the attention he gets from his enemies who watch his every move and who have "marked [him] fi death." He uses the word "special" also as a sliding signifier for the .45 special gun that symbolizes an Ogun aesthetic underlying the literal and metaphoric significance of the gun and fire that convey the extent of his lyrical force: "Dat's why mi strap wid mi .45 special bwoy a pree mi." Because of the great degree of rivalry among deejays who have close ties to gang culture, Mavado makes it known to those who say they want his head on a block ("seh dem waan mi head pon block"), as in killing him both lyrically and literally, that he will burn fire. In other words, he will fire gunshots and combative lyrics until their own heads are wet either with blood or his overflowing lyrical potency: "bun di fire til it wet pon dat." The lyrics from "So Special" display a blurring between the represented and the Real. A primary reason for this, as Norman Stolzoff explains, is that the deejays are susceptible to "armed assaults by rival performers and gangsters" in which "values and social imagination" are formed for the inner-city youths.[56] There is also a deeper psycho-social issue at play, however. The violent rivalries that Mavado engages in with other deejays stem partly from his post/neocolonial condition, especially given that Jamaican society is still steeped in the hegemonic traditions of the former British colonial regime and the neocolonial frontier of globalization brought by the United States. In this light, "So Special" seems to highlight the misdirected political agency of rival deejays who experience the omnipresent specter of the plantation system. As collective historical memory, there is a mimicry of gang life in dancehall's performance rituals, which display Ogun's combative Will. The ritualistic violence of the plantation order under the slave master is also repeated as an archetype of power. Below, Barbara Whitmer explains the significance of ritualistic practices:

> Ritual as practice has a divine model, an archetype. Rituals are practices that repeat the act believed to have been performed at the beginning of time by a god, a hero, or an ancestor. In this way, an act becomes real, or "meaningful" through repetition. The mechanism of the transformation of human into archetype through repetition can be approached through the examination of the extent to which collective memory preserves the recollection of a historic event. In the example of epic poetry, the historical character of the persons celebrated undergoes a change. To be preserved in the collective memory, the historical event approaches a mythic model. In this respect, "myth is the last—not the first—in the development of a hero."[57]

In dancehall music, the Ogun archetype functions as a mythic model—wherein new and old rituals of violence are married.

Dancehall music becomes a play of signs in the encounter of the Real of violence that simultaneously terrifies as the slave sublime (re)encounter with the plantation and pacifies with beauty in an ephemeral moment of sublimation. This is present in Mavado's song "Real Killa" about the interplay between murder and madness that represents and reflects the social reality of poverty and gang life in the West Kingston ghettos. At the end of this song, Mavado, in the persona of a don, announces that he is "mad" and "mentally sick." There is a clear link to Marlon James's novel *A Brief History* in which James describes the ghetto, the gully experience, and a similar interrelation between murder and the madness that stems from the debased, socioeconomic conditions of poverty, as discussed in chapter 4. One key difference is that James's novel gives an insight into the world of the ghetto but seems to stop short of describing in full detail and commenting upon the complete ugliness of the violence—perhaps due the readership's sensibilities and the generic limitation of the novel form in its representation of the excesses associated with the slave sublime. A *YouTube* video clip of Mavado filmed in a West Kingston garrison community helps us to understand the deeper significance of the song "Real Killa." In the video clip, which is rendered under a documentary platform, Mavado portrays himself as a gangsta (gangster) with a posse, who he refers to as his "dawgs." Along with being a gangsta, he identifies himself simultaneously as a "gully gaad" (gully god): "me as di gangsta and me as di gully gaad." In a paradoxical Ogunic fashion, he describes himself as having a "hot head," as in having a fiery temper, but is quick to mention that his music also involves "upliftment." Furthermore, he characterizes his music as a "lyrical bomb" and follows up with the declaration, "me a di gaad fi every garrison, every garrison wid a gully. A me a di gaad in deh."[58] This characterization of his music as "lyrical bomb" and his position as "gully gaad" comes out of a desire to suggest the degree of his creative force to capture the Real of ghetto life marred by gang rivalry and the don-like stature that affords him. Sonjah Stanley Niaah calls our attention to the representational and evocative power of Mavado's music for a complete understanding of the ghetto, arguing that his 2007 "debut album can be seen as a treatise on gangsta epistemology, pedagogy and ontology." Additionally, she characterizes his music as "letters from the gangsta battlefield, revealing stories, strategies and spatial philosophies from the street."[59]

In the song "Real Killa," Mavado sings, "Mek mi tell you somethin' bout real killa." The message he conveys about street life in rapid fire is that of the chilling reality behind the don persona that he portrays and what drives his crazed homicidal violence. Mavado describes the coldblooded killing with the imagery of severed heads spinning "like mi van wheel," blood running out of bodies, and a boy's face as he lies dead on the tarred pavement. One thing Mavado makes clear is that the don is part of this horrific gangsta lifestyle because "Mi dawgs hungry and dem waan real dinner." The dawgs, of course, are the members of the posse, the *shottas*. Mavado suggests, therefore, the don's role as provider and represents killing as meeting dire economic needs, as other prominent dancehall artists such as Busy Signal also insinuate. In the more recent song "Stay So," which deals with the precarious life of a gangsta, Busy Signal seems to echo Mavado's point in "Real Killa" about the economic needs that underlie the gangsta life. One line from Busy Signal's song states, "From you nah stop mi food, dawg, me no matter 'bout you and me no care 'bout that." Another line also reveals the crazed image of the *shotta* and the don's posse: "all a di dawgs dem a bare mad smaddy." This line refers to the vicious nature of gangsta life, which erupts in a frenzied and murderous madness, not only as Dionysiac, but also as Ogunic, as this god does in one Yoruba tale. In the song "Silence," another popular artist Popcaan announces Ogun's presence as a Petro spirit in his long-time friends on the warring turfs of gang life: "Long time Petro dem a hold it pon di battlefield." In a life marred by gun violence and homicides, life in the ghetto has little beauty as the awful realties of the slave sublime experience are heightened. In his song "Lef My Gun," Popcaan talks about the notion that there is nothing pretty in the ghetto but the gun. He points out in a number of songs that his "old iron" is always strapped to his waist given the rivalry and violence that sometimes occur within the music industry, which mirrors gang culture. In "Firm and Strong" Popcaan reveals that "This music biz is like a battlefield to me" and that "Old iron de pon mi waist, you know seh every clip full." Intergang warfare is a space where Ogun reigns as both positive and negative energy. Representing a composite of creativity and destruction, Ogun is thus a fit archetype for understanding the slave sublime in which the split between the mind and body and the sublime and beautiful are bridged.

From a Western point of view, it is difficult to understand why Ogun in the don/*shotta* persona that the dancehall artists render can be understood as both positive and negative. This is because "In the West, positive and negative—familiarly glossed as evil and good—can be divided into opposing parts and symbolized by Satan and God." However, in "West Africa, positive and negative power is not separate. Power is singular."[60] Western notions of duality—as in the separation between Apollonian and Dionysiac virtues, the Cartesian division of mind and body, and the Kantian split between reason and imagination as well as the sublime and beautiful—do not exist within an African epistemology. In contrast, the nature of Ogun's combative Will in Yoruba myth "exhibits two significant sides of his personality: a positive side, represented by his innovation, benevolence, and creativity, and a negative side of unpredictable, violent passion, which is indiscriminate in its effects."[61] In a paradoxical way, the manifestation of the Ogunic Will in Mavado's and other dancehall artists' music signals a transition from the abyss of social death with a singular power that also leads to the actual death of others. Put differently, the violence associated with Ogun is rendered as heroic so as to translate social death from a state of nonbeing into agency through the paradoxical Ogunic Will to combat the abyss of suffering, albeit contradictorily.

The song "Overcome" offers paradoxically Mavado's optimism while maintaining a degree of sober pessimism about the possibility of overcoming life's frustrations in the gully. After an invocation of the Rastafari figure and former Ethiopian emperor, Haile Selassie, the deejay starts off the song with the line "Brighter day," which he states with uncertainty, somewhere between declaring hope for a better day and the frustration that a better day has not come yet, as evidenced by his repeated wailing of the word "No, no, no, nooo" in the second line. In Mavado's music, there is a plurality of religious symbols enveloped in Rastafari consciousness, but beneath it Ogun lurks even with a Christian undercurrent. Mavado wails throughout this hymn-inspired track with a gospel choir singing the refrain, "We shall overcome," as he wails screechingly "Weeeeeeeee," voicing his frustrations about the violent and brutal gully life. Gully life is an extended metaphor for police brutality, poverty, gang warfare, high mortality, and the shedding of innocent blood. Although Mavado voices his own particular experiences of police harassment ("Tired a Babylon and dem damn molestation"), these individual experiences are actually collective because they typify life in the gully. The difference is that, as a deejay, Mavado is empowered with having a political platform, one that allows him to use his music as a means of offering social critique while he "talk[s] wid di nation," but more importantly as an expressive vehicle for both individual and communal catharsis. Given his political platform, it is no wonder that he characterizes the incidences he has had with the police—the various arrests, for instance—as deliberate attempts at censoring his music ("so nuh lock off the di soun"). He fears, however, that without his music to temper the *sufferahs'* frustrations, a demonstration might occur ("mi nuh want nuh demonstration").[62] These lines suggest dancehall's role as an opiate for the masses in its function not only as a secular religion[63] but also as a form of reflection and mediation.

Dancehall deejays such as Mavado who hail from Kingston ghettos are merely wordsmiths who represent the violence they have witnessed or experienced. The don/*shotta* has risen as a paradoxical figure, as both heroic and vicious, to become emblematic in dancehall music and culture as an expression of the Ogun archetype in which rituals of violence are repeated through performance. In the role of mediator, the deejay facilitates a symbiotic play between actual and performative violence by using a complex system of coded language and signification to which the audience responds in a form of call and response. The audience "indicate their ascent and identification with the powerful and deadly themes of these songs by hands raised in a pointing gun salute, waves, flags, flaring lighters and the occasional discharge of live rounds of ammunition."[64] The gun salute, flickering lighters, and gunshots are all symbols of the Ifa paradigm[65] that connect to Ogun in his modern-day incarnation. By adopting the persona of the don/*shotta* and related Ogun symbolism, many dancehall performers recreate a pantomime of linguistic symbols that are associated with this violent yet heroic figure. The symbols include a contorted and seemingly aggressive facial expression—a highly symbolic screw face that functions as a form of bodily discourse. The *screw face*, which has become normative in dancehall culture, is a fierce and unmistakably violent and masculine grimace that often includes the symbolic posture of holding a gun.[66]

By embracing the persona of the don/*shotta* and the attendant symbols of gang culture, many dancehall deejays blur the lines between playful fantasy and reality. In the essay "Representation," W. J. T. Mitchell points to the links between aesthetic/semiotic and political representation, which involve a "complex interaction between playful fantasy and serious reality in all forms of representation." Mitchell notes that there are "potential problems that come up with representations" such as when "they present a barrier that 'cuts across' . . . four lines of communication with others, presenting the possibility of misunderstanding, error, or downright falsehood."[67] Essentially, the axes of representation function as ideological sites or mirrors that distort images, suggesting a dynamic relation to other signs in the "adjacent" network of possible meanings. Representation in this manner is engaged in a metonymic process that generates meanings as a relationship of contiguity rather than as a metaphoric process of similarity. When taken out of context, the object or signifier is thus taken at face value. Mitchell points to one "crucial consideration that enters into any analysis of representation": "the relationship between the representational material and that which it represents." To address this dilemma he points to three types of representational relationships: icon, symbol, and index. The first, as he explains, is iconic representation that involves reproduction, mimesis, and imitation for which a relation of resemblance serves as the basis as it "transcend[s] the differences" between the two things that are linked together. In short, iconic representation (sound, speech act, gesture, or facial expression) can be reproduced through relations of resemblance. The second, by contrast, involves symbolic representations that "are not based on the resemblance of the sign to what it signifies but on arbitrary stipulation . . . because we have agreed to regard it this way." Linguistic representation is a prime example of this second form of representation; it is "'symbolic,' in that letters, words, and whole texts represent sounds and states of affairs without in the least resembling what they represent." As the third aspect, indexical representations are relational, taking into account issues such as "cause and effect or some 'existential' relation like physical proximity or connectedness."[68] These three aspects of representation (icon, symbol, and index) occur in dancehall music and culture.

The don/*shotta* serves as an iconic representation of an Ogun warrior, given that these figures engage in a brutal war of survival and retribution. While the resemblance is not apparent at first, the comparison bridges the difference because both are fearless, autonomous, and armed with deadly weapons that incite either fear or admiration. Keeping Mitchell's arguments in mind, it should be noted that when iconic signs such as the don/*shotta* are taken at face value (when reproduced in dancehall culture as literal representations) it becomes problematic, especially when the lines are occasionally blurred between iconic and symbolic representation. In addition to the iconography, indexical representation is also important in regard to cause and effect, given that the don/*shotta* as an icon of power emerged out of the context of globalization and the need to survive the neocolonial conditions, the 1980s neoliberal structural adjustment resulting in even more socioeconomic turmoil. The representation of the don/*shotta* as an icon of dancehall culture occurs through the processes of mimesis and imitation of a Dionysiac power structure that underlie historical and contemporary modes of oppression. Overall, dancehall music plays a key role in the perception and performance of legitimate and unsanctioned violence in Jamaica, and it operates in multiple modes as iconic, symbolic, and indexical representation—in service of representing and mediating violence, even in the function of a secular religion that seeks respite from social death.

Ogunic Will and Tragic Anguish

Afro-diasporic performance practices that grew out of slavery have provided a means of dealing with the overwhelming tragic anguish connected to the slave sublime condition involving social death and psychic despair—the Manichean delirium. In his essay "The Fourth Stage," Wole Soyinka argues that music is able to "contain tragic reality" during the heightened moments of the tragic experience. Music, he explains, arises from that tragic experience as "a language" or an "echo" of the "the stricken cry of man's blind soul as he flounders in the void and crashes through a deep abyss of spirituality and cosmic rejection."[69] In the Caribbean context of slavery, the "abyss of spirituality and cosmic rejection" is comparable to Orlando Patterson's notion of social death that stems from enslavement. In the spirit of Ogun, dancehall music deejays not only reveal the genre's secular religiosity but also capture the slave sublime paradoxes of violence that are cathartic yet irresolvable, creative yet destructive, and spectatorial yet participatory. These paradoxes, however, mask the underlying subversive and spiritual power that is associated with Ogun. Soyinka points to the fundamental disparities that Ogun embodies as the Yoruba god who functions "both as essence of anguish and as combative will."[70] The central paradox of this god, as Soyinka explains, connects to the Will, which is "the paradoxical truth of destructiveness and creativeness in acting man." In other words, Ogun embodies the tragic forces that lie within him, but his redemptive power comes from his ability to channel the destructive energies into the creative medium: "Ogun he experiences a yawning gulf within him, a menacing maul of chthonic strength yawning ever wider to annihilate his being; he is saved only by channelling the dark torrent into the plastic light of poetry and dance; not, however, as a reflection of illusion or reality, but as the celebrative aspects of the resolved crisis of his god."[71] Creative representations oftentimes convey the tragedy that is connected to the god's despair, which Soyinka characterizes as being "vast, numinous," and "always incomprehensible." The idea of vastness and incomprehensibility suggests elements of sublimity, especially given Soyinka's argument that "In vain we seek to capture it in words."[72] The author claims that only the one who experiences "disintegration" in which the "spirit has been tested" and the "psychic resources laid under stress by the forces most inimical to individual assertion" can grasp "the force of fusion between the two contradictions." The artist is one such person who is able to understand and to express this paradoxical sensibility as the "principle of destruction and re-creation."[73]

It can be argued also that the dance hall is a permissive space that functions for the artists and audience alike as an outlet for the violence they experience, allowing them momentary release in a sort of Ogunic revelry to deal with their tragic circumstances. Donna P. Hope has noted that "while staging and mimicking violence in the dancehall these artists are simultaneously involved in making meaning of social and political practices that form a part of Jamaican inner-city reality." She points out also that violence is manifested in the onstage and backstage interaction between the artists, between the artist and audience, and among members of the audience.[74] What is more, the music serves a cathartic function, although ephemeral, of allowing artists and audience alike to escape and to release the tensions of their daily life. The fact that Bunny Wailer (a founding member of Bob Marley and the Wailers) was assaulted by the audience during the 1991 Sting concert when their patience ran out with his roots reggae style of music serves to suggest that as a collective body the audience wanted to "hear about the harsh conditions that they faced in Kingston's inner cities," that "they wanted to hear gun tunes and tunes of violence," and that "they wanted to immerse themselves in the flood of dancehall stories about individuals like themselves."[75] The audience's reaction was not simply a celebration of their reality but an acknowledgment of the power to voice the slave sublime, the overwhelming pain of their material condition, and the cathartic joy of finding fulfillment in knowing that their particular experiences have communal resonance. Because many dancehall deejays emerge from the crime-infested ghettos in Kingston, their narratives about the deviant yet heroic don/*shotta* create a sense of cultural and social normalcy for those residing in the slums. Attali's notion about the "channelization of violence"[76] helps to explain why sometimes there are real acts of violence committed outside and inside the dance hall. As normative behavior, the call-and-response nature of the music (present in many Afro-diasporic forms of worship) ensures that the audience also participates in these symbolic acts. As expressions of Ogun's combative Will in dancehall culture, bodily gestures such as the screw face, rhythms, dynamics, and dance provide momentary freedom to the deejays' and the audience's embodied subjectivity, allowing them to release the terror and tensions accompanying the slave sublime experience. This experience can be characterized as a ritualistic journey through sound, enabling moments of catharsis, although ephemeral, and the reawakening of the self as "Self rather than Other" amidst the pleasure/pain paradox stemming from the superabundance of sonic and somatic stimulation.[77] Moreover, given the pleasure/pain paradox underlying the deejays' and audience's slave sublime experience, one cannot overlook the necessity of the art form for channeling tragic anguish in hopes of achieving catharsis from the spiritual abyss connected to their tragic circumstances stemming from the persistent legacies of slavery.

For dancehall music adherents, the Ogunic revelry is a mimetic response to the tragedy that occurs from slavery and contemporary forces such as globalization. In this sense, the dance hall activities are comparable to the Dionysiac rites of ancient Greece and Rome, where music functioned as a locus of subversion and transcendence of the body's limitations within sociopolitical environs. Moreover, the dance hall provides a means of articulating the tragic upheaval stemming from the cyclical histories of conquest, including globalization. Tragedy, according to David Scott, has a "dramatic ability to contain and represent moments of historical transformation, moments when possible futures seem less certain than they have been, and when heroic personalities embody both the old and new in ways that lead to both grandeur and catastrophe."[78] As Scott explains further, "the tragic narrative is cast as a dramatic confrontation between contingency and freedom, between human will and its conditioning limits."[79] Contingency in this sense is the continued perpetuation of plantation structures since emancipation, which brings forth the present tragic circumstances of the neoliberal order of globalization—its paradigmatic connection to slavery and limits imposed upon freedom after abolition. As the slave sublime suggests, the past and present commingle in a manner that captures, as Scott puts it, the idea of tragedy of having "a more respectful attitude to the past, to the often-cruel permanence of its impress."[80] Very important to understanding Scott's notion of tragedy in relation to time is the "African metaphysical system, in which time, instead of moving forward into the future, moves backward into the past, only to recur as part of a cyclical rhythm."[81] Thus, the slave sublime concept highlights an engagement with tragedy and the past that, as a way of conceptualizing the present moment as the changing same, is informed by both an African diasporic and ancestral epistemology.

Ogun operates within a tragic framework through which European notions of tragedy can be rejected by putting forth the centrality of Will as counter to a belief in a deterministic worldview—the notion that one is powerless to effect change, as the positivist myth of neoliberalism suggests in its idea of irreversibility and linear time. The Ogun Will is the kind of spiritual force and agency that is markedly different from the Greek and Shakespearean traditions. In these Western traditions, as Andrew Gurr notes, "the miseries and the injustices of human existence called for explanation, not revolution." Within this European framework of tragedy "virtue" is equated with a belief in "fatalism, in resigning oneself to the demands of one's destiny or to the will of the gods" because of the Grecian stoic tradition and Shakespearean ideas of "Christian patience."[82] A similar ethic can be ascribed to the neoliberal myth about historical progression in which our fate lies not in human ability but in a naturally operating economic system. The cosmos or god in this sense is the so-called invisible hand of market forces that cannot be altered or reversed. Ogun, however, is not the sufferer who is resigned to a deterministic and static belief in destiny; instead, the Ogunic Will foregrounds a dynamic revolutionary spirit.[83] An invocation of Ogun within the tragic context of the slave sublime condition is significant for challenging the Western neoliberal worldview, which is steeped in the Christian virtue of patience and the hope for salvation in the long run. Armed with a combative Will, Ogun is considered "as the challenger and conqueror of transition,"[84] functioning as an oppositional force to globalization and the economic dispossession and social death brought about by the transition to a neoliberal space. In his role as the "conqueror of transition," Ogun "reestablish[es] a union between being and nonbeing."[85] In essence, he forges an awakening from social death, in which the spirit is revived from the state of nonbeing. By extension, this understanding allows us to think about the significance of Ogun to the slave sublime agency, as an act overturning social death—in other words, to reclaim the self from dispossession through an act of the combative Will. Self-reclamation, Fanon argues, is a preliminary process that needs to occur before a revolution can be waged.

Damian Marley utilizes the aesthetic power of dub in "Confrontation," creating a collage that juxtaposes generations of fragmented musical and spoken word texts, ranging from Haile Selassie and Marcus Garvey to Bunny Wailer, as a form of "hypernarrative" that calls attention to the *sufferahs'* notions about violence and political agency—whether it is violence in the form of war, rebellion, uprising, revolt, or ideology. Using the phrase "Red-a-judgment a blaze" in the song "Confrontation," Damian Marley calls attention to the significance of the color red as conveyed in the Ifa paradigm with a nod to Ogun who symbolizes retributive, revolutionary violence. As Adu-Gyamfi explains, "the dominance of the colour red becomes a kind of supra-reality epitomizing the lived reality of the repetition of war in Nigeria" and elsewhere in the world.[86] Damian Marley explains why nothing has been done to stop the violence in Jamaica, a situation that is so severe that "not even superman coulda save you with him cape cause Red-a judgment a blaze." The violence in Jamaica has assumed apocalyptic proportions because the establishment created the grounds for the bloodshed with its economic policies, state religion, and accessible firearms. Damian Marley represents the incessant violence as a "War" (much like a slave uprising), in which "the new generation [is] rising up" in Kingston, a place where it is "not safe to walk about" because it is a "slaughterhouse." His lyrics are interspersed with a speech from Marcus Garvey that urges the dispossessed to fight against oppression if they want to survive: "If you cannot do it, if you are not prepared to do it, then you will die. You race of cowards, you race of imbeciles, you race of good for nothings, if you cannot do what other men have done, what other nations have done, what other races have done, then you yourself shall die." Garvey's speech, as the last verse, fades to helicopter sounds. Indeed, the sound of the music is as revolutionary as the lyrics themselves. Drumbeats sound like gunshots and Damian Marley delivers his militant lyrics as a barrage of bullets, making it known that if the violence "is a fight for freedom, sign me up."

Thrown together as a collage of sound, the dissimilar and dissonant elements in "Confrontation" produce sonic dissonance to serve as a frame for Damian Marley's revolutionary discourse. Structurally speaking, the song "Confrontation" is a collage of sounds: speeches as non-musical elements and orchestral pieces that are led by strings and military style drumming along with clashing symbols. The tonal rendition starts off in monotone by decreasing intonational dynamics and expansion of scalar structure that then moves toward lyricism. Damian Marley escalates his voice in order to demonstrate his heightened emotional state, at times even exceeding the bounds of the rhythmical structure that the instruments attempt to maintain. A similar process is exemplified in Johann Sebastian Bach's "St. John's Passion" in which atonal choral elements collide with instrumentation as a way to communicate Christ's ordeal during the Crucifixion, yet the dissonant elements find resolution as a means of conveying the religious message and promise of atonement, in all senses of the word's meaning. The dissonance in "Confrontation" is communicated by the drum and symbol sounds juxtaposed with a classical, orchestral-inspired sample called "Invasion" from Christian Poulet and Jean-Yves Rigo, which is then silenced when interstitial, militant speeches from Haile Selassie and Marcus Garvey are spliced in.[87] There is no harmony between the instrumental and vocal pieces, however, and the dissonance is fostered by the splicing together of musical and nonmusical components that have different tempi. In the structural and tonal dynamics of dancehall music, dissonance symbolizes the absence of catharsis, given Jamaica's social dissonance in the era of globalization. As Michael E. Veal points out, ethnomusicologist Veit Erlmann has "speculated that the juxtaposition of radically dissimilar and decontextualized genres in certain forms of world popular music may reflect the violent historical encounter between industrial capitalist and preindustrial societies."[88] Erlmann's speculations certainly ring true in Jamaica, as the dissonance in "Confrontation" is never resolved (unlike in "St. John's Passion") in order to suggest the continued social crisis in the new era of globalization and the absence of long-lasting catharsis during this tragic situation. Through "Confrontation's" dub aesthetic, Damian Marley symbolizes agency as Ogun's combative Will, which occurs as a sonic distortion, and as the paradox or indeterminacy that are emblematic of the Yoruba god's rebellious spirit.

As a secular religion, dancehall music and performance have the power to revive the socially dead, thereby having the potential for revolution, while paradoxically taming this revolutionary spirit because the music also functions as an opiate. Nietzsche's comment about the importance of art to "tame" the nihilistic Will when one is powerless to change their situation helps to shed light on the underlying paradox that exists within dancehall culture: "Here, at this moment of supreme danger for the will, art approaches as a saving sorceress with the power to heal. Art alone can re-direct those repulsive thoughts about the terrible or absurd nature of existence into representations with which man can live; these representations are the *sublime*, whereby the terrible is tamed by artistic means, and the comical, whereby disgust at absurdity is discharged by artistic means."[89] Although dancehall music harmonizes at times, its overwhelming social and musical dissonance suggests that performativity blurs the boundaries between symbolic performance itself and what Nietzsche would characterize as the "terrible and absurd of existence" in the inner city of West Kingston. In a Jamaican context, catharsis through performance is only temporary, as the permanent imposition of resolution would be aesthetically false to the material reality. In a way, this idea is similar to Frank B. Wilderson III's premise in *Afropessimism* that Blackness in the African American experience "emanates from a condition of suffering for which there is no imaginable strategy for redress—no narrative of social, political, or national redemption."[90] Rather than the complete foreclosure that Wilderson describes, dancehall music strives toward catharsis with the goal of dispelling violence, yet its cathartic function is sometimes displaced by actual instances of violence. This pleasure/pain paradox is at the core of the slave experience and the collective memory of their descendants. Saidiya Hartman explains that, for the slave, pain was "essential to the making of productive slave laborers" and that "the sheer enormity of this pain overwhelms or exceeds the limited forms of redress available to the enslaved." It is with this significance that the "performative lies not in the ability to overcome this condition or provide remedy but in creating a context for the collective enunciation of this pain, transforming need into politics and cultivating pleasure as a limited response to need and a desperately insufficient form of redress."[91] While many dancehall deejays such as Damian Marley do not glorify the violence, their artistic representation of the unrest is often misinterpreted as glorification. Dancehall music and violence thus become integrally linked as a conscious expression for the sublime violence from slavery and its aftermath.

Dancehall Music as Metalanguage

Although dancehall music functions as the iconic expression of the bloody turmoil in Jamaica, it was not responsible for making Kingston the "murder capital" of the world in 2005. In a Sunday edition of *The Daily Gleaner*, veteran journalist Ian Boyne criticized prominent dancehall deejays for their performative play with violence. In a June 5, 2005 article entitled "Waltzing with Wolves: Dancehall's Link to Violence," he argues that the wider Jamaican society has shown "disgust" toward the "gunman terrorist" except for the dancehall. Boyne adds that "The dancehall is the only space in which the gunman has honour, recognition and 'ratings.' In the dancehall it is no shame to be a gunman. Indeed, you have pride of place there."[92] He goes on to say that dancehall deejays "glorify nihilistic violence," which "contributes to the culture of criminality in the country."[93] Unabashedly, Boyne labels the arguments put forth in the defense of dancehall music as "fallacious," in particular arguments that suggest that the artist is "merely reflecting the injustices, inequalities and the dehumanization of his environment." He anticipates criticism that will identify him as a "middle class hypocrite" and acknowledges that the deejays are not responsible for their "dehumanising conditions" but states that "their lyrics reinforce and strengthen the negatives of their environment": "A youth oppressed by the ruling class, starved of opportunities, stigmatized as belonging to a 'worthless good for nothing' class; stereotyped as a criminal, actually participates in his own oppression. He aids the oppressor class by spouting lyrics which reinforce the prejudices toward ghetto people and which besmirch the majority of decent people who live in the inner city."[94]

Referencing B. F. Skinner's determinism theory, Boyne argues that it is not in anyone's best interest to make excuses for the artists' "uncivilised behavior and violent lyrics" and that it is a "patronizing and literally dehumanising view" of the inner-city people, the youth in particular, as "mindless automatons 'beyond freedom and dignity' who can't help but reflect their conditions."[95] He undercuts the claims of Carolyn Cooper, the leading scholar of dancehall culture at the University of the West Indies at the time, including her argument that Bob Marley's music contains violent lyrics, too. Boyne undermines Cooper by linking Marley's lyrics to "revolutionary violence to end oppression" and by characterizing dancehall music's "glorification" of the *shotta* as promoting "nihilistic violence."[96] Despite the seeming soundness of many of Boyne's claims, he nonetheless overlooks the fact that roots reggae Nyabinghi drumming draws upon the Burru music and dance that had a tradition of celebrating criminality.[97]

The violence in dancehall music is nothing new—it is part of a long historical trajectory in which a revolutionary dialectic "waltzes" with violence. Hebdige notes that, given the vast unemployment in West Kingston during the rise of the Rastas and *rudies*, the "embittered youth abandoned the society which claimed to serve them" and turned to the "locksman [Rastas] for explanations, to listen to his music, and emulate his posture of withdrawal." What is more, as Hebdige suggests, "it should hardly surprise us to find that, behind the swagger and sex, the violence and the cool of the Rude Boy music of the sixties stands the visionary Rastaman with his commodious rhetoric, his all embracing metaphors."[98] While Hebdige offers keen insights into the reception of earlier forms of Jamaican music, he, too, regards the music as "simple celebration of deviant and violent behavior."[99] He does admit, however, that "there was a trend away from undirected violence, bravado and competitive individualism of the early sixties, towards a more articulate and informed anger; and if crime continued to offer the only solution available, then there were new distinctions to be made."[100] As with dancehall music, roots reggae had suffered a great deal from the stigma of its association with nihilistic violence, thus overlooking its implicit revolutionary mission, which is distorted by the slave sublime paradox of its Ogunistic worldview and its indeterministic polysemic signs, as it performs (at times destructive) responses to state-sanctioned violence.

Boyne offers his claims during a time when Jamaica was scrambling to identify the factors contributing to the *BBC*'s labeling of West Kingston as "murder capital of the world." The notion of "waltzing with wolves" is a clever and strategic play of language to produce a highly alliterative, political sound bite that deflects attention away from state-sanctioned modes of violence.[101] In his frantic finger pointing, while acknowledging to some extent the dire social and economic circumstances, Boyne overlooks the importance of the slave sublime paradox that the music's Ogunistic worldview reveals. Although the high murder rate in Jamaica is immensely tragic,[102] by adopting an Ogunic worldview that paradoxically both mimes and challenges the Dionysiac, the deejays are able to, as Nietzsche argues, "transform those repulsive thoughts about the terrible and absurd aspects of existence into representations with which it was possible to live; these representations are the sublime, whereby the terrible is tamed by artistic means."[103] The form of expression that the Ogunic worldview adopts is indeed wedded with tragedy and is sometimes rendered under a comedic guise, which, as a result, is taken at face value as glorification of nihilistic violence.[104]

Unlike Boyne's firm stance against the violent lyrics in dancehall music, Chang and Chen state in *Reggae Route* that the mounting violence represented in dancehall music at the time was "nothing new." They question the value, however, interrogating whether an artist such as Ninjaman was simply reflecting or actually valorizing violence in his music. Despite the tentativeness of this position, Chang's and Chen's commentary seems to point to the deejay's performance as holding up a mirror to society because his "gun talk" and "badmanism" reflect the levels of violence occurring in the society.[105] Arguably, there is no clear distinction between valorization and imitation, and the conflict points to the multiple elements of mimesis that include imitation, representation, and mimicry. As a mimetic strategy, the deejay assumes the role of simulating or framing the reality of the violence that exists in Jamaica. As is well known, Aristotle pointed out that the more closely an imitation approximates reality, the more fraudulent it appears. Myth and ritual have the important symbolic function of narratology, for conveying and exhibiting "the story of trauma."[106] More precisely, the kind of imitation that Ninjaman and other artists such as Mavado undertake is further complicated by elements of both mimesis and diegesis because it involves, respectively, a *telling* (narration and report) in the lyrical sense and a *showing* (imitation and representation) in the performative sense. Essentially, at the core of Boyne's as well as Chang's and Chen's critique are the issues of *mediation* and *reflection*. Considering Andrew Salkey's prologue in *A Quality of Violence* and its representation of a shattered mirror, realistic mimesis and its forms of narrative resolution, having failed, suggest only a "mirroring" that is true to the shattering effects of the slave sublime condition it reflects, given its dissonance that mediates the social crisis and psychic despair.

The term mediation has resonance with the words intermediary, medium, and agent. As Raymond Williams has defined the term, mediation "describe[s] the process of relationship between 'society' and 'art,' or between 'the base' and 'the superstructure.'" Williams warns that we "should not expect to find (or always to find) directly 'reflected' social realities in art, since these (often or always) pass through a process of 'mediation' in which their original content is changed."[107] Through the process of mediation, dancehall deejays project the social realities but change them by adopting symbols as a means of indirect expression. As such, dancehall deejays have been criticized for promoting violence rather than being identified as commenting on or reflecting what they see. Williams notes that this process of mediation serves as a "metaphor of 'reflection'": "It is virtually impossible to sustain the metaphor of 'mediation' . . . without some sense of separate and pre-existent areas or orders of reality, between which the mediating process occurs whether independently or as determined by their prior natures. Within the inheritance of idealistic philosophy the process is usually, in practice, seen as a mediation between categories, which have been assumed to be distinct. Mediation, in this range of use, then seems little more than a sophistication of reflection."[108] Williams explains that reality (as a social process) and the act of conveying reality (as a linguistic mode of expression) when regarded as "categorically distinct" result "inevitably" in disparate concepts such as reflection and mediation, involving, respectively, the same tension between "production and reproduction of real life." There is an underlying correlation between the two terms, however. The dichotomy could be bridged, as Williams argues, by seeing "language and signification as indissoluble elements of the material process itself, involved all the time both in production and reproduction."[109] From this perspective, the deejay's role as an intermediary in the process of mediation can be seen as positive, as a necessary part of making meanings and values in the political and social process of polysemic signification through language. Given the various personas that the deejays adopt as warrior figures, including Ogun via the don/*shotta*, a clear distinction between reflection and valorization (as a form of mediation) is very difficult to evince, as both the social practices of violence and the symbolic and actual expressions of it occur simultaneously, yet ambiguously.

What has been absent until now is a reading of the dancehall art form as a metalanguage in which structures and form are imperative—both as discrete and dynamic polysemic entities that capture the ineffable aspects of language that exceed method. To put it simply, dancehall music harmonizes the turbulent into form as a metalanguage. This raises a question: Once there is a metalanguage, can violence be represented? Roland Barthes notes that the "signifier of myth presents itself in an ambiguous way: it is at the same time meaning and form, full on one side and empty on the other. As meaning, the signifier already postulates a reading ... [I]t has a sensory reality (unlike the linguistic signifier, which is purely mental)." For Barthes, when a myth (in this case, dancehall as a musical form that conveys violence through the Ogun warrior archetype) "becomes form, the meaning leaves its contingency behind; it empties itself, it becomes impoverished, history evaporates, only the letter remains." He explains that this impoverishment or erasure of history denies meaning to the form, resulting in the "paradoxical permutation in the reading operations, an abnormal regression from meaning to form, from linguistic sign to the mythical signifier."[110] In Jamaica, performance rituals (both secular and religious) have had the historical function of combating oppression.

When critics focus on form alone they empty out the history and its connected moral imperatives, leaving it with what Barthes calls a "penury" or "impoverishment" of form. Dick Hebdige references Barthes in *Subculture: The Meaning of Style* and remarks that "contemporary bourgeois societies are subject to a systematic distortion, liable at any moment to be dehistoricized, 'naturalized,' converted into myth."[111] For a complete reading, as Barthes encourages, form must be rooted in its meaning and "It is this constant game of hide-and-seek between meaning and the form which defines myth."[112] However, as Barthes insists, the function of myth is to "distort" rather than to erase. Thus, in myth, form lends itself to a "literal, immediate presence" because it is attached to a given "meaning" in which the "elements of form therefore are related as to place and proximity: the mode of presence of the form is spatial" because "elements are linked by associative relations."[113] Taking into consideration both Raymond Williams's and Roland Barthes's claims, one may argue that dancehall music and culture (as a counter-hegemonic myth) function as a mirror of society that reflects through the deejay, who functions as an intermediary, distorted messages about violence that are only taken at face value to be mere celebration. Barthes notes that the "relation which unites the concept of the myth to its meaning is essentially a relation of *deformation*."[114] As Barthes also argues in *Mythologies*, myth is a system or mode of signification that conveys discourse, which is not defined by its object but by the manner of its utterance.[115] In Jamaica, distortion is enabled by class-driven ideologies in which history is drained from the political imperatives of the dancehall form in order to attain the linguistic meaning that the genre's primary function is to incite violence. In this manner, dancehall music is perceived simply as language rather than a metalanguage. As a result, its signs are taken at face value, thus overlooking the system of distorted meanings, polysemic character, and symbolic disguise—strategies that are inherited from slavery to disguise encoded meanings from the master class. One underlying point is that there is potency in the dancehall form as a revolutionary engine in its contingency as a primary language and value system. In this sense, meaning is attached to dancehall as engaging in and connected to the historical continuum of resistance and rebellion.

As Barthes has argued, form and meaning are two discrete yet dynamic aspects of myth. Despite this, many critics of dancehall music have overlooked this multilayered characteristic by either focusing on form alone to determine a literal meaning or erroneously pointing to meaning solely in its aesthetic sense, thereby reducing dancehall music to mere reflection and not interrogating the dialectic of material and form. As I've discussed in this book, narrative structures steeped within literary realism, as inherited from the West, call for particular forms of representativity and resolution. Dancehall music, on the other hand, assumes the dissonant material of contemporary violence into its form as signified it by its very refusal of resolution. It is not merely mimetic, as it involves a reflection on form and history. By casting the performance as ritualized dramas, Cooper points to the political aspect of dancehall musical lyrics, which "urgently articulate the struggle of the celebrants in the dance to reclaim their humanity in the circumstances of grave economic hardship that force the animal out of its lair."[116] Cooper's argument, although well-intentioned, suggests that dancehall is merely an expressive outlet—not a reflective medium—another version of not interrogating form. Nonetheless, she highlights a key difference between the rhetoric of the sound and literature, that is, the multiple layers of signification that accompany a performance.[117] Yet the music has been met with harsh criticism because of the ambiguity that it is wedded to its form as a system of myth/metalanguage, which is defined by intention rather than its literal meaning. Barthes explains the "duplicity" of the signifier in a myth:

> How is a myth received? We must here come back to the duplicity of its signifier, which is at once meaning and form. I can produce three different types of reading by focusing on the one, or the other, or both at the same time. If I focus on an empty signifier, I let the concept fill the form of the myth without ambiguity . . . If I focus on a full signifier, in which I clearly distinguish the meaning and the form, and consequently the distortion which the one imposes on the other, I undo the signification of the myth, and I received the latter as an imposture . . . Finally, if I focus on the mythical signifier as an inextricable whole made of meaning and form, I receive an ambiguous signification: I respond to the constituting mechanism of myth, its own dynamics, I become a reader of myths.[118]

As such, dancehall music is seen as merely garrulous in form and functioning in the simplistic service of promoting violence, and this perception deforms the underlying meaning, thus alienating meaning from form that, in turn, lends to its negative identity.

The explicit verbal wordplay in dancehall seems to be at the heart of the contention, whereas the wordplay in literature is oftentimes stated very subtly. While the novel struggles to represent violence due to the aesthetic limitations of its form, as I have discussed in chapters 1 and 4, the issue is effectively handled by dancehall music—not merely *what* the musical artists say but *how* they talk about it deserves attention, which may suggest the possible viability of oral forms and the need to redeem them as valid forms of expression. As a performative text, the body is utilized as a means of counteracting the legacies of slavery, apprenticeship, and colonialism and the current, concomitant cultural and economic encroachments from the Global North. Paul Gilroy has argued that performance is the means by which Black artists have debated modernity, particularly on the basis of music's power to disturb both language and textuality as "preeminent expressions of human consciousness."[119] In a way, too, we must heed Julian Henriques's echoing of Gilroy when he prompts us to shift our understanding from only equating logos with word and to consider also the significance of sonic and visual semiotics within dancehall culture[120]—which, as I argue, are fundamental to dancehall's metalanguage, which revels in linguistic indeterminacy and paradoxes. This is the terrain wherein the Ogun archetype as a slave sublime aesthetic of dancehall culture can be understood as mounting a counter-hegemonic resistance in which logos is connected to somatic discourse and sonic disturbance against class/racial hierarchies and economic systems such as globalization that preserve plantation structures as the changing same from slavery. No doubt, oral forms complicate aesthetic values and threaten the long-standing hierarchical value of written texts because of the subject matter and audience they serve. It is therefore important to consider the subversive power of representing violence in musical culture while remaining cognizant of the racialist discourse that positions Black sound (and people) as violent.

Coda

"Walk and live. Talk and bombo claut dead," a line from the 1997 Jamaican dancehall movie *Dancehall Queen*, summarizes (with the expletive "bombo claut") the notion that open speech can be dangerous. Something as simple as a walk is a lively text, rich with the polysemic modes and nodes of expression, which nonetheless is bound up extralinguistically through image and iconicity as a form of cloaked speech. Coded language or "cloaked speech" is a form of "hidden transcript," a term that Tricia Rose uses to denote the openly expressed yet camouflaged codes of conduct that invert social stigmas. As Rose argues, "cloaked speech and disguised cultural codes" are used as a means of "comment[ing] on and challeng[ing] aspects of current power inequalities" as one engages in a "symbolic and ideological warfare."[1] In Jamaica and elsewhere in the African diaspora, cloaked speech is a social practice, a performative culture that can be traced back to slavery, a time when open speech was considered to be transgressive because the planters feared that communication among the slaves would lead to a rebellion. The dispossession that is fostered by historical and contemporary forms of violence has been translated to a performative context, a context in which open speech is often considered dangerous and is therefore censored. Facing the exigencies of New World slavery, colonialism, and globalization, Afro-diasporic peoples have utilized performance culture as a linguistic mode of communication.

The proposition that contemporary violence functions as a nonverbal expression of the slave sublime (a reaction to the unbroken histories of oppression) helps to explain why the deeply felt structures that underpin the legacies of violence and dispossession challenge a scribal representation in the realist novel. Drawing upon Gilroy's radical critique of modernity and its high regard for textuality, chapters 3 and 5 have explored the ways in which reggae's sonic language and the metalanguage of dancehall music (through its extralinguistic performance of violence) have the ability to disturb Western textuality. While the genre of magical realism suggests a movement toward a more suitable aesthetic form, its scribal element confronts the legacy of linguistic and psychic violence that is embedded in a colonial language. My discussion in chapter 2 of the alternative, demotic language that is present in Philip's poetry, particularly in *She Tries Her Tongue*, pinpoints the counter-hegemonic potential that lies within Afro-diasporic vernacular culture.

The viability of dancehall music as an oral form can be linked to its indeterminate lyricism and the iconic signs that are constantly in flux, as they are reimagined in relation to the latest fashion and dance trends, which immediately speak about the cultural, social, and political moment. The iconic signs' lack of fixity is connected to an emergent vernacular culture and a living language that challenges continually in its countercultural discourse the ideologies and sensibilities of middle- and upper-class Jamaicans. It is not merely what is said but how it is said that is a major point of contention. Within this context, dancehall music and culture constitute a metalanguage with codes, symbols, and icons that are expressed in the carnivalesque mode of dressing provocatively and outlandishly as well as the so-called vulgar manner of speaking *patwa*, both of which undermine middle- and upper-class sensibilities. Thus dancehall musical aesthetes can be identified physically by their manner of speaking and dressing, their bodily language, and their ideological stance. In these carnivalesque expressions, the carnival is *ever-present*, suggesting that the struggles are constant and that the field of inversion is not limited to a particular time or place. Using the body as a text, dancehall artists and aesthetes announce vociferously through polysemic symbols the installation of a new mode of social order that is both intrinsically and extrinsically connected to spectacle and exteriority. This subaltern negotiation of what is deemed acceptable within Jamaican culture is carried out on the body, which serves as a sight/site of contestation that visually expresses group belonging or cultural citizenship.

In the context of globalization and in the forced construction of global identities, the body serves as an inscription, a sight/site of performance and contestation that also expresses visually the cultural citizenship of dancehall music. Building upon the political potentialities of reggae, its musical forerunner, dancehall music functions as a *bricolage* and speech act that fill in the gaps and silences of a history and culture founded upon violence. This silencing equates with marginality by imposing alternate belief systems to legitimize conquest, as I've discussed in chapters 2 and 4, such as the salvific rhetoric underlying the nineteenth-century conquest of Africa and the neoliberal agenda underlying globalization.

Nonetheless, the problematics of dancehall music cannot be overlooked. I have argued that dancehall performers harness the creative and destructive spirit that characterizes paradoxically the subversive powers of Ogun, a Yoruba deity. In the Caribbean context, the Ogun archetype is a mimetic response to the tragedy associated with the Dionysiac nature of slavery and its afterlife. This mimetic response and symbolic form of retribution are connective tissues to the slave sublime concept that respond to the current iterations of plantation structures and their supporting myths, which enact violence while purporting to be a (divine) myth of salvation for the exploited. This "violence mythos" is connected to power and "is based upon the control as exploitative force, dualism, hierarchy, detachment, and the mind/body split, all abstracted elements of trauma experience and symbolized in a hero mythology."[2] By adopting an outlook that at times mimes the Dionysiac worldview that accompanied colonization, musical performers sometimes elide the boundaries between pleasure and pain, fantasy and reality in their performance of violence. Even though dancehall music displays every so often the dissonant material of violence into its form, it should be noted that the mode of expressing violence is not merely mimetic, given its reflection on form and history as a metalanguage that conceals its signs. Music and violence have thus become integrally related as a conscious, material expression of the slave sublime. As a means of counteracting historical and contemporary forms of dispossession and as an expression of the slave sublime, dancehall draws upon religiously based rituals (such as Pocomania and Rastafari/Nyabinghi drumming) that exist in Jamaica's cultural repository, as I've discussed in chapters 1 and 3. However, the performance ritual of dancehall has taken on a secular quality because of its strategic public discourse and modes of consumption. It fosters the practice of a radical form of democracy, given its contestation of physical and social spaces in the blurring between public and private spaces and given its viability and connection to (legitimate and illegitimate) underground economies. Dancehall is an *everyday* practice in which the body is reclaimed and articulated socially, albeit to a limited extent.

This book centers on a discussion about the ways in which violence can be socially articulated in the continued presence of plantation structures. It also explores the importance of aesthetic form and the related tensions between speech and writing, silence and speech, writing and performance. While this study is primarily centered on Jamaica, I've also addressed the larger question of violence in the Caribbean, given the shared history of slavery, colonialism, and globalization—regimes that utilize rhetorical strategies as a means of legitimizing and replicating former modes of dispossession and a way of maintaining social death through newer mechanisms of the plantation structure. Through a Foucauldian lens, I offer a new understanding of the ghetto to reveal a persisting assumption from the Enlightenment era that Africans (and their descendants) are animals incapable of reason and thus to be relegated to the category of the nonhuman "Other" and confined. The trope of madness represented in various Caribbean literary and musical texts demonstrates how historically the poor and unemployed were lumped together with those categorized as insane and confined away from "civilized" society, given that madness is also a construction based on notions about the inability to reason. The confinement in the ghetto is a slave sublime experience in which Manichean despair stems from unequal socioeconomic and physical divisions— the structural violence of inadequate housing, poor education, joblessness or underemployment—and limited avenues for escape. The ghetto is a place where the police in the role of overseer or slave driver keep the poor in confinement and at bay, a way to maintain the social and physical divide through violence to protect capital in a color-based oligopoly. This sense of a constrained Black subjectivity, similar to that of a bounded slave, allows us to think about binary terms such as human/animal, reason/imagination, sane/insane, and freedom/unfreedom in relation to the power to inflict both social and physical death. In discovering this paradigmatic aspect of violence, I've offered the unique perspective that slavery is the Real of freedom, in the Lacanian sense, and that the Real returns to its point of origin—in this case, the originary violence of conquest and slavery.[3] Reading Henry Whiteley's *Excessive Cruelty to Slaves: Three Months in Jamaica in 1832* (1832), written during slavery, and James Williams's *Narrative* (1837), written during the apprentice era, made me realize that the practices of violence under apprenticeship were no different from slavery—that the only difference was that the official nomenclature had changed. That finding allowed me to make a genealogical link between slave drivers and the contemporary Jamaican police force, which is known formally as the Jamaican Constabulary Force. These linguistic or rhetorical strategies of substitution suggest that violence operates as a language. It is within this framework that I offer the compelling argument that (post)colonial violence can be mapped on the paradigmatic axis of language because it operates through modes of substitution that denote similarity or resemblance.

As a concept, the slave sublime focuses on affect and mediation as two crucial issues. The term conveys the idea that the experience of slavery remains *ever-present*, a challenge to Kant's epistemological premise about the disinterest and transitory nature of the sublime, which he consigns to the mind while dismissing the body's importance. In my reading of Elaine Scarry's description of torture in *The Body in Pain*, I see an implicit engagement with the sublime that exceeds the cognitive basis to suggest the embodiment of pain. By defining the slave sublime, I extend Scarry's point by suggesting an interconnection between embodied pain and mobilizing the imagination so as to mediate such extreme affect, thereby unshackling and redeeming the imagination's importance to contemplations of the sublime. Although Orlando Patterson's notion of "social death" speaks to the slave's constrained agency, the slave sublime recognizes a paradoxical agency that expands our understanding of "social death" to move beyond a historiography of slavery and to consider violence from the perspective of the slave for whom the sublime is linked to interest rather than the disinterest Kant posits. The descendants of slaves articulate the continued unfreedom since emancipation in a distorted language, in a manner similar to what Roland Barthes describes in *Mythologies*, but as a metalanguage that grammaticizes violence.

As I argue, the Caribbean subject's identity stems from their entrance and embeddedness into a language of violence (given Lacan's ideas about the significance of language to subject formation), namely the physical and symbolic violence of plantation systems that are not only sustained by judicial codes but also facilitated by their transformation under neoliberalism, in which hegemonic systems such as the IMF maintain the sublime presence of slavery as the Real of freedom. Despite superficial *changes*, plantation systems remain the *same* in their rendering of dispossession and social death—as transhistorical metaphoric substitutions that reveal a paradigmatic structuring of violence similar to language. The neoliberal discourse presenting the United States as a savior disguises, for instance, that the hegemonic imperatives of substituting free market enterprise for political/economic autonomy have led to more debt and poverty—not to mention the encroachment upon national sovereignty in the economic dispossession.

The aftermath of the novel coronavirus pandemic and its COVID-19 disease, which has been wreaking havoc around the world, may have even more devastating consequences for people in both the developing and developed world. The first instance will occur when the United States decides to transfer its debts from the bailouts to countries in the Global South. The fact that the United States Treasury can manufacture money without any tangible backing (such as a gold reserve) is a subject for magical realism. This attempt to stabilize market forces and to prevent a severe economic depression certainly challenges once again the myth about the invisible hand of the market. What looms ahead for Jamaica and the rest of the Global South is that the terms of their debts from the IMF and World Bank will most likely be reassessed again with stringent measures to eke out capital—to pay off the price tag for the trillion dollar bailouts. The coronavirus pandemic has also been met with global outcries against police brutality, primarily stemming from the brutal death of George Floyd and other African Americans. The various demonstrations led by Black Lives Matter activists provide further evidence to support the broader Afro-diasporic experience of the slave sublime in relation to the continued dishonoring of black bodies by state agents who adhere to plantation-derived, racist ideologies that devalue black lives. That is to say, similar to their Caribbean counterparts, Black people who live in developed Western societies also experience the ever-present fear that marks the slave sublime experience as police agents maintain the violence that ruled over the slave plantation. Frantz Fanon has already warned us in *The Wretched of the Earth* about the fratricidal violence that normally occurs when the economically oppressed and socially dispossessed seek an outlet for the pent-up frustration stemming from such conditions. In the United States, the coronavirus pandemic disproportionately affected Black people because of the continued racial inequality since slavery. For Blacks, this slave sublime realization is further compounded by an economic recession stemming from the pandemic, continued extralegal killings that are reminiscent of Jim Crow–era lynching, and a smoldering national tension spurred on by an acrimonious president supporting iconic remnants of the Confederacy and reigniting racist rhetoric about white supremacy. We need only think about the waves of fratricidal violence among African Americans during the July 4, 2020 weekend marking the United States' independence with its foundation firmly cemented in institutionalized racism (and racialized terror) to maintain an oligopoly centered around white power. Since the incidents of July 4, the blood of young African Americans continues to color red the streets of major U.S. cities such as Chicago. What is needed is not "law and order" but a commitment to social justice to correct the inequalities stemming from the enduring legacy of plantation slavery. More than ever, this is certainly a time when the slave sublime is an apt term for denoting this continued awe and terror among Afro-diasporic people, not only in the Caribbean but also in the wider Black Atlantic region, in which the displeasure associated with the sublime does not disappear in a transcendent moment when reason polices the imagination, as Kantian philosophy suggests. The cultural output representing these troubling times and the ever-present terrors stemming from the specter of slavery will bear aesthetic markers delineating the slave sublime experience in which the imagination and body are important.

Notes

Introduction

1. Demonstrating some improvement in 2014, Jamaica ranked sixth place worldwide (Campbell and Clarke 93). As of 2018, Jamaica maintains its top three ranking in the Americas—the region with the highest per capita homicide rate in the world—coming in behind Venezuela and El Salvador (Dalby and Carranza 1).

2. BBC Caribbean, "Jamaica 'Murder Capital of the World.'"

3. According to the July 1997 Report of the National Committee on Political Tribalism, the close proximity between garrison communities in West Kingston has posed a challenge to the maintenance of law and order, impeding movement and in turn affecting "human rights, transportation, and job attendance and opportunities." To a large degree, these communities function autonomously as states within a state, leading the Jamaican State to argue that it "has no authority or power except in as far as its forces are able to invade in the form of police and military raids." Each garrison community is framed by its allegiance to one of the two leading political parties in Jamaica (the Jamaica Labour Party [JLP] and the People's National Party [PNP]) and their formation has "become central to the practice of electoral manipulation," as constituents who function as a reservoir of loyal voters. Criminal gangs within the garrison communities function both as leaders of the underground criminal economies and as "perpetrators of political violence and election malpractices." The garrison communities under their control benefit from the scant allocation of resources from the political benefactor. What happens as a result is large scale political "homogenisation" in each community and the "increasing incidence of violence and the attendant space of murders and serious bodily injuries." And despite the system of political patronage that exists, the "living conditions of the people in most of the 'tribalised' communities . . . reek of abandonment and neglect" that includes "[s]ub-standard housing, poor sanitation and numerous environmental hazards. It comes as no surprise that poverty has been identified as the main reason for both the development and the maintenance of garrison communities in Jamaica" (https://repository.arizona.edu/bitstream/handle/10150/192313/azu_etd_mr20090047_sip1_m.pdf?sequence=1&isAllowed=y).

4. My use of Paul Gilroy's term slave sublime extends the original concept by taking into account violence, the repeating histories of domination in the Caribbean, and the "rationalistic" discourse from the West that sought to legitimize brutality. This codification of the concept suggests an attempt to recuperate the mind/body split about sublimity, which informed Kant's discourse, for example.

5. Barrett, Sr., *The Rastafarians*, 29.

6. Patterson, *Slavery and Social Death*, 1.

7. Patterson, 5–13.

8. T. Lacey, *Violence and Politics in Jamaica*, 22.

9. Quijano, "Coloniality," 169.

10. In *Mythologies*, Roland Barthes argues that a myth functions as a metalanguage in that it conceals signs through the process of similarity and then dissociates the sign from its historical significance—a process through which signs may appear as natural, as a way to disguise their underlying ideology. For a myth to work in its full political deployment, it depends on the meaning(s) associated with the original sign, but in that instance it erases the historical context of the original sign. Thus, its power comes from such distortions and are not arbitrary because they translate existing signs into signifiers.

11. Brown, "Spiritual Terror," 24.

12. Brown, 28–29.

13. Brown, 24.

14. Brown, 32.

15. Patterson, *Slavery and Social Death*, 5–8.

16. Patterson, 8–10.

17. Patterson, 37.

18. Scarry, *The Body in Pain*, 28.

19. Scarry, 29.

20. Scarry, 49.

21. Scarry, 53.

22. Scarry, 54.

23. Scarry, 39.

24. Scarry, 47

25. W. E. B. DuBois makes a similar point in *The Souls of the Black Folk*, in which he links the experience of disenfranchised African Americans during the Reconstruction era to being trapped in a "prison-house" with unscalable walls.

26. Scarry, *The Body in Pain*, 28.

27. To understand the term transhistorical, Dominick LaCapra suggests that we think about history in relation to the "problem of limits" especially when there are "extreme events" that are "limit breaking" and "radically transgressive." He goes on to explain that "Any closure, terminal date, or periodization is placed in question when one addresses the mutual implication of the past, present, and future or the insistence of repetitive temporalities that may come with unsettling disorientation" (2–3).

28. Kant, *The Critique of Judgment*, 129–30.

29. Scarry, *The Body in Pain*, 3.

30. Scarry, 27.

31. Scarry, 46.

32. Scarry, 46.

33. Scarry, 12.

34. Scarry, 57.

35. Horkheimer and Adorno, *Dialectic of Enlightenment*, 1.

36. Scarry, *The Body in Pain*, 58.

37. That same violence is harnessed as agency, similar to Frantz Fanon's notions about colonial delirium and "collective autodestruction" in *The Wretched of the Earth* (52–54).

38. Scarry, *The Body in Pain*, 4.

39. Brown, "Spiritual Terror," 32.

40. Scarry, *The Body in Pain*, 28.

41. Gilligan, *Violence*, 75.

42. Gilligan, 61.

43. Archer and Gartner, *Violence and Crime*, 66, 75.

44. LaCapra, *History and Its Limits*, 1.

45. Craton, *Testing the Chains*, 325.

46. Heuman, *The Killing Time*, xiii.

47. Burton, *Afro-Creole*, 111.

48. In my discussion of Bob Marley's music in chapter 3, I talk about this trope of "fire" with its imaginative link to Armageddon. Marley's music functions as a historical memory of the violence, and in songs such as "Slave Driver" Marley reenacts this originary violence but turns the table on the master when he uses his imagination to cast himself as a transhistorical slave who has transcended time and space. I return to this trope of "fire" in chapter 5 in my discussion of the Ogun archetype that underlies Jamaican dancehall music.

49. Heuman and Trotman, *Contesting Freedom*, xxi–xxvi.

50. Heuman and Trotman, xxi–xxvi.

51. Mintz, *Sweetness and Power*, 176.

52. Lowe, *The Intimacies*, 46, 135.

53. N. Roberts, *Freedom as Marronage*, 9.

54. Iadicola and Shupe, *Violence, Inequality*, 427.

55. In *Scenes of Subjection*, Saidiya Hartman argues that "the texture of freedom is laden with the vestiges of slavery" because the "plantation system" is reorganized "through contiguous forms of subjection" (116–127).

56. The continued deferral of freedom since emancipation speaks to this tradition of European thought about the *human* in relation to ethics, affect, aesthetics, and freedom, a critique that Sylvia Wynter and Achille Mbembe both offer.

57. I offer more explanation later in this introduction on the definition of violence, particularly its linguistic and symbolic significance, from Žižek and Fanon.

58. Please note that the apprenticeship system replaced slavery and complete emancipation did not occur until 1838. Apprenticeship is often referred to as "slavery by another name."

59. Reagan, "Remarks."

60. Jones, "The Changing Same," 200.

61. Jones, 180.

62. McDowell, *The Changing Same*, xviii.

63. Mbembe, *Critique*, 113.

64. Mbembe, 131.

65. Žižek, *Violence*, 11–12.

66. Mbembe, *Critique*, 79.

67. Steger, "Ideologies," 14–19.

68. Žižek, *Violence*, 1.

69. Žižek, 2.

70. Steger, "Ideologies," 16–22.

71. Žižek, *Violence*, 2.

72. Mbembe, *Critique*, 131.

73. Ricoeur, *Oneself as Another*, 2–3.

74. Mbembe, *Critique*, 132.

75. Mbembe, 108, 107.

76. Mbembe, 131.

77. Mbembe, 131.

78. The ongoing use of the U.S. military is an overt display of American hegemony which, as well as covert missions involving the CIA, suggests the prescience of Fanon's 1957 ideas in *The Wretched of the Earth*—the idea that multinational corporations from First World countries function as capitalist masters that use their governments' military power for advantage in developing nations in the Third World.

79. Fanon, *Wretched*, 52–54.

80. Sartre, "Preface," 20.

81. In *Reflections*, Sorel addressed the relationship between myth and revolution. For him, myth is important to the consciousness of revolutionaries for it instills a heroic consciousness in the violent struggles against oppositional forces because "Myth would animate a final revolution and the creation of a fundamentally new social and moral order." On the issue of morality, for Sorel violence "moves from being the mere instrument sometimes called upon to facilitate change to being a key element in the moral transformation of the species" (Finlay 17).

82. Finlay, "Violence and Revolutionary Subjectivity," 20

83. Fanon, *Wretched*, 36–37.

84. Fanon, 43.

85. Girard, *Violence and the Sacred*, 81.

86. Lewis, *Growth of the Modern West Indies*, 29.

87. Seaga, *Revival Cults*, 13.

88. Seaga, 5.

89. Kant, *Critique*, 123.

90. Kant, 102–3.

91. Rundell, "Creativity and Judgement," 102.

92. Rundell, 103.

93. Rundell, 104.

94. Rundell, 105.

95. Kant, *Critique*, 120.

96. Kant, 120.

97. Kant, 122.

98. Kant, 124.

99. Kant, 134.

100. N. Roberts, *Freedom as Marronage*, 30.

101. Hartman, *Scenes of Subjection*, 21.

102. Hartman, 22. This is related to my previous discussion that draws upon Vincent Brown's point about the spectacular displays of violence in Jamaica during slavery.

103. Hartman, 21.

104. In a Jamaican context, one way to consider this is as a paradigmatic substitution of the slave for reconstituted peasant during the colonial era, per Sidney Mintz's argument, suggesting the contiguity between slavery and colonialism—and more importantly between slavery and a developing capitalist system.

105. Hartman, *Scenes of Subjection*, 21.

106. Hartman, 21.

107. Hartman, 21.

108. Hartman, 79.

109. Hartman, 20.

110. Burke, *A Philosophical Inquiry*, 39.

111. Burke, 86.

112. Burke, 65.

113. Burke, 58.

114. Gibbons, *Edmund Burke and Ireland*, 232–33.

115. Gibbons, 23.

116. Gibbons, 232–33.

117. Gibbons, 35.

118. Rundell, "Creativity and Judgement," 102.

119. The sublime, according to Rundell, is "always played in a minor key. While judgements of the sublime, too, are made without interest, the *condition* of sublimity is one of unease, of restlessness, of dissonance. The dissonance is experienced not between the imagination and the understanding, but between the imagination and reason which orientate themselves either to the faculty of cognition of the faculty of desire" (103).

120. Lull, "Communicative Properties," 368.

121. King and Jensen, "Bob Marley" 19.

122. Ehrlich, "The Reggae Arrangement," 52–55.

123. The racist underpinnings of the sublime, particularly the Kantian conception, should be noted. Charles W. Mills points out that Kant was "the most important ethicist of the modern period and the famous theorist of personhood and respect, [who] turn[ed] out to be one of the founders of modern scientific racism, and thus a pioneering theorist of subpersonhood and disrespect" (1382). Note also, as David Lloyd has argued in "The Pathological Sublime: Pleasure and Pain the Colonial Context," that Kant explicitly critiques Burke's mode of explaining the sublime as too "physiological"—that is, not founded on a notion of the formal person or subject but on the individual corporeal frame and its responses. In this sense, Burke, too, is a racist, but the mode of racial judgment is very different from Kant's "modern scientific racism." This is why it is crucial to consider my codification of the slave sublime as an aesthetic of the slave.

124. Henriques, *Sonic Bodies*, xix.

125. Henriques, ix–xv.

126. Henriques, 181.

127. Henriques, 137.

128. Henriques, 140.

129. Henriques, 147.

130. Grammatically speaking, a proper syntactic structure ensures coherence through a logical sequence of the subject, verb, and object.

131. James, *A Brief History*, 81.

132. Cooper, *Sound Clash*, 16.

133. Stanley Niaah, "Dis Slackness Thing," 62.

Chapter One

1. Mbembe, *Critique*, 87.

2. D. Roberts, "Sublime Theories," 178.

3. Spivak, "A Critique of Postcolonial Reason," 13.

4. Wynter, "Unsettling the Coloniality," 264–65.

5. Wynter, 266–67, 287.

6. Sepper, *Descartes's Imagination*, 1.

7. Wynter, "Unsettling the Coloniality," 287–88.

8. Kant, *Critique*, 130.

9. Mbembe, *Critique*, 13.

10. D. Roberts, "Sublime Theories," 171–72.

11. See Lacan's "The Direction of the Treatment and the Principles of its Power."

12. Mbembe, *Critique*, 86.

13. Mbembe, 17.

14. Mbembe, 89.

15. Green, *A British Slave Emancipation*, 328–29.

16. Mbembe, *Critique*, 55.

17. Knox, "British Colonial Policy," 10–11.

18. Luhmann, "European Rationality," 66–67.

19. Robbie Shilliam in his essay "Redemption from Development: Amartya Sen, Rastafari and Promises of Freedom" offers the argument that "classical political economy . . . professed a faith-based episteme" and that the "market was a new tabernacle, wherein sufferers could be blessed by Providence" (6).

20. Paton, *Cultural Politics*, 247.

21. Mignolo, "Delinking," 457.

22. Seaga, *Revival Cults*, 12–13.

23. Paton, *Cultural Politics*, 149.

24. Paton, 316.

25. Stewart, *Three Eyes*, 183.

26. Patterson, *Slavery and Social Death*, 36.

27. Browne, *Surviving Slavery*, 133.

28. American Navy ships undermined Haiti's sovereignty twenty-four times between 1849 and 1913, because, as Noam Chomsky notes, "there was little consideration for the rights of its people" on the assumption that they "'are an inferior people,' unable 'to maintain the degree of civilization left them by the French or to develop any capacity of self-government entitling them to international respect and confidence'" (200). These words spoken by President Woodrow Wilson's Assistant Secretary of State William Philips conveyed the perception that Haitians were unable to "shape" their "own world" if we recall an earlier quote from Mbembe.

29. Paton, *Cultural Politics*, 315.

30. Salkey, *A Quality of Violence*, 22.

31. Salkey, 24.

32. Salkey, 25.

33. Salkey, 48.

34. Paton, *Cultural Politics*, 1.

35. Paton, 1.

36. Seaga, *Revival Cults*, 4.

37. Salkey, *A Quality of Violence*, 44.

38. Green, *British Slave Emancipation*, 328.

39. Irobi, "The Philosophy of the Sea," 10.

40. Patten, "Dancehall Bodies," 399.

41. Henry, *Caliban's Reason*, 84.

42. Fanon, *Black Skins*, 109–10.

43. Mbembe, "Fragile Freedom," 27.

44. Salkey, *A Quality of Violence*, 154.

45. Salkey, 147.

46. Salkey, 146.

47. Stewart, *Three Eyes*, 144. Stewart uses the derivative term Kumina because of the stigma attached to Pocomania.

48. Stewart, 171.

49. Paton, *Cultural Politics*, 3.

50. Paton, 11.

51. Paton, 154.

52. Paton, 120.

53. Paton, 161.

54. Paton, 205.

55. Salkey, *A Quality of Violence*, 36.

56. Salkey, 36.

57. Supriya M. Nair characterizes Wilson Harris's language of the imagination as one that allows for a less overt "political agenda" (177).

58. McWatt, "Wilson Harris," 37.

59. Morris, "Rereading *A Quality*," 101.

60. Mays, *The Norton Introduction*, 111.

61. Stewart, *Three Eyes*, 180.

62. Salkey, *A Quality of Violence*, 37.

63. Salkey, 28.

64. Salkey, 40–41.

65. Nazareth, *In the Trickster Tradition*, 18–20.

66. Salkey, *A Quality of Violence*, 41.

67. Salkey, 10, 71.

68. In *Sweetness and Sugar*, Sidney Mintz refers to Caribbean peasants in this context of the post-slavery era as "reconstituted peasants" to suggest their transition from slaves to peasants (176).

69. Salkey, *A Quality of Violence*, 11.

70. Salkey, 104.

71. Eudell, *Political Languages of Emancipation*, 28, 79.

72. Salkey, *A Quality of Violence*, 11.

73. Salkey, 100.

74. Salkey, 91.

75. Salkey, 101.

76. Salkey, 104.

77. Salkey, 113.

78. Salkey, 123.

79. N. Roberts, *Freedom as Marronage*, 178.

80. Salkey, *A Quality of Violence*, 125.

81. Salkey, 130.

82. Salkey, 60.

83. Browne, *Surviving Slavery*, 148.

84. Browne, 145.

85. Browne, 134.

86. Marshall, "Liminal Anansi," 39.

87. Marshall, 40.

88. Salkey, *A Quality of Violence*, 161.

89. Mbembe, *Critique*, 131.

90. Salkey, *A Quality of Violence*, 175.

91. Salkey, 192.

92. Salkey, 192.

93. Rundell, "Creativity and Judgement," 110.

94. Salkey, *A Quality of Violence*, 171.

95. Rundell, "Creativity and Judgement," 89.

96. Mbembe, *Critique*, 85.

97. Carr, "A Complex Fate," 101.

98. Carr, 103.

99. V. Chang, "So Differently," 165.

100. V. Chang, 165.

101. V. Chang, 170–71.

102. Paton, *Cultural Politics*, 283.

103. D. Roberts, "Sublime Theories," 174.

104. Morris, "Rereading *A Quality*," 100.

105. Wynter qtd. in Morris, 100.

106. Carr, "A Complex Fate," 100–101.

107. Mbembe, *Critique*, 41.

108. Gayatri Spivak calls this state of becoming as a "not-yet-subject" in *A Critique of Postcolonial Reason*.

109. Mbembe, *Critique*, 41–42.

110. Mbembe, 43.

111. Mbembe, 43.

112. Paton, *Cultural Politics*, 302–3.

113. Jonas, *Anancy in the Great House*, 11.

114. Jonas, 52.

115. Jonas, 11.

116. Marshall, "Liminal Anansi," 40.

117. As historian Michael Craton notes in *Empire, Enslavement and Freedom in the Caribbean*, the "subterfuge" of Caribbean slaves against their plantation masters involved "real

life . . . stratagems" that are often attributed to Anancy, which included "exaggerated defer-
ence and disguised satire as well as outright cunning, duplicity and mendacity" (189–90).

118. Salkey qtd. in Nazareth, *In the Trickster Tradition,* 18.

119. Salkey qtd. in Nazareth, 8.

120. Pelton qtd. in Priebe, "Review of *The Trickster,*" 402.

121. Nazareth, "Reviewed Work," 548.

122. Sullivan, "The Irony of Incarnation," 402–3.

123. MacDonald, "Review of *The Trickster,*" 463.

124. McWatt, "Wilson Harris," 34–37.

125. McWatt, 36–37.

126. Rundell explains that "If the imagination is a metaphor or a condition for creativity,
it is also a metaphor or condition for the utopic and dystopic forms it takes. Because cre-
ations are often dystopic, they confront the limits of the sublime, of what is impossible.
This confrontation may force us back near the ground of the beautiful as a politics which
accepts corporeality as finitude. This form of the political is, thus, a form of the imagination
not as redemption nor reconciliation, but as a possibility to imagine differences, plurality
and the autonomy of others" ("Introduction," 11).

127. Rundell, "Introduction," 7.

128. This is Heidegger's argument in *Kant and the Problem of Metaphysics,* although he
refers implicitly to the *Critique of Judgment.*

129. Rundell, "Creativity and Judgement," 88–92.

130. Rundell, 88–92.

131. McWatt, "Wilson Harris," 41.

Chapter Two

1. We can think of Michel Foucault's "The Order of Discourse," which conveys the notion
that it is not just negative images and discourses vehiculated in Western languages but also
the hierarchy of knowledge and language itself that gets to be established. For example,
African/Caribbean languages in which the subaltern spoke were not considered as languages.

2. Sankofa is a West African word that means "We must go back and reclaim our past so
we can move forward; so we understand why and how we came to be who we are today." In
essence, Sankofa signifies a quest for knowledge based on the research and exploration of
primary sources.

3. Trouillot, *Silencing the Past,* 6.

4. Behdad, *Belated Travelers,* 40.

5. Behdad, 40–41.

6. JanMohamed, "The Economy of Manichean Allegory," 87.

7. Pratt, "Scratches," 144–46.

8. Pratt, *Imperial Eyes,* 53.

9. Slemon, "Magical Realism," 414.

10. Reitz, "Review," 363.

11. J. Foster, Jr., "Magical Realism," 271.

12. Erickson, "Metoikoi and Magical Realism," 427.

13. Slemon, "Magical Realism," 410.

14. This hesitation between the realistic and the magical is what Tzvetan Todorov identifies as being the crux of the fantastic genre and its related conventions (25). Philip's use of magical realism is different from Todorov's formulation of the fantastic, and this is particularly important given Todorov's troublesome *Conquest of America*, which deals centrally with language but in a manner that suggests European superiority in the imperial project. His later work shows how colonial attitudes toward language inflect/infect scholarly work, too.

15. Quijano, "Coloniality and Modernity," 170.

16. Philip, *Looking for Livingstone*, 14.

17. Philip, 74.

18. Philip, 11.

19. Mikics, "Derek Walcott," 372–73.

20. Zamora, "Magical Romance," 498.

21. Trouillot, *Silencing the Past*, 27.

22. Bhabha, "In a Spirit," 327.

23. Philip, *Looking for Livingstone*, 10.

24. Philip, 7. The passage displays irony by highlighting the fact that Livingstone is actually Scottish and not English. That is to say, the irony is that he himself comes from a culture in which history was almost erased by British colonization.

25. Philip, 25.

26. Philip, 11.

27. Philip, 11.

28. Philip, 11.

29. Philip, 11.

30. Philip, 12.

31. Philip, 12.

32. Trouillot, *Silencing the Past*, 5.

33. Philip, *Looking for Livingstone*, 12.

34. *The Bible*, John 1:1–3.

35. This is similar to the imagined conversation in which the word is a triplicate used to symbolize materialism, Livingstone's god.

36. *The Bible*, John 1:3–5. See *The New Oxford Annotated Bible*, edited by Bruce M. Metzger and Roland E. Murphy.

37. Kermode, "John," 446.

38. Philip, *Looking for Livingstone*, 16.

39. Henry, *Caliban's Reason*, 23.

40. Henry, 85.

41. Philip, *Looking for Livingstone*, 11.

42. Pratt, *Imperial Eyes*, 53.

43. Busia, "Silencing Sycorax," 86.

44. Spivak, "Can the Subaltern Speak?" 90.

45. Spivak, 91.

46. Spivak, 92.

47. Spivak, 104.

48. Philip, *Looking for Livingstone*, 13.

49. Philip, 13.

50. This metonymic process that Philip utilizes in poetry is a concerted counter-hegemonic strategy, a means of destructuring the paradigmatic aspect of colonial violence that is also embedded in the colonial language.

51. Here in this poetic line, Philip does violence to language by forcing verbs and prepositions to act as nouns. I will address this issue in more detail during my discussion of *She Tries Her Tongue.*

52. Philip, *Looking for Livingstone,* 8.

53. Philip, 8.

54. Philip, 9.

55. Philip, 10.

56. Philip, 10.

57. Philip, 10.

58. As I discuss later in this chapter, Philip's goal is to challenge racist Western historiography by reclaiming ancient Egypt as part of African history.

59. Dunand and Zivie-Coche, *Gods and Men,* 67.

60. Philip, *Looking for Livingstone,* 62.

61. Zamora, "Magical Romance," 500.

62. Philip, *Looking for Livingstone,* 17.

63. Philip, 17.

64. It is important to point out that the author uses words to tell the story and, thus, she reinscribes the binarity of the system she critiques. In other words, even if there are silences in her story, she is NOT silent.

65. Philip, 18.

66. Philip, 23.

67. Here again I am referencing Mbembe's phrase from *Critique of Black Reason.*

68. Leitch, "Gayatri Chakravorty Spivak," 2196.

69. Slemon, "Magical Realism," 414.

70. Dash, "Introduction," xxix.

71. Glissant, *Caribbean Discourse,* 76. Gayatri Spivak offers a similar point of view about the institutionalization and collusion between historical and literary discourses. In *A Critique of Postcolonial Reason,* she argues that "the establishment of an intimate relationship between 'literary' and the 'colonial,' the reading of literature can directly supplement the writing of history with suspicious ease" (205).

72. Glissant, 74.

73. It is similar to Anancy's strategies of dissimulation.

74. Aching, *Masking and Power,* 2.

75. Glissant, *Caribbean Discourse,* 99–100.

76. Glissant, 99–105.

77. Glissant, 82, 106.

78. Glissant, 101, 120.

79. Glissant, 120.

80. Glissant, 120.

81. Glissant, 133.

82. Glissant, 270.

83. Glissant, 270.

84. Brathwaite, *Roots*, 266.

85. Brathwaite, 260.

86. Brathwaite, 266. It should be noted, however, that Brathwaite's concept of nation language is subjected to the masculinist discourses that are embedded in the word nation.

87. Brathwaite, 277.

88. Brathwaite, 284.

89. Brathwaite, 284.

90. Rowe, *Literary Culture*, 267.

91. Fanon, *Black Skin*, 10–12.

92. Fanon, 17–18.

93. See Jacques Lacan's "The Mirror Stage" in *Literary Theory: An Anthology*. See also *Black Skin, White Masks* (chapter 6, note 25), in which Frantz Fanon discusses the significance of Lacan's theory to Black subjectivity.

94. Fanon, *Black Skin*, 161–64.

95. Resonating with Aníbal Quijano's ideas in "Coloniality and Modernity/Rationality," Stuart Hall explains that the "production of the meanings of concepts" occur "in our minds through language"—"we could not interpret the world meaningfully at all" without the "the system of concepts and images formed in our thoughts which stand for or 'represent' the world" according to "conceptual maps" (17).

96. Philip, *She Tries*, 15.

97. Edmonds, "Dread 'I,'" 32.

98. Edmonds, 33.

99. McFarlane, "The Epistemological," 107–8.

100. Referenced in McFarlane, 116.

101. Philip, *She Tries*, 14.

102. Philip, 17.

103. Philip utilizes the Rastafari wordplay that stresses the "i" in words, a technique that suggests self-empowerment.

104. Philip, 18.

105. Philip, 19.

106. An art term in French that means "to fool the eye."

107. Philip, 35.

108. Philip, 18.

109. Philip, 14.

110. Philip, 29.

111. Philip, 29.

112. Sakai, *Translation and Subjectivity*, 36.

113. Sakai, 36.

114. A term first used by Claude Levi Strauss and which, in Cultural Studies, refers to processes by which people appropriate objects from across social divisions to create new cultural identities.

115. Van Gennep, *The Rites of Passage*, 82.

116. Cuddon, *The Penguin Dictionary*, 507.

117. Jakobson, "Two Aspects of Language," 91.

118. Philip, *She Tries*, 31.

119. Freud, *The Interpretation of Dreams*, 311.

120. Freud, 330.

121. Philip, *She Tries*, 37.

122. In the introduction of *Caribbean Discourse*, J. Michael Dash explains that, for Glissant, a key attribute of the Caribbean text is not "clarity or accessibility" but rather "the articulation of a collective consciousness trying to be, to find expression. Inevitably there is something forced about this kind of writing in its striving to avoid the trap of eroded forms and self-consciously reaching for the realm of the unsaid and perhaps the unsayable" (xxvi).

123. Philip, *She Tries*, 32.

124. Philip, 33.

125. Philip, 34.

126. Bernal, *Black Athena*, 3–4.

127. Bernal, 484.

128. Bernal, 453.

129. Philip, *She Tries*, 23.

130. Philip, 13–15.

131. Philip, 12.

Chapter Three

1. Ricoeur, *Oneself as Another*, 2–3.

2. Mbembe, *Critique*, 133.

3. Holt, *The Problem of Freedom*, 5.

4. Hartman, *Scenes of Subjection*, 116–27.

5. Moten, *In the Break*, 93.

6. Ricoeur, *The Rule of Metaphor*, 204–5.

7. Gilroy, *The Black Atlantic*, 75–77.

8. Maroon armies also used the *abeng* as a war-horn to pass messages to each other. It had another function of summoning the ancestral spirits.

9. Soyinka, *Myth, Literature and the African World*, 147.

10. Chude-Sokei, "The Sound of Culture," 187.

11. During slavery, Burru musicians played a key role in the production of labor, and their music functioned as a "'work metronome' for the slaves" since it was their job "to play the music that buoyed the spirits of the slaves and made them work faster and so speed up production." When slavery ended, however, these musicians found themselves without work because they had "little experience as field hands and hence could do little with their post-slavery plots of ground in the hinterlands." It is for this reason, as Verena Reckford explains, that they migrated to the city, particularly to the Kingston and Spanish Town slums. A "natural" merging between the Rastas and the Burru people occurred in the 1930s because of their shared ethos of self-help, their belief in the importance of retaining African roots, their acceptance of communal lifestyles, and their dismissal of religious groups such as Pocomania (Reckford 234–38). A major difference between Rastafari and Afro-Christian religious groups, such as Pocomania, is that the latter center spiritual practices on the experience of possession. Rastafarians, in contrast, grounded "them in a meditative mysticism that did not reject the material world" (Henry 211). Because the Burru people had no

religious beliefs of their own, their "exchange of music for doctrine in the later 1940s resulted in the merger of these groups and the almost extinction of Burru people as a social group" (Reckford 238).

12. Edmonds, "Dread 'I,'" 30.

13. See page 176 of Sidney Mintz's *Sweetness and Power*.

14. In "Babylon System: The Continuity of Slavery" Howard Winant references the significance of Marley's metaphor of the winepress to the Bible (*The New Politics of Race: Globalism, Difference, Justice,* 81). His reference draws upon Revelation 19–20: "The angel swung his sickle on the earth, gathered its grapes and threw them into the great winepress of God's wrath. They were trampled in the winepress outside the city, and blood flowed out of the press, rising as high as the horses' bridles for a distance of 1,600 stadia."

15. Quijano, "Coloniality and Modernity," 170.

16. Edmonds, "Dread 'I,'" 24.

17. Marley qtd. in Dawes, *Bob Marley*, 243.

18. *Sufferah* is the Jamaican *patwa* word for sufferer. It refers to the very poor, marginalized people who suffer from the continued effects of slavery and its modern-day incarnations.

19. Marx qtd. in Policante, "Vampires of Capital," 7.

20. Marley, "Babylon System."

21. J. Williams, *Narrative*, 11.

22. J. Williams, 6.

23. J. Williams, 54.

24. Paton, *No Bond but the Law*, 106.

25. Paton, 106.

26. Scarry, *The Body in Pain*, 28.

27. It is the same system that Peter Tosh laments about in "Four Hundred Years," from the Wailers' *Catch A Fire* album (1973). Taking the lead on this song, Tosh sings: "Four Hundred Years (four hundred years, four hundred years) / And it's the same, the same philosophy / I've said it's four hundred years (four hundred years, four hundred years) / Look how long / And the people still can't see."

28. Dawes, *Bob Marley*, 264.

29. Marley, "Babylon System."

30. This motif of flying Africans is also present in Toni Morrison's *The Song of Solomon*.

31. Mbembe, *Critique*, 155, 165.

32. D. Roberts, "Sublime Theories," 176.

33. Rundell, "Creativity and Judgement," 103.

34. Barrett, Sr., *The Rastafarians*, 193–94.

35. Reckford, "From Burru Drums," 43.

36. Hebdige, "Reggae, Rastas and Rudies," 123.

37. Reckford "From Burru Drums," 244–45.

38. Reckford, 244–45. In a similar vein, Leonard Barrett notes that "the downbeat of the drummer symbolizes the death of the oppressive society but it is answered by the *akete* drummers with a lighter upbeat, a resurrection of the society through the power of Ras Tafari" (193).

39. Ricoeur, "Personal Identity," 227.

40. Ricoeur, 226.

41. Ricoeur, 228.

42. Atkins, "Commentary on Ricoeur," 221.

43. Atkins, 221.

44. As Edmonds explains, "I-an-I" denotes the connection or "oneness between two (or more) persons" and the "affirmation of self as an active agent in the creation of one's own reality and identity" (33). In Rastafari hermeneutics, as McFarlane explains, "the power of I lies in its ability to command the self . . . and its purpose is to create a new identity and meaning for the speaker" (108).

45. Here, I draw upon Walter D. Mignolo's concept.

46. Das qtd. in Bhabha, "In a Spirit of Calm Violence," 329.

47. Das qtd. in Bhabha, 329.

48. Das qtd. in Bhabha, 329.

49. Bhabha, 329.

50. Spivak, "Postcoloniality and Value," 228.

51. Barry Chevannes notes that ethnographic research conducted as far back as 1929 reveals the "predilection of the Jamaican peasant for the spoken word . . . a tendency not adequately explained by the absence of a tradition of literacy, since even literate people have the feeling that to address one in person is more effective than in writing" (36). This "predilection" can be explained by the fact that verbal communication, at the phonological level of discourse, correlates to ideophones, the "highly expressive linguistic elements" of sound symbolism and auditory perception that "stimulate, especially in spoken language, a sensory perception, emotion or event" (Willems and De Cuypere 4).

52. Lacan qtd. in Bhabha, "In a Spirit of Calm Violence," 329.

53. Bhabha, 330.

54. Wilden, "Lacan and the Discourse," 164.

55. The song echoes Chinua Achebe's ideas in *Things Fall Apart* and his essay "An Image of Africa," both of which convey his critique of Joseph Conrad's *The Heart of Darkness*. In many ways, too, the ideas here connect to my discussion in chapter 2 of NourbeSe Philip's travel narrative, which challenges the colonialist depiction of Livingstone as the "bearer of light."

56. The Enlightenment legacy celebrates European individualism and moral self-interest, especially in relation to modern perceptions of freedom associated with (Black) labor and (white) property rights. The Enlightenment's privileging of individualism, as influenced by Locke, is connected to "liberal individualism"—the notion that these ideas set "the individual free politically, intellectually, and economically" (Kramnick xvi). I-an-I as a Rastafari concept is about connection, which contrasts with such notions about individuality.

57. In some versions of "Concrete Jungle" Marley sings "collusion, confusion" but in other versions, for instance, the segment on Stephen Marley's 1999 production of *Chant Down Babylon*, which includes a remix of "Concrete Jungle" featuring African American rapper Rakim, Marley sings "pollution, illusion, confusion." Singing live at the Old Grey Whistle Test in 1973, Marley sings "pollution" to rhyme with "confusion" ("Bob Marley & the Wailers—Live"). The Jamaican version of the song similarly conveys "pollution," "illusion," "confusion" instead of the word "collusion." The book *Bob Marley: Songs of Freedom* also has the lyrics as "illusion" rather than "collusion" for the original 1973 *Catch A Fire* album. In his 2007 live performance at the Avalon Club in Hollywood, California, Ziggy Marley also sings "illusion, confusion" ("Concrete Jungle-Ziggy Marley").

58. In the song "Keepers of the Light" from the *Maestro* album (2015), Bob Marley's son Ky-Mani Marley, featuring his brother Damian Marley, picks up the conversation. Ky-Mani asks by using the effect of repeating rhetorical questions in the chorus, "So where is the justice (somebody tell me now) / Where is the peace you talk about / Still living in darkness, (somebody tell me now) / Tell me where are the keepers of the light?" The third verse echoes the Wailers' "Concrete Jungle" when Ky-Mani sings "Trapped here in this dark place, wish a light would shine on me / Trying to keep my faith, the one thing they can't take from me." Previous lines in the song state, "We're living in a battle, and the God is on our side." For Ky-Mani, his Rastafari faith (the idea that "the God is on our side") gives him courage to fight this "battle." It is a position that extends Marley's argument that the revolution can only be won with Rasta. Another key issue in Ky-Mani's song is that he, similar to his father, challenges the position that colonialism and the torch of Christianity were necessary for civilizing Africans and bringing them out of primitive darkness and chaos. By asking "where is the justice" and the "peace you talk about" and highlighting the fact that they are "still living in darkness" he calls attention to the continuity of oppressive practices that have morphed from slavery and colonialism. On the whole, the trope of "darkness" in this song maintains his father's representations of the paradoxical significance of "light" and "dark."

59. It should be noted that in *Enquiry*, as Meg Armstrong and other have pointed out, Edmund Burke on the issue of the physiological sublime equates it with Blackness and skin color. To a large degree, these beliefs foreground dominant philosophical ideals on the sublime, the notion that, in a European context, language fails to give representation of Blackness because it was deemed as incomprehensible: "Africa and Blackness have, since the beginning of the modern age, plunged the theory of the name as well as the status and function of the sign and of representation into deep crisis. The same is true of the relation between being and appearance, truth and falsehood, reason and unreason, even language and life. Every time it confronted the question of Blacks and Africa, reason found itself ruined and emptied, turning constantly in on itself, shipwrecked in a seemingly inaccessible place where language was destroyed and words themselves no longer had memory" (Mbembe, *Critique*, 13).

60. Moten, *In the Break*, 87.

61. The sublime and the Real are both are concerned with the unrepresentable and the failure of achieving resolution. Dennis A. Foster calls such a failure of resolution an "unresolved encounter" (12) and "formless horror" (11) that suggest a correlation between the Real and the sublime, what he coins as the "Real Sublime" (12). Thus, for him, the sublime event "is prior to and beyond the representable" (11). Here Foster invokes the Lacanian notion of the Real that is prior to the symbolic. As a means of explication, Foster references Slavoj Žižek and points out that the Real is "evoked by the implicit limits of symbolic representation, by the fact that something is always excluded: the limit creates the beyond, the prior, the silence. The triumph of the Symbolic brings with it its own mad other, its failure" (12). Foster explains further that the "Real refers to that property of experience that prevents any rational project from reaching completion, that precludes any representation of the world from being fully adequate to one's experience of it" (12).

62. Hamilton, "Jamaican String Theory," 89.

63. See Kant, *Observations*, 48.

64. The dub aesthetic was pioneered by Jamaican studio engineers such as Osbourne Ruddock ("King Tubby"), Lee Perry ("Scratch"), and Errol Thompson ("Errol T") in the 1960s and 1970s.

65. An alternate version was produced for the Jamaican audience, which does not have the rock-inspired instrumental break. My discussions of "Concrete Jungle" are based on the *Catch a Fire* (1973) album version produced by Chris Blackwell.

66. Veal, *Dub*, 75, 40, 16–17, 2, 63.

67. Hill, *Black Soundscapes*, 11.

68. Moten, *In the Break*, 107.

69. Achille Mbembe notes that "the real rarely lends itself to precise measurement or exact calculation . . . The encounter with the real can only ever be fragmentary and chopped up, ephemeral, made up of dissonance, always provisional, always starting anew . . . The event par excellence is always floating. The image, or the shadow, is not illusion but fact. Its content always exceeds its form" (*Critique*, 130).

70. Moten, *In the Break*, 92.

71. Kant, *Critique*, 100–102.

Chapter Four

1. D. Foster, *Sublime Enjoyment*, 11–12.

2. Mbembe, *Critique*, 130–31.

3. In *Cities of the Dead*, Joseph Roach gestures toward an understanding of the slave sublime and its emphasis on the imagination wherein the excesses of the sublime move in the direction of the beautiful. Roach characterizes performances in this context as the "choreography of catastrophic closure," which is fueled by "kinesthetic imagination" that "carries forward through time the memory of a movement, a 'downward turning,' redolent of violence and fatality but also of agency and decision." In such performances, Roach suggests that "the dead may speak through the bodies of the living" (33–34). Accordingly, through his music, Marley connects to his predecessors as he ventures into the imaginary realm with a political consciousness that allows him to envision himself as a postcolonial subject who exists simultaneously in the historical past, thereby allowing him to exhume the transgenerational memories and traumas as a first-person experience. Memory, in this sense, is connected to "the universe of the senses, imagination, and multiplicity" and the "coupling of the imagination and memory enriches our knowledge of both the semantics and the pragmatics of remembrance" (Mbembe, *Critique*, 121).

4. Roach, *Cities of the Dead*, 41–42.

5. Leslie qtd. in Burnard, *Mastery*, 103.

6. Burnard, 149, 104.

7. Roach, *Cities of the Dead*, 41.

8. Kant, "Selections," 51.

9. Bywater's translation qtd. in Cuddon, *The Penguin Dictionary*, 926.

10. For neither Kant nor Burke is the sublime ever-present, which suggests a major difference between the sublime and the slave sublime.

11. James, *A Brief History*, 408–9.

12. James, 9.

13. Fanon, *Wretched*, 40.

14. Pithouse, "Manichean Delirium."

15. Fanon, *Wretched*, 38.

16. Mbembe, *On the Postcolony*, 175.

17. Reyes, "Fanon's Manichean Delirium," 16–17.

18. Fanon, *Wretched*, 23.

19. Foucault, *Madness and Civilization*, 39.

20. Foucault, 46.

21. Carlyle, "Occasional Discourse." The title of this essay is often given as "Occasional Discourse on the Nigger Question" as cited in the book *Discourse, Dictators and Democrats: Russia's Place in a Global Process* by Richard D. Anderson.

22. Foucault, *Madness and Civilization*, 47.

23. Foucault, 64–85.

24. See Kelly Baker Joseph's *Disturber of the Peace* (2013), which offers a wonderful discussion about madness in Anglophone Caribbean literature between 1959 and 1980, focusing on the representation of madness in relation to the transition from colonial to postcolonial status and the project of nation building. A more recent book, *Madness in Anglophone Caribbean Literature* (2018), edited by Bénédicte Ledent, Evelyn O'Callaghan, and Daria Tunca, provides a collection of essays that link madness to "a legacy of forced servitude, displacement, and violence" that "resulted in the ontological trauma that still manifests" and highlight the "repercussions of these wounds" (5).

25. Foucault, *Madness and Civilization*, 93.

26. Foucault, 66–72.

27. Foucault, 74.

28. Foucault, 46, 75.

29. Foucault, 46–75.

30. James, *A Brief History*, 8.

31. James, 9.

32. James, 263.

33. Ellis, "Marlon James's Savage Business."

34. Eagleton, *Sweet Violence*, 1.

35. Cuddon, *The Penguin Dictionary*, 367.

36. Harrison, "Excess."

37. James, *A Brief History*, 335.

38. Ullman, "History and Tragedy," 25–27.

39. Sterling, "The Theory of Verisimilitude," 613–19.

40. Lloyd, "Violence and the Constitution of the Novel," 137.

41. This is a problem in general for modern drama, as Raymond Williams has discussed at length. C. L. R. James's *The Black Jacobins* is at best the closest Caribbean text to a tragedy—precisely because he regards colonial violence as a form of fate or destiny.

42. James, *A Brief History*, 372.

43. James, 9.

44. James, 8.

45. Kincaid, *A Small Place*, 78–79.

46. Kincaid, 79.

47. James, *A Brief History*, 3.

48. James, 282.

49. James, 8.

50. Fanon, *Wretched*, 39.

51. James, *A Brief History*, 3.

52. James, 340.

53. James, 417.

54. Marley, "Ambush in the Night."

55. Fanon, *Wretched*, 306–7.

56. Mbembe, *Critique*, 18.

57. Certainly, and not to dismiss Mbembe's point, alliances in the form of slave rebellions were forged against the slave master.

58. James, *A Brief History*, 416.

59. Marley, "Ambush in the Night."

60. James, *A Brief History*, 34.

61. James, 90.

62. James, 185.

63. James, 36.

64. James, 74.

65. James, 57.

66. Even in the United States, constables were important figures for policing slaves within the plantation order. In his 1845 *Narrative*, Frederick Douglass speaks about his fight with Covey, in the aftermath of which he was able to be escape being "taken by the constables to the whipping-post, and there regularly whipped for the crime of raising my hand against a white man in defense of myself" (138). See pages 148–49 of this text as well for additional mentions about the role of constables.

67. T. Lacey, *Violence and Politics in Jamaica*, 22.

68. J. Williams, *Narrative*, 16.

69. Mbembe, *Critique*, 131.

70. Thomas, *Exceptional Violence*, 4.

71. Fanon, *Wretched*, 309.

72. Jean-Paul Sartre, "Preface," 18.

73. James, *A Brief History*, 9.

74. James, 67.

75. James, 416.

76. James, 344.

77. Walonen, "Violence, Imperialism," 67–68.

78. James, *A Brief History*, 84.

79. James, *A Brief History*, 82.

80. Walonen, "Violence, Diasporic," 2.

81. Mbembe, *Postcolony*, 175.

82. James, *A Brief History*, 82 (emphasis in original).

Chapter Five

1. Chude-Sokei, "The Sound of Culture," 201.

2. Henriques, *Sonic Bodies*, xix.

3. Lewis, *The Growth of the Modern*, 44.

4. By referring to musical artists as a "priestly caste of organic intellectuals," Paul Gilroy states that "These people have often been intellectuals in the Gramscian sense, operating without the benefits that flow either from a relationship to the modern state or from secure institutional locations within the cultural industries. They have often pursued roles that escape categorization as the practice of either legislators or interpreters and have advanced instead as temporary custodians of a distinct and embattled cultural sensibility which has also operated as a political and philosophical resource" (76).

5. Dolby, "Popular Culture," 268.

6. Dolby, 269.

7. As an expression of radical democracy, the dancehall genre captures a range of creative expressions that are assimilated to it as spin-off genres and consumed as the social practices of dancehall theater, cinema, choreography, fashion design, and modeling. These spin-off genres have a signifying function and modality as a sum of signs or syntagmatic semiological chain of discourse that contributes to the global sign of dancehall music as a "resistive transcript." As a "resistive transcript" and a counter-hegemonic system, dancehall music conveys noise as a symbolic substitute for violence and a new ideological stance that combats the myth of liberty and the painful legacies of historical oppression. The unconscious and conspicuous consumption of dancehall in the forms of the various spin-off genres can be linked to the new underground and legitimate economies that have sprung up around the music, all of which are not supported by the established economic networks that the ruling class controls. The dancehall music industry operates independently of the commercial sector with its superimposed class consciousness. Its development and proliferation have been attributed to the popularization of sound systems such as Stone Love and the emergence of popular radio, such as Irie FM, which is devoted solely to dancehall music, and which was made possible by the divestment of the media in Jamaica. This accessibility finds a similar trend in the television industry with programming centered on a dancehall format.

8. Rose, *Black Noise*, 102.

9. Rose, 144.

10. Hope, *Inna di Dancehall*, 17.

11. Hope, 18.

12. Stolzoff, *Wake the Town*, 1.

13. Attali, *Noise*, 27.

14. Dancehall theatre, fashion, and choreography as underground economies have cropped up since the 1980s and function as viable economies.

15. Attali, 100.

16. N. Barnes, *Cultural Conundrums*, 104.

17. Nietzsche, *The Birth of Tragedy*, 19.

18. Brooks, "Manifestations of Ogun," 163.

19. McCarthy Brown, "Systematic Remembering," 68.

20. S. Barnes, "The Many Faces," 20.

21. S. Barnes, 14.

22. Babalola, "A Portrait of Ogun," 155.

23. Babalola, 156.

24. S. Barnes, "The Many Faces," 14–15.

25. S. Barnes, "Preface," ix.

26. Sridhar et al., "Disasters," 150.

27. McCarthy Brown, "Systematic Remembering," 68.

28. McCarthy Brown, 66.

29. A word-for-word translation would be as follows: Music is gal [girl] over gun / Tell them don't stop the fun / Because if they stop the fun / They must be prepared to stop the gun.

30. Mais, *The Hills Were Joyful*, 239.

31. Headley, *The Jamaican Crime Scene*, 20.

32. Barrett, *The Rastafarians*, 13–15.

33. Barrett, 13.

34. T. Lacey, *Violence and Politics*, 74.

35. Kirton, *Jamaica*, 5.

36. Fanon, *Wretched*, 61.

37. Saunders, "Is Not Everything," 101–2.

38. Here, I am invoking Antonio Benítez-Rojo's term. See note 63.

39. Fanon, *Wretched*, 84.

40. In chapter 2 on M. NourbeSe Philip, I discuss the function of language as a vehicle of violence and the fact that, given the Lacanian notion that language is transmitted from the paternal figure to the child, the institutionalization of violence during slavery and colonialism can be characterized as a paternal language that is handed down to slaves and their descendants. The father/child dichotomy between masters and slaves is suggested by the so-called system of paternalism that was used to legitimize slavery.

41. Lawson, *Religion and Race*, 8.

42. Whiteley, *Excessive Cruelty*, 7.

43. "Human Rights in Jamaica," 6.

44. "Human Rights in Jamaica," 8.

45. "Human Rights in Jamaica," 11–12.

46. Human Rights Watch, "Jamaica: Investigate Police and Military Killings."

47. Stolzoff, *Wake the Town*, 10.

48. Hussain, *The Jurisprudence of Emergency*, 102–9.

49. Gunst, *Born Fi Dead*, xv.

50. "Fighting Rages."

51. M. Lacey, "Unrest Grows in Jamaica."

52. Drewal, "Dancing for Ògun," 204.

53. Cosentino, "Repossession," 291.

54. Cosentino, 291.

55. Cosentino, 292.

56. Stolzoff, *Wake the Town*, 8.

57. Whitmer, *The Violence Mythos*, 75.

58. "Mavado vs Vybz Kartel."

59. Stanley Niaah, *Dance Hall*, 73–74.

60. S. Barnes, "Many Faces," 19.

61. Adu-Gyamfi, "Wole Soyinka's 'Dawn,'" 76–77.

62. Although this book focuses on dancehall music leading up to the 2005 declaration of Kingston as the "murder capital of the world," I focus on music in a few years surrounding that event, both before and after. My reference here to more recent songs from Busy Signal and Popcaan is in an effort to demonstrate the continued significance of the Ogun archetype in Jamaican dancehall music.

63. Dancehall music is part of the discourse and an outlet for the violence experienced throughout Jamaican history, and, despite the seemingly contradictory nature of Mavado's ideas, there is some credence to his viewpoints. The music allows dancehall adherents to channel the internalized violence that results from institutionalized forms of historical and contemporary violence. Dancehall music "has thus become a strategic consumption, an essential mode of sociality for all those who feel themselves powerless before the monologue of the great institutions" (Attali 100). In *The Repeating Island*, Antonio Benítez-Rojo argues that "performance and rhythm . . . carr[y] the desire to sublimate apocalypse and violence" (16). He argues further that "Caribbean performance . . . does not reflect back to the performer alone but rather it also diverts itself toward a public in search of a carnivalesque catharsis that proposes to divert excesses of violence and that in the final analysis was *already there*" (Benítez-Rojo 22). Arguably, Benítez-Rojo's notion about that which was "*already there*" points to the originary violence of colonization and slavery that Mbembe characterizes as Dionysiac. A noteworthy complement to Benítez-Rojo's viewpoint is Attali's idea that "a society cannot recover from a psychosis without reliving the various phases of its terror" and that music "induces a reliving of noise's fundamental endowment with form, the channelization of the essential violence" (Attali 30). By these accounts, dancehall music functions as part of the discourse and outlet for the historical violence of slavery and colonialism and newer forms of bondage such as globalization.

64. Hope, *Inna di Dancehall*, 90.

65. The "Ifa paradigm is based on the belief that certain imagery, symbolism, and thematic references in African diasporic literature are deliberately references to African culture, and it outlines specific realms of knowledge (colors, myths, etc.) allowing critics to deliver an enriched and African-centered critique" (Brooks 164).

66. Barry Chevannes notes that the "proliferation of guns as a symbol" of masculinity in Jamaica "is not a simply a function of the drug trade but the ultimate representation of what it means to be a man" (30).

67. Mitchell, "Representation," 12.

68. Mitchell, 14.

69. Soyinka, "The Fourth Stage," 366.

70. Soyinka, 369.

71. Soyinka, 374.

72. Soyinka, 367.

73. Soyinka, 369.

74. Hope, *Inna di Dancehall*, 86–87.

75. Hope, 114.

76. Attali notes that the musician functions as "one of the first catalyzers of violence and myth" and that the musician plays "an integral part of the sacrifice process, [as] a channeler of violence" (12). For Attali, "Listening to music" is comparable to "attend[ing] a ritual murder, with all the danger, guilt, but also reassurance that goes along with that; that applauding is a confirmation, after the channelization of the violence, that the spectators of the sacrifice could potentially resume practicing the essential violence" (28).

77. Henriques, *Sonic Bodies*, 137.

78. Scott, *Conscripts of Modernity*, 142.

79. Scott, 135.

80. Scott, 135.

81. Adu-Gyamfi, "Wole Soyinka's 'Dawn,'" 86.

82. Gurr, "Third-World Drama," 46.

83. Gurr, 48.

84. Adu-Gyamfi, "Wole Soyinka's 'Dawn,'" 75.

85. Adu-Gyamfi, 81.

86. Adu-Gyamfi, 85.

87. "Invasion" was used as the theme song for wrestler Bill Goldberg, who holds the record for the largest undefeated winning streak in professional wrestling. As a theme song "Invasion" has a well-established association with announcing the entrance of a great warrior and the imminent battle. Despite the fact that "Invasion" is Western-inspired, for Damian Marley it serves a similar function.

88. Veal, *Dub*, 207.

89. Nietzsche, *The Birth of Tragedy*, 40. Soyinka openly admits that these arguments about the tragic dimensions of music are not uniquely specific to Yoruba culture, given that "the embodiment of the tragic spirit has been more than perceptively exhausted in the philosophy of Europe" and that "there is little to add, much to qualify." What Soyinka is suggesting is that, despite the key difference that lies in the concomitant relationship between Yoruba musical form, myth, and poetry, there are some parallels between European and African myth and the related cultural forms (367). There are parallels, for instance, between the Yoruba deity Ogun and the Greek god Dionysus. While Soyinka admits that there are "key departures," he nonetheless argues that Ogun "is best understood in Hellenic values as a totality of the Dionysian Apollonian and Promethean virtues" (364–65). In spite of these pronounced differences between Yoruba and Greek myth, the following argument that Soyinka offers is particularly noteworthy, as he nullifies Nietzsche's racially/culturally exclusive assumptions in *The Birth of Tragedy*: "Such virtues place Ogun apart from the distorted dances to which Nietzsche's Dionysiac frenzy led him in his search for a selective 'Aryan' soul, yet do not detract from Ogun's revolutionary grandeur. Ironically, it is the depth-illumination of Nietzsche's intuition into basic universal impulses which negates his race exclusivist conclusions on the nature of art and tragedy" ("The Fourth Stage" 365).

While Nietzsche's formulation of the Dionysiac in *The Birth of Tragedy* is not an all-compassing standard, by any means, for understanding the multi-faceted and racially specific epistemologies of African or Afro-diasporic cultures, it is, nonetheless, useful. This formulation is useful primarily because of the extensive explication that Nietzsche offers and the parallels that Soyinka himself identifies. In other words, Soyinka's debunking of

Nietzsche's race-exclusive premise makes possible my occasional alignment of dancehall music with the Dionysiac as is evident in the music of dancehall deejays. While taking particular care to make the necessary qualifications, I will use the Dionysiac as a structure of thinking rather than the basis for empirical, psychological claims about the effects of dancehall; in particular, it is useful for understanding the paradoxical aspect of dancehall music in which the spirit of Ogun is very much present. In a sense, the Dionysiac functions as a kind of structuring convenience, as it offers a model of Dionysian chaos/violence versus Apollonian enlightenment that furnishes, then, a metaphor for the oppositions to dancehall culture. Also, it functions as way of explaining the status of Ogun, given Soyinka's position that Dionysus is the Hellenic parallel of Ogun. In *The Birth of Tragedy*, Nietzsche offers the following explanation for the Dionysiac structure of thinking:

> It was into a world built up and artificially protected like this that the ecstatic tones of the festival of Dionysus now penetrated, tones in which all the *excess* of pleasure and suffering and knowledge in nature revealed itself at one and the same time. Here everything which, up to this point, had been acknowledged as a limit, as a definition of measure, proved to be an artificially created illusion: "excess" unveiled itself as the truth. For the first time there roared out the daemonically fascinating song of the people in all the drunkenness of an over-mighty feeling ... The ecstasy of the Dionysian state, which destroys the usual barriers and limits of existence, contains, for as long as it lasts, a *lethargic* element in which all personal experiences from the past are submerged. (128–29)

90. Wilderson, *Afropessimism*, 15.

91. Hartman, *Scenes of Subjection*, 51–52.

92. Boyne, "Waltzing with Wolves," G1.

93. Boyne, G1. In this sense, a number of dancehall music lyrics can be compared to gangster rap in the United States or to *narcocorridos* heard on both sides of the U.S.-Mexican border.

94. Boyne, G1–G6.

95. Boyne, G6.

96. Boyne, G6.

97. I have also shown analytically the ways in which some dancehall lyrics address the causes and consequences of violence.

98. Hebdige, "Reggae, Rastas and Rudies," 120. The Rude Boys of the 1970s were considered to be young, unemployed, and underemployed men in the impoverished neighborhoods in Kingston that experienced increased violence and political rivalries. The music of this period, as Michael E. Veal describes it, changed from the ska style of music to depicting a "'darker' social mood," which was "more bottom-heavy, less concerned with abandon and more with controlled and repeated syncopations. The accompanying dancing became more controlled as well, with the halting, syncopated bass lines" (31).

99. Hebdige, 122.

100. Hebdige, 122–23.

101. In 2010, as a response to one of Boyne's articles titled "Taming the Crime Beast," a reader (Leighton) posted an online comment saying, "Mr. Boyne; you are for the most part an excellent journalist, but you are plagued with the need to plug the Government at every opportunity. Maybe one week you could write an article that has no public relations

undertone—I know it's your day job, but you write on a Sunday. Give us the views of 'Ian' one of these weeks."

102. In this same article, Boyne notes that a "giggling female at a prominent gunman's funeral was . . . featured on the front page of a newspaper with a wreath in the shape of an M-16" and that "polite society was shocked and astounded at this perversion of values." While I am in no way apologizing for or defending the "giggling female" and her behavior, it must be taken into consideration that the paradox that exists at the heart of the Dionysian worldview suggests the tragic-comic response to the "terrible."

103. Nietzsche, *The Birth of Tragedy*, 130.

104. Žižek offers "an important argument that cynicism and, in particular, the mask of cynical reason are the ruling class's response to the 'plebian rejection of the official culture by means of irony and sarcasm'" (Aching 7).

105. Chang and Chen, *Reggae Routes*, 82.

106. Whitmer, *The Violence Mythos*, 155.

107. R. Williams, *Marxism and Literature*, 593.

108. R. Williams, 594.

109. R. Williams, 594.

110. Barthes, *Mythologies*, 117.

111. Hebdige, *Subculture*, 9.

112. Barthes, *Mythologies*, 118.

113. Barthes, 121–22.

114. Barthes, 122.

115. Barthes, 109.

116. Cooper, *Sound Clash*, 17.

117. Cooper's argument came at a time when white, gay activists in New York, Canada, and England characterized dancehall music as a universal sign of homophobia and anti-gay sentiment.

118. Barthes, *Mythologies*, 127–28.

119. Gilroy, *The Black Atlantic*, 75–77.

120. Henriques, *Sonic Bodies*, xix.

Coda

1. Rose, *Black Noise*, 100.

2. Whitmer, *The Violence Mythos*, 4.

3. In the dynamic sense that dancehall is a performative act that employs the body as a vehicle of expression, violence itself can be considered as a sublexical, nonverbal language that is articulated through the body. In *Formations of Violence*, Allen Feldman argues that violence is an institution that has its own "symbolic and performative autonomy" and that the transference of this nonverbal language to the body is articulated in societies that are undergoing a national crisis. What is also noteworthy is Feldman's notion that the display of excessive violence in a society indicates its formation, its coming into being, "an incomplete project, as something to be made" from the rambles of colonial violence (5–21). In this light, there is an apparent link between the originary violence of conquest and the dispossession that the dancehall form captures in its metalinguistic representations.

Bibliography

Aching, Gerard. *Masking and Power: Carnival and Popular Culture in the Caribbean.* *Cultural Studies of the Caribbean*, 8. Minneapolis: University of Minnesota Press, 2002.

Adu-Gyamfi, Yaw. "Wole Soyinka's 'Dawn' and the Cults of Ogun." *Ariel: A Review of International English Literature* 28, no. 4 (October 1997): 73–89.

Archer, Dane, and Rosemary Gartner. *Violence and Crime in Cross-National Perspective.* New Haven, CT: Yale University Press, 1984.

Atkins, Kim. "Commentary on Ricoeur." In *Blackwell Readings in Continental Philosophy: Self and Subjectivity*, edited by Kim Atkins, 220–34. Malden, MA: Blackwell Publishing, 2005.

Attali, Jacques. *Noise: The Political Economy of Music.* Translated by Brian Massumi. *Theory of History and Literature*, vol. 16. Minneapolis: University of Minnesota Press, 1985.

Babalola, Adeboye, "A Portrait of Ogun as Reflected in Ìjálá Chants." In *Africa's Ogun: Old World and New*, expanded 2nd edition, edited by Sandra T. Barnes, 147–72. Bloomington: Indiana University Press, 1997.

Barnes, Natasha. *Cultural Conundrums: Gender, Race, Nation, and the Making of Caribbean Politics.* Ann Arbor: University of Michigan Press, 2006.

Barnes, Sandra T. "The Many Faces of Ogun: Introduction to the First Edition." In *Africa's Ogun: Old World and New*, expanded 2nd edition, edited by Sandra T. Barnes, 1–26. Bloomington: Indiana University Press, 1997.

———. Preface to *Africa's Ogun: Old World and New*, expanded 2nd edition, edited by Sandra T. Barnes, ix–x. Bloomington: Indiana University Press, 1997.

Barrett, Leonard E., Sr. *The Rastafarians.* Boston: Beacon Press, 1997.

Barthes, Roland. *Mythologies.* New York: Hill and Wang, 1957.

———. *The Responsibility of Forms: Critical Essays in Music, Art, and Representation.* Translated by Richard Howard. Berkeley and Los Angeles: University of California Press, 1991.

Behdad, Ali. *Belated Travelers: Orientalism in the Age of Colonial Dissolution.* Durham, NC, and London: Duke University Press, 1994.

Benitez-Rojo, Antonio. *The Repeating Island: The Caribbean and the Postmodern Experience.* Durham, NC, and London: Duke University Press, 1997.

Bernal, Martin. *Black Athena: The Afroasiatic Roots of Classical Civilization.* New Brunswick, NJ: Rutgers University Press, 1991.

Bhabha, Homi. "In a Spirit of Calm Violence." In *After Colonialism: Imperial Histories and Postcolonial Displacements*, edited by Gyan Prakash, 326–44. Princeton, NJ: Princeton University Press, 1995.

———. *The Location of Culture.* London and New York: Routledge, 1994.

Bounty Killer. "Look." Released November 2006. Track 20 on *Nah No Mercy: The Warlord Scrolls.* VP Records, compact disc.

Boyne, Ian. "Taming the Crime Beast." *The Gleaner* (Kingston, Jamaica), May 9, 2010. https://jamaica-gleaner.com/gleaner/20100509/focus/focus1.html.

———. "Waltzing with Wolves: Dancehall's Link to Violence." *The Gleaner* (Kingston, Jamaica), June 5, 2005.

Brathwaite, Kamau. *Roots*. Ann Arbor: University of Michigan Press, 1993.

Brooks, Robin. "Manifestations of Ogun Symbolism in Paule Marshall's *Praisesong for the Widow*." *Journal of Africana Religions* 2, no. 2 (2014): 161–83.

Brown, Vincent. "Spiritual Terror and Sacred Authority in Jamaican Slave Society." *Slavery and Abolition* 24, no. 1 (2003): 24–53.

Browne, Randy M. *Surviving Slavery in the British Caribbean*. Philadelphia: University of Pennsylvania Press, 2017.

Burke, Edmund. *A Philosophical Enquiry into the Origin of our Ideas of the Sublime and Beautiful*. Edited by J. T. Boulton. New York: Columbia University Press, 1958.

Burnard, Trevor. *Mastery, Tyranny, and Desire: Thomas Thistlewood and His Slaves in the Anglo-Jamaican World*. Chapel Hill: University of North Carolina Press, 2004.

Burton, Richard D. E. *Afro-Creole: Power, Opposition, and Play in the Caribbean*. Ithaca, NY: Cornell University Press, 1997.

Busia, Abena P. A. "Silencing Sycorax: On African Colonial Discourse and the Unvoiced Female." *Cultural Critique* 14 (Winter 1989): 81–104.

Campbell, Yonique, and Colin Clarke. "The Garrison Community in Kingston and Its Implications for Violence, Policing, De Facto Rights, and Security in Jamaica." In *Violence in Latin America and the Caribbean: Subnational Structures, Institutions, and Clientelistic Networks*, edited by Tina Hilgers and Laura Macdonald, 93–111. Cambridge: Cambridge University Press, 2017.

Carlyle, Thomas. "Occasional Discourse on the Negro Question." *Fraser's Magazine for Town and Country*, London XL (February 1849). https://babel.hathitrust.org/cgi/pt?id=inu.30000080778727&view=1up&seq=690.

Carr, Bill. "A Complex Fate: The Novels of Andrew Salkey." In *Islands in Between: Essays on West Indian Literature*, edited by Louis James, 100–108. Oxford: Oxford University Press, 1968.

Chang, Kevin O'Brien, and Wayne Chen. *Reggae Routes: The Story of Jamaican Music*. Philadelphia: Temple University Press, 1998.

Chang, Victor L. " 'So Differently from What the Heart Arranged': *Voices Under the Window, New Day* and *A Quality of Violence*." In *The Routledge Companion to Anglophone Caribbean Literature*, edited by Michael A. Bucknor and Alison Donnell, 165–72. London and New York: Routledge, 2011.

Chevannes, Barry. *What We Sow and What We Reap: Problems in the Cultivation of Male Identity in Jamaica. Grace, Kennedy Lecture Series*. Kingston, Jamaica: The Grace, Kennedy Foundation, 1999.

Childers, Joseph, and Gary Hentzi eds. *Columbia Dictionary of Modern Literary and Cultural Criticism*. New York: Columbia University Press, 1995.

Chomsky, Noam. *Year 501: The Conquest Continues*. Boston: South End Press, 1993.

Chude-Sokei, Louis. "Postnationalist Geographies: Rasta, Ragga, and Reinventing Africa." *African Arts* 27, no. 4 (Autumn 1994): 80–96. Reprinted 1997 in *Reggae Music, Rasta*,

Revolution: Jamaican Music from Ska to Dub, edited by Chris Potash. New York: Schirmer Books, 1997.

———. "The Sound of Culture: Dread Discourse and Jamaican Sound Systems." In *Language Rhythm and Sound: Black Popular Cultures into the Twenty-First Century*, edited by Joseph K. Adjaye and Adrianne R. Andrews, 185–202. Pittsburgh: University of Pittsburgh Press, 1997.

Cooke, Melville. "A State of Historical Emergency." *The Daily Gleaner* (Kingston, Jamaica). October 16, 2003. http://www.jamaicagleaner.com/gleaner/20031016/cleisure/cleisure2 .html.

Cooper, Carolyn. *Noises in the Blood: Orality, Gender, and the "Vulgar" Body of Jamaican Popular Culture*. London: Macmillan Caribbean, 1993.

———. *Sound Clash: Jamaican Dancehall Culture at Large*. New York: Palgrave Macmillan, 2004.

Cosentino, Donald J. "Repossession: Ogun in Folklore and Literature." In *Africa's Ogun: Old World and New*, expanded 2nd edition, edited by Sandra T. Barnes, 290–314. Bloomington: Indiana University Press, 1997.

Craton, Michael. *Testing the Chains: Resistance to Slavery in the British West Indies*. Ithaca, NY: Cornell University Press, 1982.

———. *Empire, Enslavement and Freedom in the Caribbean*. Princeton, NJ: Markus Wiener, 1997.

Cuddon, J. A. *The Penguin Dictionary of Literary Terms and Literary Theory*, 4th edition. London: Penguin Books, 1998.

Dalby, Chris, and Camilo Carranza. "Insight Crime's 2018 Homicide Roundup." *Insight Crime: Investigation and Analysis of Organized Crime*, January 22, 2019. https://www .insightcrime.org/news/analysis/insight-crime-2018-homicide-up.

Dash, J. Michael. Introduction to *Caribbean Discourse: Selected Essays*, by Edouard Glissant, xi–xliv. Charlottesville: University Press of Virginia, 1999.

Dawes, Kwame. *Bob Marley: Lyrical Genius*. London: Sanctuary Publishing Company, 2002.

D'haen, Theo L. "Magical Realism and Postmodernism: Decentering Privileged Centers." In *Magical Realism: Theory, History, Community*, edited by Lois Parkinson Zamora and Wendy B. Faris, 191–208. Durham, NC, and London: Duke University Press, 1995.

Dolby, Nadine. "Popular Culture and Democratic Practice." *Harvard Educational Review* 73, no. 3 (Fall 2003): 258–84.

Douglass, Frederick. *Narrative of the Life of Frederick Douglass, an American Slave*. Peterborough, Canada: Broadview, 2018.

Drewal, Margaret Thompson. "Dancing for Ògun in in Yorubaland and in Brazil." In *Africa's Ogun: Old World and New*, expanded 2nd edition, edited by Sandra T. Barnes, 199–234. Bloomington: Indiana University Press, 1997.

Dunand, Francoise, and Christiane Zivie-Coche. *Gods and Men in Egypt 3000 BCE to 395 CE*. Translated by David Lorton. Ithaca, NY: Cornell University Press, 2004.

Eagleton, Terry. *Sweet Violence: The Idea of the Tragic*. Oxford: Blackwell Publishing, 2003.

Edmonds, Ennis B. "Dread 'I' In-a-Babylon: Ideological Resistance and Cultural Revitalization." In *Chanting Down Babylon: The Rastafari Reader*, edited by Nathaniel

Samuel Murrell, William David Spencer, and Adrian Anthony McFarlane, 23–35. Philadelphia: Temple University Press, 1998.

Ehrlich, Luke. "The Reggae Arrangement." In *Reggae International*, edited by Stephen Davis and Peter Simon, 52–55. New York: Rogner and Bernhard, 1982.

Ellis, Nadia. "Marlon James's Savage Business." *Public Books*, n.d. Posted March 1, 2015. http://www.publicbooks.org/fiction/marlon-jamess-savage-business.

Erickson, John. "Metoikoi and Magical Realism in the Maghrebian Narratives of Tahoar ben Jelloun and Abdelkebir Khatibi." In *Magical Realism: Theory, History, Community*, edited by Lois Parkinson Zamora and Wendy B. Faris, 427–50. Durham, NC, and London: Duke University Press, 1995.

Eudell, Demetrius L. *Political Languages of Emancipation in the British Caribbean and U.S. South.* Chapel Hill: University of North Carolina Press, 2002.

Fanon, Frantz. *Black Skins, White Masks.* Translated by Charles Lam Markmann. New York: Grove Press, 1967.

———. *The Wretched of the Earth.* Translated by Constance Farrington. New York: Grove Press, 1963.

Feld, Steven, and Aaron A. Fox. "Music and Language." *Annual Review of Anthropology* 23 (1994): 25–53.

Feldman, Allen. *Formations of Violence: The Narrative of the Body and Political Terror in Northern Ireland.* Chicago: University of Chicago Press, 1991.

"Fighting Rages in Jamaica." *Al Jazeera.* May 2, 2010. *YouTube.* http://www.youtube.com/watch?v=u29vXEsSp7c.

Finlay, Christopher J. "Violence and Revolutionary Subjectivity, from Marx to Zizek." *UCD Geary Institute Discussion Paper Series.* January 1, 2006. University College Dublin. http://www.ucd.ie/geary/static/publications/workingpapers/GearyWp200601.pdf.

Foster, Dennis A. *Sublime Enjoyment: On the Perverse Motive in American Literature.* Cambridge: Cambridge University Press, 1997.

Foster, John Burt, Jr. "Magical Realism, Compensatory Vision, and Felt History: Classical Realism Transformed in *The White Hotel*." In *Magical Realism: Theory, History, Community*, edited by Lois Parkinson Zamora and Wendy B. Faris, 267–83. Durham, NC, and London: Duke University Press, 1995.

Foucault, Michel. *Madness and Civilization: A History of Insanity in the Age of Reason.* Translated by Richard Howard. New York: Vintage Books, 1988.

Freud, Sigmund. *The Interpretation of Dreams.* Translated by James Strachey. New York: Avon Books, 1998.

———. "The 'Uncanny.'" In *The Norton Anthology of Theory and Criticism*, edited by Vincent B. Lietch, 929–52. New York: W. W. Norton & Company, 2001.

Gennep, Arnold van. *The Rites of Passage.* London: Routledge, 1960.

Gibbons, Luke. *Edmund Burke and Ireland: Aesthetics, Politics and the Colonial Sublime.* Cambridge: Cambridge University Press, 2003.

Gilligan, James. *Violence: Our Deadly Epidemic and Its Causes.* New York: G. P. Putnam's Sons, 1996.

Gilroy, Paul. *The Black Atlantic: Modernity and Double Consciousness.* New York: Verso, 1993.

Girard, René. *Violence and the Sacred.* Translated by Patrick Gregory. Baltimore: Johns Hopkins University Press, 1977.

Glissant, Edouard. *Caribbean Discourse: Selected Essays.* Translated by J. Michael Dash. Charlottesville: University Press of Virginia, 1999.

Green, William A. *British Slave Emancipation: The Sugar Colonies and the Great Experiment 1830–1865.* Oxford: Clarendon Press, 1976.

Gunst, Laurie. *Born Fi Dead: A Journey Through the Jamaican Posse Underworld.* New York: Henry Holt and Company, 1995.

Gurr, Andrew. "Third-World Drama: Soyinka and Tragedy." *The Journal of Commonwealth Literature* 3, no. 3 (April 1976): 45–52.

Hall, Stuart. "The Work of Representation." In *Representation: Cultural Representation and Signifying Practices,* edited by Stuart Hall, 13–74. Thousand Oaks, CA: Sage Publications, 2000.

Hamilton, Njelle W. "Jamaican String Theory: Quantum Sounds and Postcolonial Spacetime in Marcia Douglas's *The Marvellous Equations of the Dread.*" *Journal of West Indian Literature* 27, no. 1 (2019): 88–105.

Harrison, Sheri-Marie. "Excess in *A Brief History of Seven Killings.*" *Contemporaries,* post45. October 24, 2015. http://post45.org/2015/10/excess-in-a-brief-history-of -seven-killings.

Hartman, Saidiya. *Scenes of Subjection: Terror, Slavery, and Self-Making in Nineteenth Century America.* New York and Oxford: Oxford University Press, 1997.

Headley, Bernard. *The Jamaican Crime Scene.* Washington, DC: Howard University Press, 1996.

Hebdige, Dick. "Reggae, Rastas and Rudies." In *Resistance through Rituals: Youth Subcultures in Post-war Britain,* 2nd edition, edited by Stuart Hall and Tony Jefferson, 113–28. London and New York: Routledge, 2006.

———. *Subculture: The Meaning of Style.* New York: Methuen & Company, 1979.

Henriques, Julian. *Sonic Bodies: Reggae Sound Systems, Performance Techniques, and Ways of Knowing.* London: Continuum International Publishing Group, 2011.

Henry, Paget. *Caliban's Reason: Introducing Afro-Caribbean Philosophy.* New York and London: Routledge, 2000.

Heuman, Gad. *"The Killing Time": The Morant Bay Rebellion in Jamaica.* Knoxville: University of Tennessee Press, 1994.

Heuman, Gad, and David Vincent Trotman. *Contesting Freedom: Control and Resistance in the Post-Emancipation Caribbean.* London: Macmillan Caribbean, 2005.

Hewan, Clinton G. *Jamaica and the United States Caribbean Basin Initiative: Showpiece or Failure? American University Studies, Series X: Political Science,* vol. 44. New York: Peter Lang, 1994.

Higman, Barry W. "Slave Populations of the British Caribbean, 1807–1834." *Journal of Interdisciplinary History* 16, no. 2 (Autumn 1985): 365–67.

Hill, Edwin C. *Black Soundscapes White Stages: The Meaning of Francophone Sound in the Black Atlantic.* Baltimore: Johns Hopkins University Press, 2013.

Holt, Thomas C. *The Problem of Freedom: Race, Labor, and Politics in Jamaica and Britain, 1832–1938.* Baltimore: Johns Hopkins University Press, 1992.

Hope, Donna P. *Inna di Dancehall: Popular Culture and the Politics of Identity in Jamaica.* Kingston, Jamaica: University of the West Indies Press, 2006.

Horkheimer, Max, and Theodore Adorno. *Dialectic of Enlightenment: Philosophical Fragments.* Edited by Gunzelin Schmid Noerr and translated by Edmund Jeffcott. Stanford: Stanford University Press, 2002.

"Human Rights in Jamaica: Death Penalty, Prison Conditions and Police Violence." *News From America's Watch* 5, no. 3 (March 1993): 1–16. https://www.hrw.org/reports /JAMAICA934.PDF.

Human Rights Watch. "Jamaica: Investigate Killings in Tivoli Gardens: Reports of Unarmed Men Shot by Soldiers." Accessed June 6, 2010. http://hrw.org/en/news/2010 /06/04/jamaica-investigate-killings-tivoli-gardens.

Hussain, Nasser. *The Jurisprudence of Emergency: Colonialism and the Rule of Law.* Ann Arbor: University of Michigan Press, 2003.

Hutton, Clinton, and Nathaniel Samuel Murrell. "Rastas' Psychology of Blackness, Resistance, and Somebodiness." In *Chanting Down Babylon: The Rastafari Reader,* edited by Nathaniel Samuel Murrell, David Spencer, and Adrian Anthony McFarlane, 36–54. Philadelphia: Temple University Press, 1998.

Iadicola, Peter, and Anson Shupe. *Violence, Inequality, and Human Freedom,* 3rd edition, Lanham, MD: Rowman and Littlefield, 2013.

Irobi, Esiaba. "The Philosophy of the Sea: History, Economics and Reason in the Caribbean Basin." *Worlds & Knowledge Otherwise* (Fall 2006): 1–14.

Jakobson, Roman. "Two Aspects of Language." In *Literary Theory: An Anthology,* edited by Julie Rivkin and Michael Ryan, 76–80. Malden, MA: Blackwell Publishers, 1998.

"Jamaica 'Murder Capital of the World.'" *BBC Caribbean.* January 3, 2006. http://www.bbc .co.uk/caribbean/news/story/2006/01/060103_murderlist.shtml.

James, Marlon. *A Brief History of Seven Killings: A Novel.* New York: Riverhead Books, 2014.

Jameson, Fredric. "Third-World Literature in the Era of Multinational Capitalism." *Social Text* 15 (Autumn 1986): 65–88.

JanMohamed, Abdul R. "The Economy of Manichean Allegory: The Function of Racial Difference in The Colonialist Literature." In *"Race," Writing, and Difference,* edited by Henry Louis Gates, Jr., and Kwame Appiah, 78–106. Chicago: University of Chicago Press, 1986.

Jeyifo, Biodun. *Wole Soyinka: Politics, Poetics and Postcolonialism.* Cambridge: Cambridge University Press, 2004.

Jonas, Joyce. *Anancy in the Great House: Ways of Reading West Indian Fiction.* New York: Greenwood Press, 1990.

Jones, LeRoi. "The Changing Same (R&B and the New Black Music)." In *Black Music,* 180–211. New York: Da Capo Press, 1998. https://www.amherst.edu/media/view /104652/original/Baraka%252B-%252BThe%252BChanging%252BSame.pdf.

Josephs, Kelly Baker. *Disturbers of the Peace: Representations of Madness in Anglophone Caribbean Literature.* Charlottesville: University of Virginia Press, 2013.

Kant, Immanuel. *The Critique of Judgment.* Translated by J. H. Bernard. Amherst, MA: Prometheus Books, 2000.

———. *Observations on the Feeling of the Beautiful and the Sublime.* Translated by John T. Goldthwait. Berkeley: University of California Press, 1960.

———. "Selections from *The Critique of Judgement.*" In *German Aesthetic and Literary Criticism: Kant, Fichte, Schelling, Schopenhauer, Hegel,* edited by David Simpson, 35–70. Cambridge: Cambridge University Press, 1984.

Kermode, Frank. "John." In *The Literary Guide to the Bible,* edited by Robert Alter and Frank Kermode, 440–66. Cambridge, MA: Belknap Press of Harvard University Press, 1987.

Kerr, Hon. Justice James. "Behind Jamaica's Garrisons." Excerpts from the *Report of the National Committee on Political Tribalism.* Kingston, Jamaica, 1997.

Kincaid, Jamaica. *A Small Place.* New York: Farrar, Straus and Giroux, 1988.

King, Stephen, and Richard J. Jensen. "Bob Marley's 'Redemption Song': The Rhetoric of Reggae and Rastafari." *Journal of Popular Culture* 29, no. 3 (December 1995): 17–36.

Kirton, Claremont. *Jamaica: Debt and Poverty.* Oxford: Oxfam, 1992.

Knox, Graham. "British Colonial Policy and the Problem of Establishing a Free Society in Jamaica, 1838–1865." *Caribbean Studies* 2, no. 4 (January 1963): 3–13.

Kramnick, Isaac. *The Portable Enlightenment Reader.* New York: Penguin Books, 1995.

Lacan, Jacques. "The Direction of the Treatment and the Principles of its Power." *Écrits: The First Complete Edition in English.* Translated by Bruce Fink. New York: W. W. Norton & Company, 2007.

———. "The Mirror Stage." In *Literary Theory: An Anthology,* edited by Julie Rivkin and Michael Ryan, 618–23. Malden, MA: Blackwell Publishers, 1998.

LaCapra, Dominick. *History and Its Limits: Human, Animal, Violence,* Cornell University Press, 2010. ProQuest Ebook Central. Accessed March 3, 2019. http://ebookcentral .proquest.com/lib/fau/detail.action?docID=3137929.

Lacey, Marc. "Unrest Grows in Jamaica in 3rd Day of Standoff." *New York Times,* May 25, 2010. https://www.nytimes.com/2010/05/26/world/americas/26jamaica.html.

Lacey, Terry. *Violence and Politics in Jamaica, 1960–70: Internal Security in a Developing Country.* Manchester: Manchester University Press, 1977.

Lawson, Winston Arthur. *Religion and Race: African and European Roots in Conflict— A Jamaican Testament.* New York: Peter Lang, 1998.

Ledent, Bénédicte et al. *Madness in Anglophone Caribbean Literature: On the Edge.* New York: Palgrave Macmillan, 2018.

Leitch, Vincent B. "Guyatri Chakravorty Spivak." In *The Norton Anthology of Theory and Criticism,* edited by Vincent B. Leitch, 2193–97. New York: W. W. Norton & Company, 2001.

Leland, John. "When Rap Meets Reggae Music." In *Reggae Music, Rasta, Revolution: Jamaican Music from Ska to Dub,* edited by Chris Potash, 187–88. New York: Schirmer Books, 1997.

Lewis, Gordon K. *The Growth of the Modern West Indies.* Kingston, Jamaica: Ian Randle Publishers, 1968.

Libnitz, Gottfried Wilhelm von. "On the Radical Origination of Things" (1697). In *Philosophical Papers and Letters,* 2nd edition, edited and translated by Leroy Loemker, 486–91. Dordrecht: D. Reidel, 1969.

Liefeld, David R. "God's Word or Male Words? Postmodern Conspiracy Culture and Feminist Myths of Christian Origins." *Journal of Evangelical Theological Society* 48, no. 3 (2005): 449–73.

Lloyd, David. "The Pathological Sublime: Pleasure and Pain in the Colonial Context."
In *Postcolonial Enlightenment: Eighteenth-Century Colonialism and Postcolonial Theory*,
edited by Daniel Carey and Lynn Festa, 71–95. New York: Oxford University Press,
2003.

———. "Violence and the Constitution of the Novel." In *Anomalous States: Irish Writing
and the Postcolonial Moment*, 125–62. Durham, NC: Duke University Press, 1993.

Lowe, Lisa. *The Intimacies of Four Continents*. Durham, NC: Duke University Press, 2015.

Luhmann, Niklas. "European Rationality." In *Rethinking Imagination: Culture and
Creativity*, edited by Gillian Robinson and John Rundell, 65–85. London and New York:
Routledge, 1994.

Lull, James. "On the Communicative Properties of Music." *Communication Research* 12
(1985): 363–72.

MacDonald, Mary N. "Review of *The Trickster in West Africa: A Study of Irony and Sacred
Delight* by Robert D. Pelton." *The Journal of Religion* 71, no. 3 (July 1, 1991): 463–64.

Mack, Burton. "Introduction: Religion and Ritual." In *Violent Origins: Walter Burkert, René
Girard, and Jonathan Z. Smith on Ritual Killing and Cultural Formation*, edited by
Robert G. Hamerton-Kelly. Stanford: Stanford University Press, 1987.

Mais, Roger. *The Hills Were Joyful*. Portsmouth: Heinemann Educational Books, 1953.

Marley, Bob, and the Wailers. "Ambush in the Night." Recorded January–February 1979.
Track 9 on *Survival*. Island/Tuff Gong, compact disc.

———. "Babylon System." Recorded January–February 1979. Track 4 on *Survival*. Island/
Tuff Gong, compact disc.

Marley, Damian. "Confrontation." Released September 12, 2005. Track 1 on *Welcome to
Jamrock*. Universal and Tuff Gong, compact disc.

Marley, Ky-Mani. "Keepers of the Light." Released June 30, 2015. Track 5 on *Maestro*.
Konfrontation Muzik, compact disc.

Marshall, Emily Zobel. "Liminal Anansi: Symbol of Order and Chaos: An Exploration of
Anansi's Roots Amongst the Asante of Ghana." *Caribbean Quarterly* 53, no. 3 (2007):
30–40.

Mavado. *Mr. Brooks . . . A Better Tomorrow*. Released March 3, 2009. VP Records,
compact disc.

"Mavado vs Vybz Kartel - Talks about his long dancehall feud with Vybz Kartel." Posted by
LyricDVD. October 14, 2013. Accessed April 3, 2020. *YouTube*. https://youtu.be/Thsb
-5SWKWY.

Mays, Kelly J., editor. *The Norton Introduction to Literature, Portable 12th Edition*. New
York: W. W. Norton & Company, 2016.

Mbembe, Achille. *Critique of Black Reason*. Translated by Laurent Dubois. Durham, NC:
Duke University Press, 2017.

———. "Fragile Freedom." In *Experiences of Freedom in Postcolonial Literatures and
Cultures*, edited by Shaul Bassi and Annalisa Oboe, 13–31. London and New York:
Routledge, 2011.

———. *On the Postcolony*. Berkeley: University of California Press, 2001.

McCarthy Brown, Karen. "Systematic Remembering, Systematic Forgetting: Ogou in
Haiti." In *Africa's Ogun: Old World and New*, expanded 2nd edition, edited by Sandra T.
Barnes, 65–89. Bloomington: Indiana University Press, 1997.

McDowell, Deborah. *"The Changing Same": Black Women's Literature, Criticism, and Theory*. Bloomington: Indiana University Press, 1995.

McFarlane, Adrian Anthony. "The Epistemological Significance of 'I-an-I' as a Response to Quashie and Anancyism in Jamaican Culture." In *Chanting Down Babylon: The Rastafari Reader*, edited by Nathaniel Samuel Murrell, David Spencer, and Adrian Anthony McFarlane, 107–21. Philadelphia: Temple University Press, 1998.

McWatt, Mark. "Wilson Harris: The Language of the Imagination." In *The Routledge Companion to Anglophone Caribbean Literature*, edited by Michael A. Bucknor and Allison Donnell, 34–42. New York and London: Routledge, 2011.

Memmi, Albert. *Decolonization and the Decolonized*. Translated by Roberto Bononno. Minneapolis: University of Minnesota Press, 2006.

Metzger, Bruce M., and Roland E. Murphy eds. *The New Oxford Annotated Bible with the Apocryphal/Deuterocanonical Books: New Revised Standard Version*. Oxford: Oxford University Press, 1994.

Mignolo, Walter D. "Delinking: The Rhetoric of Modernity, The Logic of Coloniality and the Grammar of De-coloniality." *Cultural Studies* 21, nos. 2–3 (March/May 2017): 449–514.

Mikics, David. "Derek Walcott and Alejo Carpentier: Nature, History, and the Caribbean Writer." In *Magical Realism: Theory, History, Community*, edited by Lois Parkinson Zamora and Wendy B. Faris, 371–404. Durham, NC, and London: Duke University Press, 1995.

Mills, Charles W. "Racial Liberalism." *PMLA* 123, no. 5 (October 2008): 1380–97.

Mintz, Sidney W. *Sweetness and Power: The Place of Sugar in Modern History*. New York: Penguin Books, 1985.

Mitchell, W. J. T. "Representation." In *Critical Terms for Literary Study*, edited by Frank Lentricchia and Thomas McLaughlin, 147–62. Chicago: University of Chicago Press, 1990.

Morris, Mervyn. "Rereading *A Quality of Violence*." In *Is English We Speaking and Other Essays*, 98–101. Kingston, Jamaica: Ian Randle Publishers, 1999.

Moten, Fred. *In the Break: The Aesthetics of the Black Radical Tradition*. Minneapolis: University of Minnesota Press, 2003.

Murrell, Nathaniel Samuel. *Afro-Caribbean Religions: An Introduction to Their Historical, Cultural, and Sacred Traditions*. Philadelphia: Temple University Press, 2010.

Nair, Supriya M. *Pathologies of Paradise: Caribbean Detours*. Charlottesville: University of Virginia Press, 2013.

Nazareth, Peter. *In the Trickster Tradition: The Novels of Andrew Salkey, Francis Ebejar and Ishmael Reed*. London: Bogle-L'Ouverture Press, 1994.

———. "Reviewed Work: *A Quality of Violence* by Andrew Salkey." *World Literature Today* 53, no. 3 (Summer 1979): 547–48.

Nietzsche, Friedrich. *The Birth of Tragedy and Other Writings*. Edited by Raymond Geuss and Ronald Speirs. Translated by Ronald Speirs. Cambridge: Cambridge University Press, 1999.

Ogunba, Oyin. "Stage and Staging in Yoruba Ritual Drama." In *African Theatre in Performance: A Festschrift in Honour of Martin Banham*, edited by Dele Layiwola, 53–66. London and New York: Routledge, 2000.

Paton, Diana. *The Cultural Politics of Obeah: Religion, Colonialism and Modernity in the Caribbean World*. Cambridge: Cambridge University Press, 2015.

———. *No Bond but the Law: Punishment, Race, and Gender in Jamaican State Formation, 1780–1870*. Durham, NC: Duke University Press, 2004.

Patten, "H." "Dancehall Bodies: Performing In/Securities." In *Dancehall: A Reader on Jamaican Music and Culture*, edited by Sonjah Stanley Niaah, 398–405. Kingston, Jamaica: University of the West Indies Press, 2020.

Patterson, Orlando. *Slavery and Social Death: A Comparative Study*. Cambridge, MA: Harvard University Press, 1985.

Philip, Marlene NourbeSe. *Looking for Livingstone: An Odyssey of Silence*. Toronto: Mercury Press, 1991.

———. *She Tries Her Tongue: Her Silence Softly Breaks*. Charles Town: Ragweed Press, 1989.

Pithouse, Richard. "Manichean Delirium (In the Time of Jacob Zuma)." *The Con*, March 30, 2017. http://www.theconmag.co.za/2017/03/30/manicheandeliriuminthetimeofjacobzuma.

Policante, Amedeo. "Vampires of Capital: Gothic Reflections between Horror and Hope." *Cultural Logic: An Electronic Journal of Marxist Theory & Practice* (January 2010): 1–20. *EBSCOhost*, http://search.ebscohost.com/login.aspx?direct=true&AuthType=ip,cookie,url,uid&db=hus&AN=77479187&site=eds-live&scope=site.

Popcaan. "Firm and Strong." *Firm and Strong*. Mixpak Records. June 25, 2018. *YouTube*. https://youtu.be/FvnWIJX9Y1g.

———. "Lef My Gun." Posted by Seed. July 19, 2018. *YouTube*. https://www.youtube.com/watch?v=ebrAgwEoViUhttps://www.youtube.com/watch?v=4OZcxNZZuqY.

———. "Silence (Lyric Video)." Mixpak Records. July 20, 2018. *YouTube*. https://www.youtube.com/watch?v=UjisomXrBVI.

Poulet, Christian, and Jean-Yves Rigo. "Invasion." Posted by Jay Michaels Ramirez. August 1, 2014. *WCW: Invasion (Goldberg)—Single*. *YouTube*. https://youtu.be/YyJTCdPX8Cs.

Pratt, Mary Louise. *Imperial Eyes: Travel Writing and Transculturation*. London and New York: Routledge, 1992.

———. "Scratches on the Face of the Country; or, What Mr. Barrow Saw in the Land of the Bushmen." In *"Race," Writing, and Difference*, edited by Henry Louis Gates, Jr., 138–62. Chicago: University of Chicago Press, 1986.

Priebe, Richard K. "Review of *The Trickster in West Africa: A Study of Mythic Irony and Sacred Delight*." *Research in African Literatures* 14, no. 3. Special Issue on Epic and Panegyric Poetry in Africa (Autumn 1983): 401–5.

Quijano, Aníbal. "Coloniality and Modernity/Rationality." *Cultural Studies* 21, no. 2/3 (March/May 2007): 168–78.

Reagan, Ronald. "Remarks on the Caribbean Basin Initiative at a White House Briefing for Chief Executive Officers of United States Corporations." April 28, 1982. http://www.reagan.utexas.edu/resource/speeches/1982/42882a.html.

Reckford, Verena. "From Burru Drums to Reggae Riddims: The Evolution of Rasta Music." In *Chanting Down Babylon: The Rastafari Reader*, edited by Nathaniel Samuel Murrell, David Spencer, and Adrian Anthony McFarlane, 231–52. Philadelphia: Temple University Press, 1998.

Reitz, Caroline. "Review: Narratives of/as Travel." *NOVEL: A Forum on Fiction* 28, no. 3 (Spring 1995): 363–66.

Reyes, Alvaro. "On Fanon's Manichean Delirium." *The Black Scholar: Journal of Black Studies and Research* 42, nos. 3–4 (Fall–Winter 2012): 13–20.

Ricoeur, Paul. *Oneself as Another.* Translated by Kathleen Blamey. Chicago: University of Chicago Press, 1992.

———. "Personal Identity and Narrative Identity." In *Blackwell Readings in Continental Philosophy: Self and Subjectivity,* edited by Kim Atkins, 225–34. Malden, MA: Blackwell Publishing, 2005.

———. *The Rule of Metaphor: The Creation of Meaning in Language.* Translated by Robert Czerny, Kathleen McLaughlin, and John Costello, SJ. London and New York: Routledge, 1977.

Roach, Joseph. *Cities of the Dead: Circum-Atlantic Performance.* New York: Columbia University Press, 1996.

Roberts, David. "Sublime Theories: Reason and Imagination in Modernity." In *Rethinking Imagination: Culture and Creativity,* edited by Gillian Robinson and John Rundell, 171–85. London and New York: Routledge, 1994.

Roberts, Neil. *Freedom as Marronage.* Chicago: University of Chicago Press, 2015.

Rose, Tricia. *Black Noise: Rap Music and Black Culture in Contemporary America.* Middletown, CT: Wesleyan University Press, 1994.

Rowe, John Carlos. *Literary Culture and U.S. Imperialism: From the Revolution to World War II.* Oxford: Oxford University Press, 2000.

Rundell, John. "Creativity and Judgement: Kant on Reason and Imagination." In *Rethinking Imagination: Culture and Creativity,* edited by Gillian Robinson and John Rundell, 87–117. London and New York: Routledge, 1994.

———. Introduction to *Rethinking Imagination: Culture and Creativity,* edited by Gillian Robinson and John Rundell, 1–14. London and New York: Routledge, 1994.

Sakai, Naoki. *Translation and Subjectivity: On Japan and Cultural Nationalism.* Minneapolis: University of Minnesota Press, 1997.

Salkey, Andrew. *A Quality of Violence.* London: New Beacon Books, 1978.

Sartre, Jean-Paul. Preface to *The Wretched of the Earth,* by Frantz Fanon. Translated by Constance Farrington. New York: Grove Press, 1963.

Saunders, Patricia J. "Is Not Everything Good to Eat, Good to Talk: Sexual Economy and Dancehall Music in the Global Marketplace." *Small Axe* 7, no. 1 (March 2003): 95–115.

Scarry, Elaine. *The Making and Unmaking of the World.* Oxford: Oxford University Press, 1985.

Scott, David. *Conscripts of Modernity: The Tragedy of Colonial Enlightenment.* Durham, NC, and London: Duke University Press, 2004.

Seaga, Edward. *Revival Cults in Jamaica: Notes towards a Sociology of Religion.* Kingston, Jamaica: The Institute of Jamaica, 1982.

Sepper, Dennis L. *Descartes's Imagination: Proportion, Images, and the Activity of Thinking.* Berkeley: University of California Press, 1996.

Shilliam, Robbie. "Redemption from Development: Amartya Sen, Rastafari and Promises of Freedom." *Postcolonial Studies* 15, no. 3 (2012): 331–50.

Signal, Busy. "Stay So." December 20, 2017. *YouTube.* https://www.youtube.com/watch?v=h6DwAox2hF8.

Slemon, Steven. "Magical Realism as Postcolonial Discourse." In *Magical Realism: Theory, History, Community*, edited by Lois Parkinson Zamora and Wendy B. Faris, 407–26. Durham, NC, and London: Duke University Press, 1995.

Soyinka, Wole. "The Fourth Stage: (Through the Mysteries of Ogun to the Origin of Yoruba Tragedy)." In *African Literature: An Anthology of Criticism and Theory*, edited by Tejumola Olaniyan and Oto Quayson, 364–74. Malden, MA: Blackwell Publishing, 2007.

———. *Myth, Literature and the African World*. Cambridge: Cambridge University Press, 1995.

Spivak, Gayatri Chakravorty. "Can the Subaltern Speak?" In *Colonial Discourse and Postcolonial Theory: A Reader*, edited by Patrick Williams and Laura Chrisman, 66–111. New York: Columbia University Press, 1994.

———. *A Critique of Postcolonial Reason: Toward a History of the Vanishing Present*. Cambridge, MA: Harvard University Press, 1999.

———. "Poststructuralism, Marginality, Postcoloniality and Value." In *Literary Theory Today*, edited by Peter Collier and Helga Geyer-Ryan, 219–44. Ithaca, NY: Cornell University Press, 1990.

Sridhar, M. K. C., et al. "Disasters and the Coping Mechanism in Nigeria." *Journal of the Royal Society of Health* 113, no. 3 (June 1, 1993): 149–51.

Stanley Niaah, Sonjah. *DanceHall: From Slave Ship to Ghetto*. Ottawa: University of Ottawa Press, 2010.

———. "'Dis Slackness Ting': Dichotomizing Master Narrative in Jamaican Dancehall." *Caribbean Quarterly* 51, nos. 3–4 (September–December 2005): 55–76.

Steger, Manuel B. "Ideologies of Globalization." *Journal of Political Ideologies* 10, no. 1 (February 2005): 11–30.

Sterling, Elwyn F. "The Theory of Verisimilitude in the French Novel prior to 1830." *The French Review* 40, no. 5 (April 1967): 613–19.

Stewart, Diane M. *Three Eyes for the Journey: African Dimensions of the Jamaican Religious Experience*. Oxford: Oxford University Press, 2005.

Stolzoff, Norman C. *Wake the Town and Tell the People: Dancehall Culture in Jamaica*. Durham, NC, and London: Duke University Press, 2000.

Sullivan, Lawrence E. "The Irony of Incarnation: The Comedy of Kenosis." Review of *The Trickster in West Africa: A Study of Mythic Irony and Sacred Delight* by Robert D. Pelton. *Journal of Religion* 62, no. 4 (October 1982): 412–17.

Thomas, Deborah A. *Exceptional Violence: Embodied Citizenship in Transnational Jamaica*. Durham, NC, and London: Duke University Press, 2011.

Todorov, Tzvetan. *The Fantastic: A Structural Approach to a Literary Genre*. Ithaca, NY: Cornell University Press, 1975.

Traunecker, Claude. *The Gods of Egypt*. Translated by David Lorton. Ithaca, NY: Cornell University Press, 2001.

Trouillot, Michel-Rolph. *Silencing the Past: Power and the Production of History*. New York: Beacon Press, 1995.

Ullman, B. L. "History and Tragedy." *Transactions and Proceedings of the American Philological Association* 73 (1942): 25–53. JSTOR, http://www.jstor.org/stable/283535.

Veal, Michael E. *Dub: Soundscapes and Shattered Songs in Jamaican Reggae*. Middletown, CT: Wesleyan University Press 2007.

The Wailers. "Burnin' & Lootin'." Recorded April 1973. Track 4 on *Burnin'*. Island/Tuff Gong, compact disc.

———. "Concrete Jungle." *Catch A Fire*. Recorded May–October 1972. Track 1 on *Catch A Fire*. Island/Tuff Gong, compact disc.

———. "Rastaman Chant." Recorded April 1973. Track 10 on *Burnin'*. Island/Tuff Gong, compact disc.

———. "Slave Driver." Recorded May–October 1972. Track 2 on *Catch A Fire*. Island/Tuff Gong, compact disc.

Walonen, Michael, K. "Violence, Diasporic Transnationalism, and Neo-imperialism in *A Brief History of Seven Killings*." *Small Axe* 22, no. 3 (November 2018): 1–12.

———. "Violence, Imperialism and Male Socialization in Cormac McCarthy's *Blood Meridian* and Marlon James' *A Brief History of Seven Killings*." *The Journal of West Indian Literature* 26, no. 2, special issue on Marlon James (November 2018): 66–79.

White, Timothy. *Catch a Fire: The Life of Bob Marley*. New York: Henry Holt & Co., 1996.

Whiteley, Henry. *Excessive Cruelty to Slaves: Three Months in Jamaica, in 1832: Comprising A Residence of Seven Weeks on a Sugar Plantation*. London: J. Hatchard and Son, 1833.

Whitmer, Barbara. *The Violence Mythos*. Albany: State University of New York Press, 1997.

Wilden, Anthony. "Lacan and the Discourse of the Other." In *Speech and Language in Psychoanalysis*, translated by Anthony Wilden. Baltimore: Johns Hopkins University Press, 1968.

Wilderson III, Frank B. *Afropessimism*. New York: W. W. Norton and Company, 2020.

Willems, Klass, and Ludovic De Cuypere. *Naturalness and Iconicity in Language*. Amsterdam: John Benjamins Publishing Company, 2008.

Williams, James. *A Narrative of the Events, Since the First of August, 1834, by James Williams, An Apprenticed Labourer in Jamaica*. Edited by Diana Paton. Durham, NC: Duke University Press, 2001.

Williams, Raymond. *Marxism and Literature*. Oxford: Oxford University Press, 1977.

Wynter, Sylvia. "Unsettling the Coloniality of Being/Power/Truth/Freedom: Towards the Human, After Man, Its Overrepresentation—An Argument." *The New Centennial Review* 3, no. 3 (Fall 2003): 257–337.

Zamora, Lois Parkinson. "Magical Romance/Magical Realism: Ghosts in U.S. and Latin American Fiction." In *Magical Realism: Theory, History, Community*, edited by Lois Parkinson Zamora and Wendy B. Faris, 497–549. Durham, NC, and London: Duke University Press, 1995.

Zamora, Lois Parkinson, and Wendy B. Faris. "Introduction: Daiquiri Birds and Flaubertian Parrot(ie)s." In *Magical Realism: Theory, History, Community*, edited by Lois Parkinson Zamora and Wendy B. Faris, 1–11. Durham, NC, and London: Duke University Press, 1995.

Žižek, Slavoj. *Violence: Six Sideways Reflections*. New York: Picador, 2008.

Index

CPSIA information can be obtained
at www.ICGtesting.com
Printed in the USA
LVHW110617130722
723385LV00005B/481